ALL OUR STORIES ARE HERE

ALL OUR STORIES ARE HERE

Critical Perspectives on Montana Literature

Edited by Brady Harrison

University of Nebraska Press

Lincoln and London

Acknowledgments for the use of previously published material appear on page vii, which constitute an extension of the copyright page.

Manufactured in the United States of America

∞

Library of Congress Cataloging-in-Publication Data

All our stories are here : critical perspectives on Montana literature / edited by Brady Harrison.
p. cm.
Includes bibliographical references and index.
ISBN 978-0-8032-1390-6 (cl.: alk. paper)
1. American literature—Montana—History and criticism. 2. Authors, American—Homes and haunts—Montana. 3. Montana—In literature. 4. Montana—Intellectual life.
I. Harrison, Brady, 1963–
PS283.M9A45 2009
810.9'9786—dc22 2008048471

Set in Minion by Kim Essman.
Designed by Ashley Muehlbauer.

CONTENTS

ACKNOWLEDGMENTS

First and foremost, I would like to thank all of the contributors to *All Our Stories Are Here: Critical Perspectives on Montana Literature* for their diligence, hard work, and faith in this project. In particular, this book would not exist without the support and guidance of Alan Weltzien. He has been a truly tremendous mentor, advisor, and friend.

I would also like to thank Ladette Randolph, our editor, and the anonymous readers for their time, energy, and goodwill. The book is much stronger and smarter for their guidance and careful criticisms; they have been the best sort of participants in the growth and development of this collective study of Montana writing. More, I am grateful for all the hard work of the staff at the University of Nebraska Press—they have taken a rather monstrous manuscript and made it into this fine book. My thanks, as well, to Colleen Pierce, my research assistant, who expertly prepared the Select Bibliography.

This project also could not have been realized without the support of Casey Charles, chair of the Department of English, Jerry Fetz, dean of the College of Arts and Sciences, and George Dennison, president of the University of Montana.

The editor and authors would also like to thank the following individuals and organizations for permission to reprint earlier versions of chapters included in this work:

William W. Bevis's "Feminism and Postmodernism in the New West: Mary Blew and Montana Women's Writing Since 1990" first appeared, in different form, in *Ten Tough Trips: Montana Writers and the West,* New Edition (Norman: University of Oklahoma Press, 2004).

Roger Dunsmore's "All My Stories Are Here: Four Montana Poets" first appeared online in *Drumlummon Views* 1, 1–2 (2006) (www.drumlummon.org).

A early draft of Andrea Opitz's "A Haunted Nation: Cultural Narratives and the Persistence of the Indigenous Subject in James Welch's *The Heartsong of Charging Elk*" first appeared as "'The Primitive Has Escaped Control': Narrating the Nation in *The Heartsong of Charging Elk*." *Studies in American Indian Literature* 18, 3 (2006): 98–106.

INTRODUCTION
Toward a Postpopulist Criticism

As even a casual scholar of Montana writing will note, the production of fine writing far outstrips the critical inquiry into the state's extraordinary literary corpus. If a handful of Montana writers such as Richard Hugo, A. B. Guthrie Jr., D'Arcy McNickle, Wallace Stegner, and especially James Welch have received considerable and diverse critical attention, there remain sizable gaps in the analysis of the state's ever-growing and ever-evolving canon. *All Our Stories Are Here: Critical Perspectives on Montana Literature* seeks, therefore, not only to build on the exemplary, foundational work of William Bevis, Ken Egan Jr., Sue Hart, Rick Newby, Julia Watson, and others, but also to open further interpretative and critical conversations. Building on the critical paradigms of the past and bringing to bear some of the latest developments in literary and cultural studies, the contributors raise questions and foreground issues that have not been widely addressed in the study of Montana literature, explore the work of writers who have not received their critical due, take new looks at old friends, and offer some of the first explorations of recent works by well-established artists. However, before turning to a brief analysis of what has been perhaps the dominant paradigm in Montana scholarship—call it the "populist tradition"—and the contributors' particular celebrations of and challenges to this tradition via their analyses of gender and genre; desire, masculinity, and queerness; history (and the unreliability of history) and identity; region and desire; place and poetry; and much more, a brief overview of the Big Sky's literary tradition will help stake the territory.

As the bookshelf of Montana writing reveals, the state possesses not only a vibrant contemporary literary scene (reaching from the Yaak to Yellowstone, from the Bitterroot to the High Line), but also a rich and diverse tradition reaching back, as Welch puts it, to "a long time ago" (3). If the publishing of Montana writing began in the 1860s, the poet-novelist reminds us that Native American stories and myths come to us from a far deeper past, from the memories and oral traditions of the Assiniboine, Blackfeet, Cheyenne, Crow, Flathead, Gros Ventre, Kutenai, and Pend d'Oreille of Montana: "How far back do these stories go? All the way to creation—of the heavens, earth, the birds and animals, the mountains and streams, the humans" (3). Stories and storytelling seem as much a part of Montana as its mountains, forests, rivers, and sweeping plains, and the voices have been many: Indian and Euro-American, female and male, gay and straight, poor and wealthy, civilian and military, truth-teller and scoundrel. Moreover, Montana writers have excelled in about every genre: epistle, diary, journal, screenplay, poem, short story, novel, western, adventure, mystery, memoir, column, essay, article, history, polemic, jeremiad, screed, bald-faced lie, and still others. In fact, Montana boasts such a long and diverse literary tradition that the bookshelf looks, the closer one investigates, more and more like a well-stocked library.

From Blackfeet and Salish creation stories to the poetry and novels of Welch and Debra Magpie Earling, from the journals of Meriwether Lewis and William Clark to the memoirs of Mary Clearman Blew and Judy Blunt, and from the semifictions of Thomas J. Dimsdale and Yellowstone Kelly to the stories, novellas, and masterworks of Mildred Walker, Norman Maclean, and Richard Ford, the canon of Montana writing includes some of the best-known and most celebrated works about the American West. Some of the most famous—and infamous—chroniclers of westward expansion and the conflicts between Indians and whites, for example, were born and raised in Montana or wrote about their experiences as explorers, sojourners, trappers, settlers, or soldiers in the territory. The oral narratives and tales of George Bird Grinnell, Mourning Dove, Plenty-coups, Pretty-shield, and Two-Leggings, among others, provide insight into diverse Indian experiences and beliefs, and while some eloquently describe tribal cultures, histories, and cosmologies, others angrily recount the encroachment and violence of Euro-Americans. On the other hand, E. C. "Teddy Blue" Abbott, Nannie T. Alderson, Andrew Garcia, Luther S. "Yellowstone" Kelly, and Frank B. Linderman offer detailed accounts of their adventures and lives among Indians, fur traders, farmers, and ranchers. Indian or white, their works remain some of the most widely read and studied accounts of life in the West in the late nineteenth and early twentieth centuries.

Since the days of loss, broken treaties, tough trips, cowpunchers, and brides going west, Montana has enjoyed several generations of regionally, nationally, and even internationally recognized writers. In the 1920s and 1930s novelists such as Myron Brinig, Dashiell Hammett, and Clyde Murphy put Butte on the literary map; in 1926 D'Arcy McNickle published *The Surrounded*, one of the seminal texts of Native American literature and a masterpiece of late naturalism; in the 1940s and 1950s A. B. Guthrie Jr., Dorothy M. Johnson, Wallace Stegner, and Mildred Walker wrote some of the most memorable—and filmable—works of Montana and western fiction.[1] In 1960 Leslie Fiedler, one of the first great wildmen of American literary criticism, put the University of Montana (then called Montana State University) on the nation's intellectual map with the publication of *Love and Death in the American Novel.*

In the 1970s Montana—and particularly Missoula and the University of Montana—experienced what some have called the "Montana Renaissance": in 1973 Richard Hugo published his fourth, and perhaps greatest, collection of poetry, *The Lady in Kicking Horse Reservoir*; a year later, his friend and former student, James Welch, brought out his surrealist masterpiece, *Winter in the Blood*, and two years later published, to critical acclaim, a revised edition of his first book, *Riding the Earthboy 40*; in the same year, at the age of seventy-three, Norman Maclean published *A River Runs Through It and Other Stories*; 1977 saw the release of Hugo's brilliant *31 Letters and 13 Dreams*; and Welch capped off the '70s with *The Death of Jim Loney*. At the university in some of the same years were William Bevis, Madeline DeFrees, and William Kittredge; coming and going through town or the state were James Crumley, Ivan Doig, Jim Harrison, and many, many others. The writers in Montana in the 1970s shared ideas, read one another's works, and shaped the writing not only of their own time but of the future as well.

If a jury on the contemporary scene cannot yet be convened, the evidence suggests a strong, albeit somewhat conservative continuation of Montana's rich legacy. Although Montana writers and readers, as Rick Newby argues, seem to "expect Montana writers to be conservative in their aesthetic approach" and therefore seem unwilling "to acknowledge the contributions of those whose works are ribald, experimental, rigorously modernist (discontinuous, constructed of fragments, rich in visual as well as verbal play), and bookish" (316–17), the realist and naturalist traditions remain vibrant. Writers such as Kevin Canty, Rick DeMarinis, David Long, and Deirdre McNamer continue to explore the dark, often bleak undercurrents of middle- and working-class lives. If Hugo yet looms large on Montana's poetic landscape, the state's history, the vastness of the West, and the individual's relationship to nature and the environment remain powerful themes in the work of Sandra Alcosser, Roger Dunsmore, Newby, and others. Most vital of all, perhaps, continues to be the Montana tradition of the memoir, where writers such as Mary Clearman Blew, Judy Blunt, Ivan Doig, and William Kittredge have seen deeply into matters of cultural history, gender, family, and property—intellectual and material—in the West. For good measure, we can also add that Montana writers have excelled in the writing of mysteries and thrillers (see, for example, the work of James Lee Burke, James Crumley, Jenny Siler, and others), natural history, popular science, and ecology (Rick Bass, Janine Benyus, Phil Condon, David Quammen, Kim Todd, and more), outdoor and adventure writing (Tim Cahill and Peter Stark, among others), and Montana and western history (Harry Fritz, Joseph Kinsey Howard, Michael Malone, K. Ross Toole, and many more).

If this catalog of Montana writers is to go on, we should perhaps pause and ask a necessary question: who qualifies as a "Montana" writer? A vexed question, indeed. For example, Hugo—a writer as closely identified with the state as any other—was born in White Center, Washington, in 1923, and after serving in the air force in World War II, returned to Seattle to study at the University of Washington and to work for Boeing as a technical writer from 1951 to 1963. Only then, nearing age forty, did he move to Montana. Kittredge, to take another example, was born in Portland in 1932, grew up on his family's vast ranch in Oregon, and earned an MFA from the Iowa Writers Workshop in 1969. Like Hugo, Kittredge was in his late thirties when he came to Montana, and one could easily claim him as an Oregon or, better, western writer. We could also consider short story writer and novelist Melanie Rae Thon: originally from Montana, she was educated at the University of Michigan and Boston College and has taught creative writing at Emerson College, Syracuse University, the University of Massachusetts, Ohio State University, and the University of Utah. Thon writes about Montana—see, for example, her extraordinary novel, *Sweet Hearts* (2000)—but doesn't live full-time in the state. Maclean, though born and raised in Missoula, spent most of his professional life in Chicago, yet he wrote what must be one of the most Montanan of all tales. As these examples suggest, the question of who "counts" as a Montana writer quickly becomes difficult to answer: no litmus test, genealogy, badge, or residency card can settle the matter. Yet for those readers dissatisfied with such a deferral, we always have recourse to common sense: a Montana writer is somebody who self-identifies as a Montana writer or who has lived, at least for part of her or his life, in Montana, who sets at least some of her or his work in Montana, and who engages one or more of the hallmark Montana themes: fighting the invaders, trapping the beaver, staking the homestead, facing the fire, wrestling the bear, pulling the calf, catching the fish, working the ranch, returning to the reserve, leaving the middle of nowhere, driving the gumbo, building the trophy home, and more. Could someone who never set foot in the state be a Montana writer? Maybe.

While the curious question of who counts will lead us, a few pages hence, to another equally curious (and keenly debated) question in western studies—does place matter?—we turn for the moment to the matter of Montana scholarship and the populist tradition of literary and cultural criticism: just as much of the best creative writing about Montana and its places and peoples has tended (with exceptions, of course) to be conservative in terms of formal or stylistic experimentation and complexity, much of the best homegrown scholarship has also tended (again, with exceptions) to be conservative in its applications and investigations of literary and cultural theory. Simply put, Montana scholars have tended to read Montana writing in terms accessible to scholars and lay readers alike.

A middling, centripetal, even folksy force of plainspokenness, no-nonsenseness, and no-putting-on-airsness seems to guide both the literature and criticism, and several factors have doubtlessly contributed to this critical style. For one, many of the most celebrated Montana writers and scholars over the latter half of the twentieth century have been determined populists. Most famously, perhaps, Hugo and historian Joseph Kinsey Howard were staunch spokespeople for the dispossessed, the underclasses, the small towners. In their efforts to write about and to speak to and for the marginalized, Hugo, Howard, and others cultivated straightforward, accessible, and seemingly traditional styles and forms. In the main, they operated from the conviction that the vernacular can be used just as effectively to explore and dissect the most entrenched historical, political, and cultural problems as the highest scholarly or poetic languages.[2] At the same time, as Bevis notes, even while "Hugo did not wish to be part of an elite; he would have been happy if everyone enjoyed his work," he knew that "poetry is not easy" (152). The same could be said, perhaps, for literary history and literary and cultural criticism.

Nevertheless, the populist approach has worked very well, and the response of Montana readers has perhaps also contributed to the populism of both the writing and the scholarship: many Montanans take a proprietary interest in Montana writing. As the in-state popularity of *The Last Best Place* (1988), the massive anthology of Montana writing, and the sheer, ever-expanding number of readings and regionally, nationally, and even internationally recognized public celebrations such as the Montana Festival of the Book attest, Montanans identify strongly with the state's literary legacy and take a particular pride in the state's many voices. As one of the few cross-cultural and cross-class bonds in a geographically vast, economically precarious, politically polarized, and scarcely populated state, the canon enjoys a prominence perhaps unequaled in other states. Projects such as "One Book Montana" and "Missoula Reads"—where organizers encourage participants to read a particular text and then to join in publicly staged events such as readings, panel presentations, and discussions—open texts to dialogue and a sense of collective ownership that encourages appreciation, interpretation, and critique. Given the state's history of populist intellectuals and its widespread yet enthusiastic readership, we should not be surprised if the homegrown scholarship has also been populist and aimed, at least in part, at interested lay readers.

The best energies of Montana populism can be seen in the urtext of Montana literary scholarship, William Bevis's *Ten Tough Trips* (1990). Understanding the state's intellectual and populist traditions as well as anyone, Bevis opts for a relatively informal approach, mixing interpretation with anecdote, personal experience, and elegant musings on the myths and realities of the West. In chapters on Guthrie, Hugo, Welch, and others, he offers trenchant readings open, he hopes, to anyone interested in the literature. As he remarks in the introduction, "The Montana literature is so various and interesting, and the West is so intertwined with American national identity, that I thought many who do not usually read criticism or history might enjoy hearing a discussion of the books. These are personal essays, then, for a general audience. For a scholar, the writing has been a most enjoyable break from the objectivity and impersonality of professional publication" (ix).

Bevis may write for anyone interested in Montana writing, but like any good scholar he pushes his audience as well, offering sustained critiques of many western myths, ones that may still resonate with readers. As he remarks, he critiques "the pastoral and primitivist pursuits of innocence and their rejections of society, psychology, and experience; attack[s] myths of the rugged individual, especially conceived as the lone rogue male; and point[s] out flaws . . . in cherished authors" (201–2). Bevis knows the books and the writers and his readers, and he performs the best sort of public intellectual work: he shares what he knows and elevates not only the critical conversation but the community conversation as well. As he recounts, "I have had men on both sides of me reciting lines from 'The Only Bar in Dixon,' in that bar. Then they told me to tell Hugo to keep his butt out" (152–53).

Perhaps another factor influencing the relative conservativism of Montana literary scholarship has been the prominence of the writers themselves in discussions of the literature. In *Writing Montana: Literature Under the Big Sky* (1996), for example, the editors, Rick Newby and Suzanne Hunger, are poets, and the majority of the contributors, including Blew, Bill Borneman, Earl Ganz, Greg Keeler, Melissa Kwasny, Lise McClendon, Maile Meloy, Gwen

Petersen, Noelle Sullivan, Wilbur Wood, and Paul Zarzyski, are best known as poets, short story writers, novelists, and memoirists. Yet even as their essays reveal, one could argue, some disinterest in contemporary literary and cultural theory and theorists, they open vast areas of Montana writing for further study. In "Brinig: The Truth Game," for example, Ganz offers one of the first critical considerations of queerness in Brinig's work; in "Exquisite Magazine Corpses," Sullivan explores the history of literary magazines in Montana and sees old issues "as a testimonial to others' language, if not mine. I can hope, against proof, that some words endure" (72). The scholarly works likewise address writers who have not received enough attention—Hart, for example, looks through "'Eyes to See': The Writers of Eastern Montana," while Watson considers "Engendering Montana Lives: Women's Autobiographical Writing"—and likewise seek as wide an audience as possible.[3] The collection's determinedly populist bent suggests, in an enlivening manner, that writers and scholars share both a keen interest in Montana literature and a cross-disciplinary openness calculated to expand the critical and public conversations.

The next step in homegrown criticism can be found in Ken Egan Jr.'s *Hope and Dread in Montana Literature* (2003). A clear successor to Bevis and Hart, Egan sees deeply into what he dubs the "Montana identity" (3). Undertaking readings of writers from the 1860s to the present, he offers a persuasive diachronic analysis and argues for a powerful dialectic of dread and hope at work in Montana literature and culture. In particular, his analysis of how the "tragic sensibility" of McNickle and Hugo gives way to the "provisional hope" of Welch and Doig shows not only mastery of the texts but also of Montana history. Thoroughly steeped in western and Native American studies, *Hope and Dread* constitutes a landmark in the field. Nevertheless, Egan's work appears to retain a measure of Montana critical populism: even as his analysis draws on Hegelian and Marxist concepts such as the dialectic and political unconscious and applies them to Montana literary, cultural, political, and economic history, he keeps his work reader-friendly and, like Bevis, available to anyone interested in Montana writing. With the history of Montana populist criticism in mind, we can now turn to the present interventions.

The contributors to *All Our Stories Are Here* come along at a fortuitous time: the fields of literary and cultural criticism could not be more open. If, over the past decade or so, some of the more ferocious energies of such schools of theory and criticism as poststructuralism and postmodernism have waned—and been the subject of robust critiques and attacks as can be found in such antitheory/antitheorist tomes as *Literature Lost: Social Agendas and the Corruption of the*

Humanities (1999) and *Theory's Empire: An Anthology of Dissent* (2005)—literary and cultural criticism and many schools of theory such as feminism, gender studies, queer theory, and more have continued to flourish. Readers of the present volume will find a remarkable range of critical practices: some of the contributors work proudly and steadfastly in the tradition of Montana populist criticism; others unapologetically engage in high theory; still others work in the tried-and-true tradition of biographical criticism; a number build on the critical practices and provocations of regional studies, western studies, Native American studies, queer theory, and more; at least one of the contributors blends the energies of postcolonial theory with those of the personal essay. Collectively, the contributors follow no one critical school or methodology, and they participate in a wide range of ongoing discussions and debates in multiple fields. Those looking for a unified field theory of Montana criticism or Montana writing will not find it here; if we contradict ourselves, very well then, we contradict ourselves.

Although the contributors to *All Our Stories Are Here* disagree on critical strategies and practices, they nevertheless agree on a few matters. For one, all agree that Montana literature merits far more critical consideration; they all share a determination to expand, complicate, and celebrate the study of Montana and western writing. More complexly, each of the scholars—whether implicitly or explicitly—engages an abiding issue in western studies: does place or region matter? In the introduction to one of the best collections on western writing, *Reading the West* (1996), Michael Kowalewski argues, for example, that "region," as a critical category, needs to be central in western studies. He remarks, "Finding region an important factor in literary studies is still often seen as the equivalent of being an overenthusiastic salesman with a special marketing territory. Regionalism, it seems, is often next to boosterism, a puffing of 'merely' local talent—a kind of literary chamber of commerce juxtaposed to the three national congressional houses of race, class, and gender" (8). Scholars, he argues, must pay particular attention to place and its influences on consciousness and literary practice; criticism of western writing, he contends, must emphasize region, attending to all its cultural, racial, gendered, sexual, historical, and literary complexities.

Although most of the contributors would agree—in spirit *and* in practice—with Kowalewski that place matters, that region matters, that the very materiality of the state's geography (or, given its natural diversity, *geographies*) and history (or, given its cultural diversity, *histories*) impacts and gives weight and substance to Montana writing (even as Montana writing in turn gives weight and substance back to an understanding and experience of place and history), can we then take the additional step and assert that from this place (these places) and this history (these histories) we get something distinct, a body of literature that we can clearly and confidently name "Montana" writing? If one were to take all place names and references to historical events from, say, *Fools Crow* or *A River Runs Through It* or *Winter Wheat*, could one still say on the basis of plot or way of telling or thematics that these masterpieces were by and of Montana? Does something hold all the works and writers we consider here together in something like a coherent or cohesive whole? The answer to these superloaded questions must, no doubt, be "no." There cannot be any single "Montana" of the imagination. Rather, however many themes one identifies (as I did earlier in this Introduction), or however extensive or limited a list of writers one evokes, or however many definitions, categories, or tropes one offers, the arguments must remain happily provisional—Montana's too big, too complex, too full of competing histories and stories to be neatly summed up (though some have tried and done well: think "Big Sky" or "The Last Best Place"). Yet even if one cannot say that such a thing as a distinctly Montanan literature exists, writers and scholars can still explore and argue over the implications and nuances of place, nature, history, memory, self, desire, and more in the lived and imaginative experiences of Montana and the West.

Part I of this collection, "Does Place Matter?" begins with a provocation. In direct challenge to some of the assumptions about place that we have just touched on, Tamas Dobozy, in an adroitly theorized reading of regionalism, "Burning Montana: Richard Ford's *Wildlife* and Regional Crisis," argues that for Ford, region does not determine or define literature or culture but rather becomes "one of the many options for voicing desire." At the same time as Ford denies the importance of region, *Wildlife* "enacts a drama of regionalism by commenting on the ways in which various 'needs' find articulation via a landscape that is not exactly commensurable with either need or articulation, and which therefore continually exceeds, or 'burns away,' the categories that structure it in communal myths and beliefs." Dobozy, via Ford, not only unsettles romantic and commonsense notions of region, but also nicely works against both established arguments about place in western studies and in the next contribution.

Next in Part I, Roger Dunsmore, an unapologetic old-school Montana populist, finds a much different understanding of region in his poets: for Mark Gibbons, Vic Charlo, Ed Lahey, and David Thomas, few things in life matter more than place and taking possession of a place. The region—its land, people, and history—sinks into people if they work hard enough to know the place where they live; as Dunsmore writes, for these poets "human wholeness and sanity have historically required that there be something essential between the 'you and any place' where we would live well. And the name of this something essential is 'home.'" Like Nancy Cook, Karl Olson, Alan Weltzien, Gregory Morris, and others in this collection, Dunsmore foregrounds the work of writers who have not received a great deal of critical or popular attention; like Hugo and Howard, he brings a populist passion to his analysis, writing in a style of criticism open to anyone who cares about Montana poetry.

In "West of Éire: Butte's Irish Ethos," Matthew Jockers offers a literary history of Butte's Irish Americans and argues for precise cultural and historical understandings of place. Focusing on an array of writers, he argues that Butte's literature differs not only from the majority of western writing but also from the majority of Irish American writing: on the one hand, and in antithesis to much western writing, Butte's prose and poetry foregrounds community over the individual; on the other hand, where Irish American writing from the Midwest and East often documents the struggles of the Irish against poverty and discrimination, Butte's Irish writing displays an exuberance over the opportunities, cultural diversity, and wealth of Montana's glittering hill-town: "This exuberance manifests itself in a literature that takes success for granted while largely ignoring the fact that the mining lifestyle was anything but easy." If place and region matter, Dobozy's, Dunsmore's, and Jockers's writers by no means agree on how or why it matters; the question remains very much open and vital.

As Mary Clearman Blew, Julia Watson, Caroline Patterson, and others have argued, Montana's women writers have not received their critical due, and in Part II, "Women Writing Montana," we begin with a perfect segue from considerations of place to a consideration of women writers, place, and more.[4] In "Home on the Range: Montana Romances and Geographies of Hope," Nancy Cook, working in the best traditions of cultural studies, foregrounds the study of mass market romances set in Montana, analyzing the cultural work of what some consider a "low" or (too) "popular" literary form aimed primarily at women readers. Building on the research of such scholars as Janice Radway, Melody Graulich, and others, Cook argues that in these romances, "Montana serves as a place conducive to the seemingly 'natural' linkage between finding love and finding a place to love, meaningful and remunerative work, a commitment to a cohesive and supportive community, partnership with one's spouse, and a stable and safe home."

From Cook and romances we turn to the venerable Bevis and his analysis of Blew's postmodern yet distinctly western feminism in *All but the Waltz*. Building directly on his arguments in *Ten Tough Trips* and bringing to bear currents of feminist theory (and thereby extending and complicating his engagement with the populist tradition), Bevis argues in "Feminism and Postmodernism in the New West: Mary Blew and Montana Women's Writing Since 1990" that the memoirist relies on a fragmented, skeptical, "quilted" narrative style as a means of speaking against "the dominant western male voice of terse certainty, common sense, natural authority." Like Judy Blunt and other second-generation western feminist writers, he argues, Blew critiques the masculinist cowboy tradition but does not wholly reject it either, opting instead for a tough-minded generosity toward others and their stories.

In Part III, "Gay and Lesbian Literature Under a Big Sky," Karl Olson and Alan Weltzien bring the latest developments in gender and queer studies to bear on Montana writing. In "West of Desire: Queer Ambivalence in Montana Literature," Olson, building on the work of Bernard DeVoto, Ken Egan, and others, explores the abiding ambivalence in Montana and western writing between loving the West and its promise and hating the damage humanity has done to the land and its people: "It is here, on the love/hate equipoise westerners maintain with the West, that I detect the queer edge." Offering some of the first detailed readings of the landmark fictions of Myron Brinig and Thomas Savage, Olson argues that these two lesser-known contemporaries of McNickle and Guthrie "make explicit the connection between the degradation of the West and the deprivation of the queer." For Olson, as for Kittredge and others, stories matter a great deal: we know ourselves through the stories we read and tell.

In "'Just Regular Guys': Homophobia, the Code of the West, and Constructions of Male Identity in Thomas Savage and Annie Proulx," Weltzien offers a trenchant dissection of the politics of literary reputation and the very real, very worldly politics of exclusion and violence toward gays and lesbians. Finding Savage's exclusion from *The Last Best Place* and from Bevis's and Egan's studies "inexplicable," he argues that the masculine codes and values of the West have worked to silence the voices of sexual minorities. Nevertheless, even as Savage and Proulx "do not offer much hope for gay men," they "courageously insist on the need for change: for a more inclusive masculinity that embraces, rather than shuns and despises, gay men."

If D'Arcy McNickle and James Welch have received perhaps more critical attention than any other Montana writers, Jim Rains and Andrea Opitz demonstrate that their complex, masterful fictions continue to invite elegant and sophisticated analyses. Building on the latest trends in Native American studies, Jim Rains opens Part IV, "Native Revisions/The Problems of History," with "'He Never Wanted to Forget It': Contesting the Idea of History in D'Arcy McNickle's *The Surrounded*." Deeply concerned with alterity and the ability of Native Americans to write their own histories, McNickle, as Rains argues, also relied on his fiction as a means "to explore and contest the very idea of history." Reopening "the book of the past" through Archilde's quest for identity, the novelist "demonstrates the way in which America's history could—and should—be forced to accommodate the individual histories of the disparate cultures that comprise the nation." Like Paula Gunn Allen, Arnold Krupat, David Moore, and others, Rains foregrounds a distinctly Native American epistemology and historicity.

Opitz, drawing on the work of diverse literary and cultural theorists such as Stuart Hall and Lisa Lowe, argues in "A Haunted Nation: Cultural Narratives and the Persistence of the Indigenous Subject in James Welch's *The Heartsong of Charging Elk*" that Welch, like McNickle, focuses on the problems of history and self-representation and continues, in *Heartsong*, the process of revisioning history that he began in *Fools Crow*: in Welch's final novel "what is produced by the Wild West show as the 'vanishing Indian' emerges as a 'ghost' in an alternative space—outside the 'historical' narrative and thus outside the nation space—and reveals that 'other' material and social histories indeed leave traces that are in excess of U.S. cultural and national narratives."

In "'I Have Had Some Satisfactory Times': The Yellowstone Kelly Novels of Peter Bowen," Gregory Morris demonstrates that Native American writers are not the only ones concerned with the legitimacy and authority of history, storytelling, and myth-making. Offering the first critical treatment of Bowen's rewrites of the historical Yellowstone Kelly's adventures and exploits, Morris argues that Bowen, like many of his postmodern peers, distrusts history and mocks the claims that historical fiction makes to historical veracity. Rather, Bowen plays fast and loose with the events of Kelly's life in order to critique the Euro-American metanarratives underlying westward—and overseas—expansionism: "Bowen's historical mode is powerfully comic, but beneath that ludic, playful history lies a more subversive ideological critique of the American mythos and of the American identity."

Finally, in Part V, "Hugo-Land," Steve Davenport and Lois Welch investigate the impact and lasting importance of Richard Hugo and the creative writing program at the University of Montana. In "Richard Hugo's Montana Poems: Blue Collars, Indians, and Tough Style," Davenport, drawing on recent work in men's and literary studies and analyzing Hugo as both a teacher and a poet, locates class, racial, and gender anxieties at the heart of Hugo's aesthetic: although the teacher-poet wanted to be tough, wanted to live and write as hard as Jack London or Ernest Hemingway, he leavened his portraits of the dispossessed and abandoned towns with sympathy and sentiment. Davenport contends, "It is, in fact, the failure of his flight from sentiment, his self-imposed prohibition against melancholy, that makes his poetry so powerful, so affecting, so human." These same qualities, he suggests, also made Hugo a great friend and mentor to students and colleagues like James Welch and William Kittredge.

In "Semicolonial Moments: The History and Influence of the University of Montana Creative Writing Program," Lois Welch takes a step back and surveys the crucial part the creative writing program has played in the formation of Montana writing. Analyzing the roles played by such key figures as H. G. Merriam, Warren Carrier, Fiedler, Hugo, and others, she traces the growth of the program into a regional—and then national—powerhouse and reads, if with wry edges, the program's success in terms of postcolonial theory. As Welch argues, "we could examine the development of Montana writing in a postcolonial light: as resistance to eastern hegemony, as primarily representational, as historically grounded, as reversing the relative advantages of center and margin. The fascination of the hegemonic (eastern, urban) culture with the indigenous and the remote (consider the Western Myth, Mythic Montana, and the Noble Savage) has increased from the 1970s through the end of the century."

As these critical investigations in Montana literature reveal, this is a good time to be working in Montana and western studies: not only are there many more writers and texts to be explored but the battles over methods and approaches continue unabated. Much more work remains to be done—many articles and books remain to be written about, say, Montana's women writers or about the state's postcolonial condition—and still more critical practices need to be brought to bear on the state's extraordinary literary corpus. Nevertheless, these contributors, building on the work of their predecessors, fill in a few more pages on the literary history and culture of Montana. Collectively, they suggest that the criticism will engage still other critical practices and methodologies, and that there can only be an increase in critical interest in Montana writing. In true Montana tradition, the work will continue.

NOTES

1. Howard Hawks, for example, directed Kirk Douglas in *The Big Sky*, and Guthrie received an Academy Award nomination for the screenplay for *Shane*; several of Johnson's stories, including "A Man Called Horse," "The Hanging Tree," and "The

Man Who Shot Liberty Valence," were made into critically acclaimed films starring such Hollywood icons as Gary Cooper, James Stewart, and John Wayne.

2. As Guthrie wrote in 1959, "When Joseph Kinsey Howard died in August, 1951, I said that Montana had lost her conscience. Who but he could push and lead us to a recognition of our shortcomings? Who would tackle prejudice and privilege and so awaken us to them? What voice would speak for the neglected, the oppressed, the victimized? Or for our misused inheritance of soil and water and timber?" (x–xi). As one measure of the power of Howard's voice, recall that in 1981 the readers of *Montana: The Magazine of Western History* selected Howard's *Montana: High, Wide, and Handsome* as "the most significant book on the state." Egan writes, "Think about it—a political diatribe that assaults big business, false dreams, and foolish settlement prospects, chosen as the most telling, most important book about the region" (95).
3. Hart, a celebrated professor of English at Montana State University–Billings, is well known to many Montanans via her "Montana Books and Authors" program on Billings public access TV. She is also the author of *Thomas and Elizabeth Savage* (Boise State University Press, 1995).
4. As Watson writes in "Engendering Women's Lives: Women's Autobiographical Writing," "women's histories and lives have too often been erased in official documentary, cinematic, and narrative histories of the West, where the prevailing trope of rugged individualism celebrating solitary selfhood in mountain grandeur has a decidedly masculine cast" (122). In "Writing and Fire," Blew offers a similar argument on Montana and western women: "The women have always been writing but have gone unheard until lately" (332).

WORKS CITED

Bevis, William W. *Ten Tough Trips*. Seattle: University of Washington Press, 1990.

Blew, Mary Clearman. "Writing and Fire." *Writing Montana: Literature Under the Big Sky*. Ed. Rick Newby and Suzanne Hunger. Helena: Montana Center for the Book, 1996. 329–43.

Egan, Ken, Jr. *Hope and Dread in Montana Literature*. Reno: University of Nevada Press, 2003.

Guthrie, A. B., Jr. Preface. *Montana: High, Wide, and Handsome*. By Joseph Kinsey Howard. Lincoln: University of Nebraska Press, 1959. ix–xiv.

Kowalewski, Michael. "Introduction." *Reading the West: New Essays on the Literature of the American West*. Ed. Michael Kowalewski. Cambridge: Cambridge University Press, 1996. 1–18.

Newby, Rick. "The Montana-Paris Axis, or Unpacking My Grandfather's Library: On the Track of a Bookish Tradition." *Writing Montana: Literature Under the Big Sky*. Ed. Rick Newby and Suzanne Hunger. Helena: Montana Center for the Book, 1996. 300–328.

Sullivan, Noelle. "Exquisite Magazine Corpses." *Writing Montana: Literature Under the Big Sky*. Ed. Rick Newby and Suzanne Hunger. Helena: Montana Center for the Book, 1996. 72–88.

Watson, Julia. "Engendering Montana Lives: Women's Autobiographical Writing." *Writing Montana: Literature Under the Big Sky*. Ed. Rick Newby and Suzanne Hunger. Helena: Montana Center for the Book, 1996. 121–62.

Welch, James. "Long Time Ago." *The Last Best Place*. Ed. William Kittredge and Annick Smith. Seattle: University of Washington Press, 1988. 2–8.

PART I Does Place Matter?

CHAPTER ONE

Burning Montana: Richard Ford's *Wildlife* and Regional Crisis

TAMAS DOBOZY

CRITICAL REGIONS

Richard Ford's position on regionalism is well known to his scholars. In an interview with Gregory L. Morris, Ford denies region an essentialist impact on character and community; instead, he prefers to articulate human behavior in spite of geographic determinants:

> I shouldn't say I have *no* relationship with landscape. But . . . saying I miss Montana is just expressing a feeling of need of mine in terms of place, likewise saying Mississippi is my home. I could express that need differently, but for some reason, something like instinct, I express it in terms of place, landscape.
>
> This is [why] I so strongly resist the notion of regionalism—in literature, in defining culture. My life has simply shown me that we're more in the same boat wherever we are, and that recognizing that fact might enable us to adapt to our situations more successfully. (Morris 109)

Here, Ford raises a number of key points for understanding landscape in his writing in general and in his novel *Wildlife* (1990) in particular. He does not deny a "relationship" with landscape, but qualifies this by disengaging the terms of region—"Montana," "Mississippi"—from the need that expresses them. Region becomes an "instinctual" expression, verging on the arbitrary, since the need from which it originates could as easily find a different outlet. Region, rather than determining literature or culture—rather than forming the basis of the need that in turn articulates it—becomes, instead, not antecedent but ancillary to need. Region is simply one of the many options for voicing desire. At the same time, Ford complicates his notion of region by suggesting that our "situations," their variable signification notwithstanding, require "adaptation," though the key to adaptation comes not with attachment to regional specifics but with the recognition that the universal character of human need is often obscured—and thus limited—by geographic reference.

It is this "universal condition" (material need), as far as *Wildlife* and Ford's depiction of Montana are concerned, that determines how region is signified in the discourse that enables our individual and communal existence. While Ford counters any notion of regionalism as "definitive," *Wildlife* nonetheless enacts a drama of regionalism by commenting on the ways in which various "needs" find articulation via a landscape that is not exactly commensurable with either need or articulation, and which therefore continually exceeds, or burns away, the categories that structure it in communal myths and beliefs.

By "burns away," I am referring to the forest fire that consumes much of Montana in *Wildlife*, but which, by supposedly threatening to overcome Ford's protagonist (48), also demonstrates how our categories of knowing are insufficient for containing the volatility of the real: "[The fire] takes you outside yourself. . . . You see everything from outside. You're up against so big a thing out there. . . . Everything seems arbitrary. . . . It's probably hard to understand" (138). Outside our understanding is the fire, which is external to, and too vast to account for within, a system of ordering. The fire instantiates the arbitrary as an external condition we try to regulate with conceptual categories and systems.

At the same time, the fire permits a realization of agency. The inability of Ford's characters to sustain region as a fixed category—and thus a fixed sense of themselves *within* region—enables them to realize that any sense of ourselves is subject to alteration, not only by conditions in the real but by ourselves, in the way we discourse on those conditions. Because knowing occurs in relation to the real, we understand, as Joe Brinson does, that there are "no final answers" (171), only a set of provisional, shifting, and contingent "answers" whose source is not the real *itself* but our *disposition* to the displacements—such as wildfires—eventuated by it. The arbitrariness of such displacements demonstrates the inadequacy, over the long term, of any single definitive cultural or political (or regionalist) framework. There are answers, but no *final* ones, since alternating social relations are themselves *determined by* as well as *determinants of* the real. It is within this radical, two-way contingency that I situate Ford's discourse on region.

I am, of course, not the first critic to tackle Ford's complex view of regionalism. Huey Guagliardo sees in Ford's writing the "breakdown of such cultural institutions as marriage, family, and community, the very institutions which give purpose and meaning to one's life" ("Introduction" xiv). We can include regionalism in this list, since regionalism is itself a cultural institution that arises out of community, one no less important in giving purpose and meaning to one's life. Guagliardo also examines how Mexico, in Ford's novel, *The Ultimate Good Luck*, "serves as a metaphor" ("Marginal" 12), suggesting a symbolic rather than essentialist function for landscape. Robert N. Funk likewise argues that *The Ultimate Good Luck* "incorporates the regional concern with the influences of the larger popular culture" (53). Region is thus a "concern" derived from "larger popular culture," suggesting that regionalism is a consensus, at the service of communal need. It is not an outgrowth of geospatial essence. Importantly, Funk sees Ford exploring the tension "between meaning (the anticipated revelation of a coherent narrative pattern) and meaninglessness (the fear that no such pattern exists)" (57). This tension also appears in *Wildlife,* where Joe confronts the disorder of his family life. Here, going further than Funk and borrowing from Maurice Blanchot, I argue that the development of meaning is inevitable: "People categorize other people. . . . But you shouldn't do that. They should teach you that in school" (30). As Joe's father says, awareness—even awareness of awareness—always ends in instruction. The knowledge of the impossibility of devising adequate metaphors ends in the devising of "adequate" metaphors: thus "wildfire" comes to serve as a metaphor for the inadequacy of metaphor.

Yet, in Ford, the mediating subject's recognition of the inevitability of metaphor does not mean a loss of agency. While metaphor may be inevitable, our choice of metaphors is not necessarily so. The inevitable displacement of the real by metaphors—i.e., language and meaning—does not mean that metaphors cannot serve individuals and communities. In reminding us, as Joe's father does, of the need to exceed categories, or interrogate the categorical impulse, Ford is not advocating nihilism but rather an awareness that meaning is never fixed, and can thus be changed.

Joanna Price, in "Richard Ford: The Postmodern Exile and the Vanishing South," and Fred Hobson, in "Richard Ford and Josephine Humphreys: Walker Percy in New Jersey and Charleston,"[1] argue that Ford's regionalism refers less to a locale than the discourse (Hobson 42) attending a specific populace in a specific place: "Ford's two novels [*The Sportswriter* and *Independence Day*] are largely concerned with exploring how an individual . . . can accommodate himself to the way in which such concepts are changing as they have ceased to be defined by regionally specific traditions and are increasingly being reshaped by the cultural and economic formations of postmodernity" (Price 261). In other words, Price views the "specific traditions" of region as already provisional, distinct from the landscape from which they purportedly emerge, since they are shaped here not by transformations in the landscape but in the American cultural milieu. Price contends that regionalism, in the form of "regionally specific traditions," is, to begin with, a set of social practices formed in relation to geography rather than granted by it. This is exactly the universalism that Ford's interview suggests: that regionalism, no matter where it forms, is a matter of adapting what we bring to what is present, of what we are running *from* to what we are running *to*, of the ways that we make the world conform to expectation and desire, as Ford indicates in the same interview:

> Well I suppose [landscape contributes to human action] in one way or another. If it's cold where you live, then you tend to stay in a lot and get cabin fever. If it's hot, then maybe you wear fewer clothes and have more sexual adventures. But I think, more commonly, that *we* say it contributes in our attempts to explain our lives to ourselves: why this happened, why we feel this way, why we're having this problem. The drama is in us, not the mountain range to the west of here. I think landscape is inert, and that we attribute to it qualities, strengths that we say affect our lives. If the explanations persuade us and others, then the relationship to landscape which we've advanced becomes true. (109)

Ford does not deny the significance of region but is quick to point out that its attributes, or "truths," say more about the community that voices them, and the forms necessitated by that voicing, than about the landscape itself. Regionalism is thus important in defining a community, but only as it allows us to regard, in the form of its signifiers and myths, the way a community embodies its sense of itself by projecting its "dramas" onto the landscape, in attributing to the landscape those metaphors whose persuasive force links community.

The opening paragraph of *Wildlife* addresses the negotiations involved in regional affiliation: "This was in Great Falls, Montana, at the time of the Gypsy Basin oil boom, and my father had brought us there in the spring that year from Lewiston, Idaho, in the belief that people—small people like him—were making money in Montana or soon would be, and he wanted a piece of that good luck before all of it collapsed and was gone in the wind" (1). This quote suggests that—like Ford's representation of the South, at least according to the criticism of Price and Hobson—Montana is essentially an economic prospect. Montana is a place where "small people" have managed to derive financial gain. It is a place, at best, defined by provisionality (i.e., by "luck"). However, the relationship to landscape changes immediately, as the fires burning in the hills to the west of Great Falls cause Joe to reflect: "Such a fire could not help changing things, and there was a feeling in Great Falls, some attitude in general, that was like discouragement. There were stories in the paper, wild stories. Indians were said to have set fires to get the jobs putting them out" (6). Though the fire is too far from Great Falls to affect the townspeople, its "reading" suggests that, far from the fire "changing things," it is rather the townspeople who change their views on a landscape beset by "too much bad luck falling one way" (6). The reappearance of fire—though it is not a threat—provides for "wild stories" that expose *other* regional concerns, for instance racial anxieties, here represented in the rumors of "Indian" arsonists. In other cases, the "wild stories" reveal a fear of lawlessness and vandalism or poachers (6). The fire is thus a metaphor for anxiety over social disorder, on the lapse of a discourse that all abide by, or on the fact that the discourse is not adequate to reality. At the same time, these "wild stories" indicate just who does and doesn't—which "small people" do and don't—profit from the "good luck" of Montana. The fire reveals the biases and assumptions that force their way to the surface in the form of a variable "reading" of landscape. This is not to deny that fire is burning in the mountains of Montana, but to show that the fire is never merely an annual aspect of region, but that its occurrence is inscribed with regional stories that have little to do with the fire itself. The drama is never in the landscape, but always in "us."

With regard to the stories of regionalism, Jeffrey J. Folks's essay, "Richard Ford: Postmodern Cowboys," argues—as elsewhere Price (260) and Ford do ("Percy" 562)—that environment is an "economic" rather than geographic "force" (214), and that Montana, in particular, is a place of "deterritorialization." By this, Folks means a place stripped of natural resources and "abandoned" (214), where characters are unable to reterritorialize themselves through "amassing of local myths, legends and folktales," instead turning to possibilities offered by "exploring the gaps and incongruities of language" (216). The characters are cut off from any definitive discourse of region. Folks's critique is important because it zeroes in on exactly what Joe comes to appreciate in *Wildlife*: that "territory" is both created and effaced via language, that territory turns oppressive not so much because of what threatens it—such as the wildfire—but because of what a community *thinks* threatens it: namely the "wild stories" that turn upon a metaphoric treatment of geography. As Folks suggests, Joe's survival depends not on an "amassing" of regional myths (Indians, lawlessness, vandals, poachers), but on recognizing those places in the discourse that are incongruous, paradoxical, open to appropriation. By seeing regionalism in terms of "persuasion," Joe can opt *not to be persuaded*, or to be persuaded by *something else*, and thereby come to a more flexible vision of his place, which enables him to better survive an existence that is, at best *and* worst, an unfathomable "mystery."

STARTING THE FIRE IN THE ACT OF PUTTING IT OUT

To borrow a title from Maurice Blanchot—while alluding to the brush fires of Montana—Joe comes to view the articulation of region as a "work of fire":

> I watched a tall spruce tree catch fire high in the dark. A spark had found it, and it exploded in a bright, steepling yellow flame that leaped and shot out bits of fire into the night toward other trees, and swirled its own white smoke, flaming and then dying quickly as the wind on the hillside—a wind that did not blow where we were—changed and died. It all happened in an instant, and I knew it was dangerous though in a beautiful way. And I understood, just as I sat there in the car with my mother, what I thought dangerous was: it was a thing that did not seem able to hurt you, but quickly and deceivingly would. (50)

Here, Ford explicitly renders the process whereby metaphor displaces landscape. Significantly, he couples this transformation with an aesthetic response: Joe finds the sight of the fire "beautiful," that is, he attributes to it a measure of aesthetic attainment, and, from that, aestheticizes the landscape itself, turning the fire into a metaphor for "danger," for the hidden forces of life that can, in an instant, and under the cover of deception, "hurt you." He infuses the appearance of the fire with not only personal implication but also artistic worth. The transition is seamless in that the landscape of Montana, at the start of the story, is already a metaphor, already seen as a place of "good luck" and economic prospects even before the family has moved there. The novel suggests that region is indeed the sum of our "predicaments," of our interior dramas, and that the rightness of our reading of landscape is always accompanied by an act of persuasion, of putting the matter into a language that will affect and effect community. This act of communication is necessarily aesthetic for the purposes of appeal.

In his essay "Literature and the Right to Death" Blanchot regards language as the inevitable consequence of consciousness, since the process of knowing insists on the transference of the thing *perceived* into the thing *known*, a movement of the object of perception into the awareness of consciousness, taking residence there, as only it can, in the form of a sign (323). What consciousness arrives at in its movement toward knowing is not the thing itself but rather the thing as *a place in consciousness*: as a symbol or word. In his way, Blanchot—like Ford—argues that language forms on the basis of a passion to know, an inexplicable need, or, as Blanchot puts it, a meaning "man" "*ha[s] to create*." There is no escaping the transference of perception into meaning, and knowledge is a play of signs. When we come to landscape then, we are "always already" situated in the midst of this "play," which is essentially an aesthetic enterprise, the arrangement of symbols into the most compelling configuration. Joe's father, in using the word "arbitrary," provides a determinate sign for a condition that is anything but determinate. Similarly, Joe's aestheticized reading of the fire, above, conflates the work of consciousness with the work of fire: leveling what it labors toward through the very means by which it labors. For Joe, and for his community, the fire is never the thing in itself, but always an appealing knowledge.

However, Ford's text is not only marked by the appeal of language but also by the terror of its autonomy, by which I mean its independence from the signified: "I didn't want to be the last one to talk. Because if I spoke anything at all, my mother would stay quiet as if she hadn't heard me, and I would have my own words—whatever they were—to live with, maybe forever. And there are words, significant words, you do not want to say, words that account for busted-up lives, words that try to fix something ruined that shouldn't be ruined, and that words can't fix anyway" (115–16). Articulation here confronts Joe with "forever." The final word, the "last one" spoken, is fearsome for Joe because he realizes that the quiet of the world means that his words are impressed on rather than arising from it. The "forever" implies a distance and isolation of indefinite duration from the real. Language is not able to "fix" the real, since it is not spoken by the real but by us. Here, I am using "fix" not only in the contextual sense of "repair," but also in the sense of identification, as in "getting a fix on" someone or something. Words do, finally, arise from scenes of "bust-up," but because they are not homologous to such scenes, they are powerless to "fix" them. Thus, to lack a "fix" is to be unable to "fix." However, Ford draws our attention to the fact that words are significant despite their incapacity to eventuate the repair Joe desires. He indicates that language is enabling and comforting not in its attachment to the real but insofar as it evokes a response, in this case from Joe's mother. Language use—if it is not to be accompanied by the twin terrors of its inadequacy to, and isolation within, the real—demands a social context. Ford at once addresses Blanchot's poststructuralism and indicates that significance, and signification, are "adequate" not because they instantiate the real but rather because they instantiate a social relation.

This view of language and significance puts Ford's work at odds with regionalist authors and critics who would think of Montana in materialist terms. Ford is well aware that his "universalism" militates against his categorization as a regionalist author. Nonetheless, *Wildlife* argues that the recognition of regionalism as a discursive rather than materialist practice is key to enabling not only survival but also success. My reading of Ford via Blanchot is therefore not much different from the "existential" reading of Elinor Ann Walker in *Perspectives on Richard Ford*, who regards *Wildlife* as a meditation on Joe's recognition—again occasioned by the wildfires in the hills—of the failure of language in capturing the real (130). Walker articulates the problem for critics wanting to read Ford as a regionalist: "Significantly, Ford and his narrators do not call attention to moments in their stories that might be named metaphorical or symbolic, as if to suggest that meaning must be derived from language, not dictated by it" (138). In other words, Ford does not produce the symbolic associations that make regionalism possible, since the text everywhere reminds us that meaning does not arise via language—it does not mediate or dictate the region—but is "derived" from language itself, from the life of words rather than from what those words stand for. The meanings arrived at are generated as a result of the process of language, from the action of words themselves.

In Ford, the words that describe our predicaments are less metaphors of region than metaphors of metaphors, language "derived from language":

> "The Lady said people want to swim in Montana. Why do you think that is? These things always signify a meaning."
>
> "What does it mean?" I said, holding my school books.
>
> She hugged her arms and turned herself a little back and forth as she stood in the window frame watching out. "Oh, that we're all going to be washed away in a big flood. Though I don't believe that. So. Some of us will not be washed away and will float to the top. That's better, isn't it?" She took a drink of coffee.
>
> "It should have a happy ending for the right people," I said.
>
> "That's easy," she said. "Everyone doesn't do it that way, though." (22)

Jeanette, Joe's mother, tackles the inevitability of meaning evident throughout the novel. In saying that things "always signify a meaning," Jeanette suggests, like Blanchot, that perception always ends in meaning, objects in signs. In this way, Ford's "literature," or literary language, witnesses "the meaning of the meaninglessness embedded in the word as expression of the obscurity of existence" (Blanchot 329). Here, literary language reflects upon signification itself, so that signification, rather than the thing signified, appears in the name. This is only a high-theoretical way of pointing out what Jeanette says: that signification, because it "always" takes place, because we always transfer "obscurity" into some register of sense, takes place in spite of the "obscurity" it signifies. The many readings Jeanette gives the "obscure" statement by "the Lady" on Montana is less relevant for what people may or may not do in Montana than for the many different "senses" we "derive from language." In effect, and as occurs elsewhere in *Wildlife*, Ford illuminates the derivation of signification *from* signification, the way we create further meaning out of what is already meaning, further language out of language. In doing so, we perceive that language itself is a concrete object that is infinitely interpretable, no less than the "obscurity" Blanchot sees as the occasion of literature. Jeanette's contention, that "everyone doesn't do it that way," nails home the point that meaning arises not from the object of meaning but from a social tendency toward that object, the way particular groups of people "do" things. Thus, language itself becomes an object of "obscurity." The phrase "people want to swim in Montana" inaugurates a proliferation of signification, language piling atop language, until the meaning becomes a play of shifting interpretations, and language is revealed as one meaning standing in for something that was already a "standing-in": metaphor of metaphor. The symbolic is inevitable.

In *Wildlife*, meaning resides not on the other side of language—to *be mediated by language*—but in the movement that is language. Meaning is already there, prior to any foray into the world. We arrive only at meaning when our real desire is to arrive at the world, and language becomes an activity in itself, consoling not for what it obtains but for its ability to double back on itself, endlessly, in its seeking to obtain: to illuminate itself as seeking. We never get what is symbolized, only symbolizing itself. Regionalism is an endless ("forever") discursive activity.

PARTING THE SMOKE CURTAIN ONTO A CURTAIN OF SMOKE

This endless recurrence, this continual fall into signification, is the central issue Joe grapples with. *Wildlife* examines the progress from need to articulation to the insufficiency of any final articulation, locating the "consolation" of language in its activity rather than its arrival at the definitive. For language to be consoling it must never stop arriving, must never fall into the mistake of equating its fixity, its totality, with the world, since the world is always only "approached" rather than "fixed." Throughout the novel, Ford addresses what happens when desire fixes on and consumes a point of reference, and the careful vigilance required to negotiate a world that continually becomes obscured under the symbols of the constant "need" for meaning that is consciousness: "Though out ahead of us, beyond the town of Augusta where the mountains commenced, smoke rose like a screen that drifted northward up the front to Canada, thick and white at the bottom but thinner and drifting above, so that as . . . the peaks became hidden by smoke, it came to seem that there were no mountains, and where the dense smoke began the plains and even the world itself came to an end" (45).

For Joe there is nothing beyond the fire, which presents both the formation of symbol and the failure of mediation that is symbolic formation. The fire is at once what Joe sees and what prevents him from seeing. As such it serves as both a metaphor—a representation—and the denial of metaphor—the impossibility of representing. The fire makes it possible to think of the landscape, and the very thing that makes the landscape unthinkable. The smoke, finally, turns into a "screen" on which Joe projects meaning. In this sense the fire, and the smoke it creates, is itself the "world . . . [come] to an end." There is no world, in other words, beyond that of the symbol.

This is not, however, to deny reality, since the fire does burn Montana, as well as occupying Joe's father, who finds work as a firefighter, suggesting the role of the patriarch in countering the instability of language by offering a definitive point of authority. Rather, it is to suggest that by the time we make contact with the real, by the time we become conscious of it, it has already become symbol, has, as it were, taken residence in our consciousness as idea-concept rather than actuality, its irreproducible specificity. Joe thus becomes aware that his projections proceed from himself rather than coming at him from what sits beyond that screen. The world beyond *does* exist, but it is forever hidden by the process of its perception by the mind. In *Wildlife*, Montana becomes a term for Joe's one-sided negotiations with his environment, the place he seeks to secure for himself in the midst of insecurity, and which functions in illustrating how we accommodate to the world as language, or how we accommodate to language itself.

And language, for Ford, is very much a communal prospect, which is where the significance of regionalism truly emerges, since regionalism, rather than being an essential relation between people and geography, is the record of a relationship between persons in a particular geospatial locale. This relationship is most clearly delineated in the middle of the novel, when Joe and Jeanette travel to the mountains to get near the fires. In contrast to his father's job, Joe comes to appreciate the "goodness" of the destruction caused by the fire and the futility of attempting to stop it:

> Our food came and we ate it and talked about forest fires, that they were like cities or factories, and went on and on and on by themselves. That there was something good about them, that they replenished where they burned, and that for humans, my mother said, it was sometimes a good thing to be near a thing so uncontrollable and out of all scale that you felt reduced and knew your position in the world. . . . That was nature's way . . . she said. People were drawn to things they shouldn't be. I thought she seemed happy to be there with me and to see the fire, happy to have said all the things we'd said. (53–54)

Here, the straight symbolic reading of the fire by Jeanette affirms the existence of an external reality at the same time as it affirms the way in which we "read" that external reality and thereby obscure it. In this case the fire signifies the lesson Jeanette wishes Joe to take from the disruptions in their family life. She uses the fire to suggest to Joe that the temporary separation of his father and mother is not to be blown out of proportion; it should be seen as a very small event in no way imbued with the significance Joe places on it. The fire becomes a yardstick by which the boy should measure a definitely *social* concern. Joe's sense of his own insignificance is important because it liberates him from the threat of solipsism: defining the world in terms of his own fixations. Rather than projecting his problems onto a landscape he has no power over, that he is "reduced" in the face of, Joe realizes how he has conceived his place in the world, and has conceived the world itself, via the social relations among his mother, father, and the larger community. The sense of his insignificance makes Joe aware of where power and agency reside: not in the fact that our concepts are equal to the real, but that our concepts, and the language in which we articulate them, are subject to alteration precisely because they are *not sufficient or affixed to the real.* In this passage, affirmation arises not because language succeeds at capturing the real but because in saying "all the things [they'd] said," the two characters draw together, alleviating their isolation and powerlessness through the consensual gesture of dialogue. Language is itself the possibility of community in the face of a threatening, inexplicable "region."

In addition to this, Jeanette's speech, in speaking of the "replenishing" work of fire, suggests something similar to Blanchot. If, as I'm arguing, fire becomes a metaphor for the inevitability of metaphor, then it is, as Jeanette suggests, "replenishing," since it suggests that an outmoded metaphoric structure—such as the one plaguing Joe, that is, the family as a structure signifying security and temporal continuance—can, by the way language reveals its always metaphoric nature, the way it signifies itself rather than the world, open itself up to being used *differently*, to enabling new, more affirming metaphoric structures. Jeanette's "eloquence"—in the words Elizabeth Hardwick uses to describe Ford's writing—provides "a sort of balance for the unstable inner and natural landscape" (161). Recognizing the failure of language to attain the thing it seeks—reality—can service a more flexible language use, which in turn allows recrafting of social relations along different lines of meaning. Language is *our* "position," and if it is malleable and changeable, if it is not anchored to externals, if it can be made to signify otherwise, then our "positions" need not be viewed in terms of insufficiency (the inability of language to render the real), but rather in terms of enabling (altering the lexicon to open up new modes of thought). Finally, the excerpt ends with Joe's observation that what constitutes "happiness" is not what *is* said, but to "have said," that is, to have been given a chance to convey meaning to a receptive audience, which engages that meaning. If language has any power it is in the process of conveyance and reception, which is only possible if there is a consensus on the language used—returning us to the notion that the language of a given people in a given place, of a regional community, has efficacy insofar as it is, as Ford says, "persuasive," appealing, aesthetically or otherwise.

The shifting relations embodied by language use are therefore an inversion of Hardwick's observation that "shifts in direction, improvisations, sleepwalking into calamitous consequences seem to be in the fiction part of the effect the Western states have upon the mind" (161). Hardwick argues that the "Western states" have an "effect upon the mind," suggesting that the "place" of western states in Ford's fiction is deterministic. They cause a "mental effect." This seems at odds with Hardwick's later suggestion that the relationship between character and landscape in *Wildlife* is one of "compromise" (162). My contention is that the compromise evinced by the novel is not so much a denial of that landscape but a reading and defining of it as a social relation. The reading of the western states in terms of "shifts of direction" and "improvisations" is a result not of a landscape that is "shifty" or necessarily any more demanding of "improvisation" than any other, but because that landscape has been the setting for social migrations that demanded, a priori, an ability to improvise, shift easily, and compromise. As Hardwick suggests, this view of Montana is derived from the history of Montana's settlement: "The characters are still pulling the wagon across the frontier, looking for a place to settle" (161). The landscape is always in place; it is the people who are on the move and unable to "settle." The landscape has been, and continues to be, read in terms of human movement rather than geographic presence: frontier and resettlement. In this sense, regionalism is indeed, as Hardwick says, "predatory" (162), since, to pun on the word, it "predates" the place settled into—migrating *from* somewhere; the "frontier" being defined in relation to places and life back East—as well as sustaining itself, as it were, in spite of locale.

Simply put, how one accommodates to region has much to do with the geographic characteristics, but the meanings and associations governing that accommodation depend on where one has come from, what one has expected to find, and the possibilities of accommodation afforded by the society in which one chooses from among them. As Ford says in conversation with Bruce Weber, "What I do is imagine a place and call it a name" (64). Place is—to invert Hardwick's order of presentation—an expression of need based on the "imagination" of a place, an expression of the demand to "shift" and "improvise" and to move uncertainly into "calamitous consequences," precisely the defining points of the family life that govern relations, including relations to locale, in *Wildlife*. The reading of Montana as the situation of people in a given place is therefore Ford's expression of regionalism, not according to a geospatial myth but according to a determining set of social concerns. We never pierce the smoke of the fire, but the beliefs projected on it tell an important story.

THE CONSOLING SOUND OF TIME

The notion of language as consolation is never distant in Ford's work. Ford himself openly states that language is as important in itself as for what it might mean:

> But I think language is consoling in other ways, is always able to give us pleasure by its sonorities, its poetical qualities, by simply the way it pleasures our ears, and so far as it comes from another, sweetens our view of that other, sweetens our view of the world, a world that can give us literature, that can give us the telling of stories. I think the telling of stories is in and of itself a way of persuading the reader away from whatever is plaguing her or him, and of asking the reader to believe that another and more felicitous order can be put on experience, and that this order has a structure that is, in an almost abstract way, pleasurable, and beautiful to behold. ("Conversation" 152)

Ford has never advocated "nonsense," by which I do not mean bad logic or incorrect thinking but rather sound that conveys itself rather than "sense" or meaning. Yet, here he comes close to advocating a view of language based entirely on a visceral, intuitive, and nonrational response. This comment approaches Blanchot's notion of literary language turning back on itself in attempting to grasp its essence, and for that one instant appreciating or viewing sound not as representing something else but in itself. For Ford, sound is important because it is the form that need takes and thus allows us to pinpoint—though not define—the other as a being of need. Moreover, Ford views the "telling of stories," narrative, as a means of restructuring "whatever is plaguing" us, of creating a different order and structure that enable greater pleasure.

Wildlife, then, enacts regionalism on the level of sound and "pleasurable" structure, while undercutting any sense that these structures are more than aesthetic configurations or "felicitous" forms "put on experience." As Ford suggests to Bonnie Lyons: "When I've written about Montana some people . . . have said to me, 'God, you really got it right.' And my answer always is, 'Well thanks, but I never tried to get it right, if by right you mean that I got it the way Montana is on earth.' I mostly just want to make it interesting on the page and to ignite the reader's imagination" (63). Ford advocates the "beautiful" in shifting cognitive and aesthetic forms not because he believes in a belated "art for art's sake," but because this is, quite simply, how one survives in the world, how one manages expectation and the world's failure to accord with it. We use language to make experience bearable, to explain and comprehend experience in "felicitous" ways. Imagination is key to Ford's process because it is through imagination that one arrives at new configurations, new stories, in which to better embody experience.

Regionalism becomes one of the many "inventions" whereby a community secures not only survival but also self-worth. When asked about characters accommodating themselves to the unforeseen, Ford responds: "That you can believe in the efficacy of things you can't predict or see the evidence of, in the faith that if you invent them they will cause you to survive, literally survive. And maybe more: survive with dignity, survive with pleasure, survive with a sense of life's being worthwhile" ("Conversation" 615). Ford's writing—and its focus on language and the artifice of storytelling—is about much more than survival. It is a metaphysical preoccupation, though one that posits metaphysics not in a spiritual "beyond," but in the here and now, in the present, in the ways in which belief can serve the moment. As discussed earlier, in the excerpt involving the anecdote on swimming, "belief" in Ford is always provisional, subject to present demand. If Jeanette does not want to believe in any one given meaning of the "Lady's" anecdote, it is because withholding her belief—and, by extension, granting it—permits her a greater variety of means of processing experience. The shifting, or play, of belief belies a response to, and a means of surviving, the contingencies of the world.

As Folks says, Ford's writing on Montana is about "the control of consciousness through the processing of cultural images and linguistic authority" (213). But rather than simply abandoning hope to the deterministic matrices impinging on the characters, Ford's writing reveals the ways in which they, through linguistic manipulations and a certain disposition toward the authority embodied in language, assume some control over their situations and realize a limited agency. Because language is not "given" by the world but imposed upon it, any given situation is open to a variety of linguistic embodiments, and thus meanings.

In *Wildlife*, Joe ponders two structures for ordering experience, which leave him poised between accepting his own agency and relinquishing it:

> I wondered if there was some pattern or an order to things in your life—not one you knew but that worked on you and made events when they happened seem correct, or made you confident about them or willing to accept them even if they seemed like wrong things. Or was everything just happening all the time, in a whirl without anything to stop it or cause it—the way we think of ants, or molecules under the microscope, or the way others would think of us, not knowing our difficulties, watching us from another planet? (96)

Here, the wonder that occupies Joe arises not from coming down on either side of the binary—choosing between "pattern" and "happening all the time"—but rather from a position in between, of not knowing which side is correct and choosing to occupy the interstice. The external "order" Joe speaks of is theological, existing beyond individual agency, and working "on you" rather than being susceptible to human activity. By contrast, the idea that the universe might be a "whirl" of events without cause, a "happening all the time," is equally inscrutable. Joe's two choices are the same: in either case a universe in which individual agency cannot influence or understand occurrence. What Joe comes to appreciate is the unknowability of circumstance, or, in the words of Michael Trussler, the fact that "temporality [is] a force which disperses whatever frail sense of meaning [Joe] can create" (39). Trussler investigates the "reductive limitations" (38) by which we create narrative out of the "random nature of events" (39).

What Ford underlines are the various choices we make in the process of putting a "felicitous order" on experience, and the above excerpt indicates Joe's growing awareness of—and reluctance to endorse—the limitations that proceed from choice, from "shaping time" (Trussler 38) according to the personal and social perspectives that dominate his life. He refuses either of the two options available to him, knowing that a story will emerge, but that it will only be one of the many possible stories, and whether he regards this story in terms of theology or existentialist absurdity will depend entirely on his needs of the moment. In a sense, then, Joe realizes his detachment from the regions in which he has hitherto located himself, recognizes, in the words of *Independence Day*, that "we . . . are anchored only to contingency" (439)—to the needs that we articulate in various terms, which in turn inform how we think of those needs.

Keeping with Trussler's recognition of Ford's concern with the means whereby we enable survival, *Wildlife* critiques how our expectations influence the diachronic narratives through which we regulate and manage the synchronic occurrences of time. Having traced the temporary dissolution of the Brinson family—the disappearance of Joe's father, Jerry, into the forest fires; Jeanette's liaison with Warren Miller—the novel does not end where we think it would: on the permanent separation of Jerry and Jeanette, and Joe's subsequent isolation. Instead, the novel includes a coda in which the two parents are ultimately reconciled and continue "being together, much as they had done before" (176). Ford indicates that Joe's story—the story of *Wildlife*—is, as Jerry says, not "important forever" (171), by which Ford underscores the articulation of *all* narrative on the basis of needs that change over time. The story of the marital breakup, and Joe's experience of it, is only one possible version of events from a particular vantage (his own). The coda hints at possibilities, at factors beyond Joe's perception, for his parents' difficulties and reconciliation. There are other story patterns, other sequences of cause and effect, that may have construed the tale differently: "And then at the end of March, in 1961, just as it was beginning to be spring, my mother came back from wherever she had been" (176). The abruptness of Jeanette's return underscores for the reader just how little Joe knows about his parents' difficulties and the reasons behind their actions. As he says in speaking of the "something" that eventuates their reunion: "I do not know exactly what that something was" (176). In other words, *Wildlife* returns us to the notion of storytelling as a contingent exercise, based on the needs of the moment, but which, given our changing needs, can always be articulated "differently." In the end, there is, as Joe tells us, so much that we "cannot fully claim to understand" (177). For our good, and the good of others, the novel suggests, it's best to remember this.

Wildlife is a novel about "claims," both those we make on each other and those we make on the land itself. In it, region emerges as an enactment of a local imaginary, and regionalism as the name given to the dramas articulated by specific communities in a specific locale. While this is hardly original, Ford is original in contending that region and regionalism are not fixed categories or determining facets of habitation; rather, they are temporary and provisional and, most importantly, social in character and thus susceptible to manipulation. In this way, regionalism becomes another possible consolation in a world always outside the frameworks—narrative and epistemological and cultural—that we bring to bear upon it.

NOTE

1. Reprinted, in somewhat altered form, as "*The Sportswriter*: Post-Faulkner, Post-Southern?" in *Perspectives on Richard Ford*. Ed. Huey Guagliardo. 83–96. Jackson: University Press of Mississippi, 2000.

WORKS CITED

Blanchot, Maurice. "Literature and the Right to Death." *The Work of Fire*. Trans. Charlotte Mandell. Stanford CA: Stanford University Press, 1995. 300–344.

Folks, Jeffrey J. "Richard Ford: Postmodern Cowboys." *Southern Writers at Century's End*. Ed. Jeffrey J. Folks and James A. Perkins. Lexington KY: University Press of Kentucky, 1997. 212–25.

Ford, Richard. *Independence Day*. New York: Vintage, 1995.

———. "Walker Percy: Not Just Whistling Dixie." *National Review* 29 (13 May 1977): 558–64.

———. *Wildlife*. New York: Atlantic Monthly, 1990.

Funk, Robert N. "The Tissue of Everyone's Loneliness: Expectation, Reality, and Alienation in *The Ultimate Good Luck*." *Perspectives on Richard Ford*. Ed. Huey Guagliardo. Jackson: University Press of Mississippi, 2000. 53–69.

Guagliardo, Huey. "A Conversation with Richard Ford." *Conversations with Richard Ford*. Ed. Huey Guagliardo. Jackson: University Press of Mississippi, 2001. 147–64.

———. "Introduction." *Perspectives on Richard Ford*. Ed. Huey Guagliardo. Jackson: University Press of Mississippi, 2000. xi–xvii.

———. "Marginal People in the Novels of Richard Ford." *Perspectives on Richard Ford*. Ed. Huey Guagliardo. Jackson: University Press of Mississippi, 2000. 3–32.

Hardwick, Elizabeth. *Sight Readings: American Fictions*. New York: Random House, 1998.

Hobson, Fred. *The Southern Writer in the Postmodern World*. Athens: University of Georgia Press, 1991.

Lyons, Bonnie. "Richard Ford: The Art of Fiction CXLVII." *Paris Review* 140 (1996): 42–77.

Morris, Gregory L. Interview with Richard Ford. "Richard Ford." *Talking Up a Storm: Voices of the New West*. Ed. Gregory J. Morris. Lincoln: University of Nebraska Press, 1994. 102–19.

Price, Joanna. "Richard Ford: The Postmodern Exile and the Vanishing South." *The World Is Our Home: Society and Culture in Contemporary Southern Writing*. Ed. Jeffrey J. Folks and Nancy Summers Folks. Lexington KY: University Press of Kentucky, 2000. 259–72.

Trussler, Michael. "'Famous Times': Historicity in the Short Fiction of Richard Ford and Raymond Carver." *Wascana Review* 28, 2 (1994): 35–53.

Walker, Elinor Ann. "Redeeming Loneliness in Richard Ford's 'Great Falls' and *Wildlife*." *Perspectives on Richard Ford*. Ed. Huey Guagliardo. Jackson: University Press of Mississippi, 2000. 121–39.

Weber, Bruce. "Richard Ford's Uncommon Characters." *The New York Times Magazine* 10 (April 1988): 50–51, 59–65.

CHAPTER TWO
All My Stories Are Here: Four Montana Poets

ROGER DUNSMORE

Considering the written work of four Montana poets, Mark Gibbons, Vic Charlo, Ed Lahey, and David Thomas, it is apparent that that hackneyed, overused phrase, "a sense of place," still does have power and reality here in Montana. For these four poets, all of whom have been here for at least three generations (probably a thousand generations in Charlo's case), their deepest identity is not separate from the life of this place, all the way back to the geologic, tectonic collisions that formed the "Backbone of the World," as the Blackfeet prefer to call the Continental Divide. Hence, some comments about poetry, identity, and place, in order to frame a context from which to examine their work.

John Haines, the Alaskan poet now living in Missoula, has written often and intensely about the necessity for a literature that is worthy of those places we can honestly come to call our homelands. How might we become genuinely native to our home places is a central question implicit in his work and in the work of many other writers from or about the American West. In his 1981 book, *Living Off the Country*, Haines asked, "How long might it take a people living here to be at home in their landscape, and to produce from that experience things that could be recognized anywhere as literature of the first rank? Several hundred years? A few generations? . . . Closeness is needed, long residence, intimacy of a sort that demands a certain daring and risk: a surrender, an abandonment, or just a sense of somehow being stuck with it. Whatever it is that is needed, it can't be merely willed" (15). Perhaps the Inuit girl speaking of her life on the Arctic coast reveals much of what has happened to diminish our life with places: "She said one day about the snowmobile: 'It gets you from here to anywhere in a few seconds. There's no space left; you just get inside, and the machine goes, and you sit and watch the land go by, and there's nothing left between you and any place" (Fables 183).

What's apparent from this quote is that human wholeness and sanity have historically required that there be something essential between the "you and any place" where we would live well. And the name of this something essential is "home."

Mark Gibbons, in his poem "In the Blood," gives the details, physically, emotionally, even spiritually, of undiminished life here in this place, Montana, the western slope of the divide:

> . . . Have these shadowed blue
> mountains put a spell on me?
> . . . .
> Somehow this ground inhabits me.
> For no reason, I refuse to leave
> like the Ponderosa snapped off at its trunk.
> No wind, no storm can drive me away
> from this place I call my journey.
> . . . .
> All my stories are here. Why do I think
> if I left, I would leave them behind,
> as if I could lose dirt & memory like luggage.
> When I'm alone I hear voices whisper.
> I'm afraid of losing my grip.
> The ospreys have returned to their nest.
> Even they would move on if the river ran dry.
> Have I become the blood of the deer?
> Tied to a rhythm I cannot name?
> Stay, stay the course, the buck whispers,
>
> We are waiting in the river,
> your father and me. We are
> shimmering in the aspen leaves.
> Listen to our voices, the water and the wind.
> Close your eyes and you will see.
> (*Connemara* 42)

This poem serves as a credo for the way a place, a landscape, may come to reside within a person, a family, or a community. Something unnamable has come into the poet, something from the blood of parents and grandparents, something from the blood of deer that he has killed, carried out of the mountains, eaten, something from the blood of these "shadowed blue mountains." "All my stories are here." These stories are the generations of connective tissue to this place. In all this imagery of blood and family and mountain death and life he expresses the way connection to place can cast a spell, beyond rationality, yet nurturing. And that spell involves those things as basic as killing for food, pouring his father's ashes into this ground, carrying the place-stories in his blood, his blood not flowing separately from the mountains—mountain blood, it has been called. Here we are in the presence of a place intimacy that "demands a certain daring and risk: a surrender, an abandonment," to return to Haines's words. Here there is no snowmobile equivalent devouring everything between "you" and the place.

Work, how one gains one's living, mountain blood, colonization, anger, and awe—these are the major stories in Gibbons's poetry of this place. Of course it isn't all about the gritty life of shanty Irish immigrants and growing up along the tracks. There is his wonderfully funny poem of early eroticism, "Swinging for the Fences." And that tremendous reach into the darkness of the suicide of the French-Irish, Modoc writer Michael Dorris in "Suicide Note." There is the honesty of confessed lust for another woman in the midst of the warmth of a strong marriage in "Smothered in Ash," and the great poem at the birth of his son, "A Letter to My First Born Son," among others. There is the astonishingly deep affection for his sister, suffering from Parkinson's disease but giving him music as basic as clean water, in "Music My Sister Gave Me." And there is the gallows humor and love of "Pissed at Potter's Funeral," or the love/hate relationship to a brother expressed through the death of their dog in "Still Waters." I breathe a little easier knowing that Mark Gibbons is there, writing his great-hearted poems into the face of those trophy homes and hot pools from heaven that smear the Montana landscape.

As a result of the family history of mining, his own years spent in the mines, and his first book, *The Blind Horses*, which won the first-ever Montana Arts Council First Book Award in 1979, Ed Lahey's poems have been closely associated with Butte and with mining. But his poems go well beyond narrating the dark and light of the miner's world. They skillfully use that world to speak about the life any of us might struggle with. He makes explicit that a poem he wrote to honor his miner father is also a poet's statement about the difficulties and values necessary to carry on the work of writing.

GIMP O'LEARY'S IRON WORKS
(for Big Ed)
You hear a lot of lies about O'Leary
but he could seal a crack in steel
no matter what the size.
His arc welder would strike
white fire and a bead
of blue-black rod would slide
along between cherry streaks,
and acrid smoke would curl away
to leave clean married steel,
not too frail, or buttered up
but straight and strong,
hard as mill forged rail.
. . . .
Often others would say to him,
"Damn good job," or some such thing.
If it was, he'd grin, and look again,
as if he thought the natural light
would show a flaw, or bridge
that didn't fuse—convinced, I guess,
that in his struggle with the steel
he could seldom really win.
He knew perfection could
conceal the wound
beneath the arc of his art.
I liked him for that.
(*Horses* 29)

The greatness of this poem lies in its fusion of creative and utilitarian work, in Lahey's affection and respect for the unassuming artistry of O'Leary, in their shared knowledge of the way "perfection could conceal the wound," not only "beneath the arc of his art" but also in his heart. And in the attitude toward what one might accomplish, knowing the tricks one plays on oneself in order to maintain the illusion of wholeness or competence, knowing that men's lives depend on the soundness of the weld, knowing men's lives depend on the soundness of the poet's word-welds as well. The metaphor for poetry contained in the poem never violates, abandons, or sacrifices the sheer reality of O'Leary in his work.

But it has been a mistake to see Lahey's work primarily in terms of Butte and his mining poems, fine as they are. Especially in his later work, Lahey expresses an emotional capacity—in poems about his grandchildren, a meeting with his ex-wife, his dying mother, a cold pony in a field outside his apartment, a torn orange in the street, the chewing power of beavers—that expands beyond and balances the tough reality of the mining poems.

I have always considered poetry a form of sanity. Its sanity is the reality of something beyond dollar power. If one does not belong to the Church of Commerce, then one had better have something besides drugs, alcohol, sex, Jesus, patriotism, or work to hang onto. I believe Lahey's struggle with what has come to be called mental illness has something essential to do with the risk and necessity out of which his poetry is written. It is part of the price he has paid in the process of earning his poetry, part of the price of creating a poetry that is as real Montana as the mines, the magpies, or the Salish. And it is part of our sanity. One thinks of Leslie Fiedler's (an important mentor for Lahey) comments on "the western" and the West in his essay "The Higher Sentimentality":

> [I]t seems clear that in it [*One Flew Over the Cuckoo's Nest*] for the first time the New West was clearly defined: the West of Here and Now, rather than There and Then—the West of Madness. . . . It is only a step from thinking of the West as madness to regarding madness as the true West. . . . But only in Leonard Cohen . . . and in Kesey is the final identification made, and in Kesey at last combined with the archetype of the love that binds the lonely white man to his Indian comrade—to his mad Indian comrade, perhaps even to the madness of his Indian comrade. . . . If a myth of America is to exist in the future, it is incumbent on our writers, no matter how square and scared they may be in their deepest hearts, to conduct with the mad just such a dialogue as their predecessors learned long ago to conduct with the aboriginal dwellers in the Western Wilderness. (254–56)

Although I would dispute Fiedler's claim that our "predecessors" conducted an exemplary "dialogue" with the "aboriginal dwellers in the Western Wilderness," Lahey's poetry can be seen as just such a dialogue with the mad, as a piece of the truer sanity of such "madness." His poem, "Birds of a Feather," for his ex-wife Marylor, whom he has run into by chance in the new Safeway with their infant granddaughter, contains his desire to tell her he loves her more than he hates her, which is blocked by his emotional attachment to the sparrow flying above them in the store, which evokes this pure image of honest, broken-down emotion:

. . . but all
I could think of was a bird
I once saw shredded
by an exhaust fan.

Feathers floating willy nilly.

She looked so fey
upon hearing my story, shyly,
so shyly, walking away,
pushing the stroller down
another aisle.

Leaving me again, again,
dead feathers gathering
about my feet. (135)

When I came back from my first teaching stint in China, in July 1991, Ed was up in the mental ward on Three North. Then, one day he just wasn't there. The nurses said he had been released and was living downtown on Pine Street. I was worried. I did not think he was ready to leave the hospital, did not know how he would manage with himself. But he surprised me. Ed brought himself back, through the work of finishing a novel. Now, as I write this piece, his novel, *The Thin Air Gang*, has found a publisher in Russell Chatham of Clark City Press.

Rereading once again the title poem from Lahey's first book, *The Blind Horses*, I am struck by the powerfully apt imagery for the working life of this place. It is all there—the blind groping underground after riches, the harnessed, overworked, blinded innocence of the horses, the green flames in which they are devoured, all the promise of that first Lexington in our first colonies come to this smoldering hole in the earth, the old miner lending his own dying dignity to it—Lahey has written a poetry worthy of all that.

Vic Charlo's poetry is testimony to the difficulties many native people, even "successful" ones, have living with two minds, one for navigating in the so-called dominant culture, and one for the continuance of traditional tribal culture. Victor is the great-great-grandson of Charlot, the holdout chief who was finally forced to lead the last Salish people out of their ancestral homeland in the beautiful Bitterroot Valley in western Montana in 1891. Vic expressed the ongoing pain of that removal in remarks made to the Twenty-second Annual Wilderness Lecture Series at the University of Montana in 2001, saying that "even though the Bitterroot is really a part of us, a lot of us never grew up there." He also spoke about removal from the language: "My name is Chetleh Skyeeme, that means Three Eagles . . . I hope. After all these Salish speakers . . . I'm not a Salish speaker. My folks, when they grew up, they experienced a lot of problems going to school, just knowing their native languages. . . . So when we were growing up, one of the things that they made sure was going to happen in our family was that nobody was going to learn the language. And isn't that too bad. . . . But that's the way it is. You make the best of it." And make the best of it he did, graduating as the salutatorian of Loyola High School in Missoula, and as cocaptain of the football team, going six years to a Jesuit seminary, then graduating from the University of Montana and becoming the principal of the Two Eagle River School up at the old Dixon Agency on the Flathead Reservation. But his poetry tells of the trickiness and difficulty of such living in two worlds. It contains a rhythm that is different, odd even, that does not lie on the ear the way most of the poetry I read does. I have to reach further than I normally would in order to hear it for and as itself. There is something fractured in these rhythms, something that inhabits a space in between the unrealized memory of the Salish his parents purposely chose not to teach him, and the English of the reservation and the white school, and the Latin of the Catholic Church and the Jesuit seminary where he spent those six years. It is just this space in between, this need to do well in the world that has come to them, while at the same time remembering, honoring, and continuing the older world of the ancestors and spirits here, that gives to his voice its fractured courage.

In a poem from his early experience of the white world and how every gain in it entailed a loss of something else, something from the world of his ancestors, Charlo makes clear this difficulty of living with "two minds."

> . . .
> Leaves are falling like they sing in song
> yet my song doesn't sing. This school strange
> and I need friends and places that have heart.
> I'm caught by priest and parent who want me here.
>
> I want to quit this football, this lie,
> and lonely wind should blow me from this tree.
> (from "Last Leave of Loyola," unpublished)

This poem expresses the loneliness of facing the lie of, what? His identity as a white person? The lie that nothing will be at stake or lost in taking up with white culture?

> I realize now if you
> sing Gregorian chant,
> you forget the stickgame songs.
> (from "St. Francis Xavier Novitiate, Sheridan, Oregon 1957," unpublished)

In his family, in other elders, in the lives of his children and his students, Charlo discovers and fosters a continuity between past and future that allows him to recover from this life lived in between the cultures. That recovery probably will not be total or complete in a person of his honesty and courage, but more and more the poems express an acceptance and an understanding, a net gain in the ability to live with the trickiness of being in between. In "Moving In (fast wind)," "I have new house that is half-assed put together, / half-assed moved into and half-assed lived in," he tells us:

> I'm trying to get my second wind . . .
> . . . coyote song
> and trail of grizzly at our front door are
> richer than all need since we touch ancestors living here
> and I must live perfect fantasy and find fast wind.

The old rhythms and cycles of life, the bear-ancestors at the front door are "richer than all need," even though the place is "half-assed." Even so, at times, the lessons and presence of a respected, beloved elder, the process of renewal of the old ways, ironically, deepens the sense of in-between existence:

> AGNES, 1979
> We hide tan here at Agency Creek
> and at Valley Creek. Hard work
> that lets your mind go as you wait
> for the rest of your life. Soft hide,
> so soft wind blows like cloth.
> Hair white with hide.
>
> She, Agnes, watches and lets us know in old
> Salish tongue. Word for scraper that I
> remember now. So hard. So to the point.

Why did I learn how to write? Why did I want to?
Is it worth the loss of your world going away?
(full poem, unpublished)

That last stanza is worth pondering. These questions coming amidst tanning hides at Agnes Vanderburg's camp up Valley Creek, "as you wait for the rest of your life." This waiting and wondering is what it means to be the great-great-grandson of the holdout chief, right here where we newcomers live now too. Part of what accentuates the whole in-between situation for Victor is his role as the son and grandson, the great-grandson, of chiefs. Being in a position of leadership during a time of rapid, confusing, forced change has to be radically unsettling. What does it mean to be a leader of the Bitterroot Salish people in western Montana today? Vic turns to his father in poems that honor his capacities as a gambler and that suggest the gambling skill itself as a metaphor for the luck, risk taking, and ability to lose without becoming lost that he embodied. His father's ability to lose big, to laugh at that, to go on leading the people in traditional ways amidst the loss, this form of richness is his responsibility to continue in his own generation and hand on to his children.

Children, his own four children and all the children of the Bitterroot Salish, are the other side of the continuance he seeks and expresses in his written work as well as in his life. When Vic looks at his son's face he sees the faces of all the old chiefs in him.

GENERATIONS OF NEED
Generations find focus in my little boy's face
when thoughts of old times and old folks creep
into that need to delve deep into who
we are. He is the little chief without saying.

I read worry of Moiese who states that we
have too much schooling, and now we think
more than we should. He says the people
used to send a young boy to the top of Red

Mountain for the good of all of our people
and we were well. I follow DeSmet's dream
as I try to freeze a focus on unfamiliar
feelings except that we do belong to mountains

and my boy is the face of our grandfathers
who hold both of us true to cottonwood and stone.
(full poem, unpublished)

The need for continuity, for old ones to keep coming back to them in the children, to recognize and honor the gift of that stream of old/new life flowing through them, carrying them, the presence of that read in his child's face, this Martin, Antoine, Victor, Paul Charlo who has come back to them and who at the same time is new.

In Charlo's 1987 trip to Churchill, upper Manitoba, in the sub-Arctic, he asks in his great bear poem, "Churchill Bear Jail," "What about all of us who know jail for bear / is truly bizarre, do we know that spirit is on trial . . . ?" It is a decisive question and expresses a departure from the earlier trouble at living between the two cultures. Of course it is rhetorical, for the evidence of "spirit on trial" is the history of every empire for the past eight thousand years. He leads us with a new sureness in his identification with the imprisoned bears:

. . .
But what is bear's offense? That he can smell
food for twenty miles? That a town is built on ancient

rendezvous ground that was his so long that genes
are imprinted with a map where every stone is turned?
That he can be trapped because there is ring seal
meat in bear trap and he is hungry before the hunt?

Is this justice? You can't help but think of all native
people in the same fix. You hear odd story about
a three, four time, many time loser bear who would
stretch his neck and close his eyes waiting for the dart.
What do bears dream of when they are all tranked
up? Dreaming of ancient ice to cover Hudson's Bay?
Can they be let out when ice does come before
their thirty, sixty days are up? What about incorrigibles?
(*Swift Current Time*)

That last question is a dead giveaway, for Charlo himself is the incorrigible, as was his father before him. Their genes are imprinted with maps of old gambling songs that allow them to win with a dime, to lose big, and not to get lost.

True memory is the capacity to presence what has been experienced before, and must be experienced again, to call up into the present older states of mind, being, spirit that one must never relinquish but always renew. This occurs most clearly in Charlo's work when, during a reading and before the "Walking Bear Song" poem, he closes his eyes and sings an old Salish song, the voice coming through him every bit as much as coming from him. Listening, we know we have witnessed something very old called up into this time, something that can be made present as long as there is someone who can sing it with the sort of connection coming through much more than his or her voice, coming through everything that he or she is, through everything that the Salish people here have lived and dreamed. It is kinship with mountains and bears being sung out. It is geologic memory. It is the Salish homeland. It is the "physical presence and spiritual resonance" of this place.

Like the other poets in this essay, Dave Thomas is a Montana original. This means that the place is etched deeply into him. Thomas was born on the Hi-line in Havre in north central Montana. His father was the Montana district court judge in Chinook, in the shadow of the Bears Paw Mountains where Chief Joseph and the Nez Perce had been forced to surrender to the U.S. Army just miles from the Medicine Line, the Canadian border. Dave came down to the University of Montana in 1965 as an enthusiastic ROTC cadet and won an army scholarship for his junior and senior years. But the Vietnam War pricked his conscience, and his classes in political science raised questions about both the morality and the rationality of the war and led to his decision to leave the military path for the psychedelic movement on the streets of San Francisco.

Real work has been another of those "streets" where Dave has traveled: on railroad gangs or big construction projects like Libby Dam, but also picking cherries on Flathead Lake, painting houses in Missoula, and performing odd jobs out of the Labor Hall, wheeling endless barrows of concrete. In his most famous poem, "The Ten Thousand Things" (read by Garrison Keillor on his National Public Radio show, "The Writer's Almanac"), a poem that purports to be a list of all the things a common laborer on the Libby Dam must move amongst, sort out, and keep track of, the poet-worker's attitude is fundamentally Taoist:

> There's times when I wander
> about picking up
> and sorting bolts

there's times when a chance glance
at a star
trying to outshine
the lamps
is all the rest I get. . . .

Sorting bolts on the edge
of artificial light
the tune of an engine
the shadow of the dam.

"Close to Halloween," a gandy dancer poem from eighteen years later, celebrates the feeling for heavy work going on into middle age, no white-collar position for this poet, and few regrets either:

I recall my first
gandy dancer
spring
sliding down river bank
mud
trying to hold tie high
enough for the diesel
machine
the "Scarfire" to pull
beneath the rail
now the weight
no longer a surprise
middle aged
muscles and joints
creak
in crisp air
the heavy breathing
of being still alive.

But all of Dave's work wasn't in Missoula or on the railroad or some big construction job. There are a number of poems from his work up in Glacier National Park, digging holes for outhouses or working for the carpenters at McDonald Lake Lodge and Sperry Chalet. The mountain sense in them is strong as only a person of "prairie blood" can muster. In "Face to Face on Apgar," the most well known of these:

a nameless
terror grabs
me as I stand
with more
before my eyes
than I can
stand to see
peaks so jagged. . . .
I have no mind
I want
to escape
this voidness
the beauty
it holds
is more
than any word
The Ground
Squirrel Buddha
of this place
keeps an eye
on us all
. . . .
this wind
this wind!
keeps us
all alive
like a broken
down medicine
man I can hardly
stand
I must bow
to the Four Directions
and love
the wind
. . . .
the sun listens
like chlorophyll
coursing leafy veins

in a huckleberry
patch grizzly shit
on the switchback
trail. 8 June 1980

The poem actually begins to "ef" the ineffable. The line breaks and overall structure are such that it is as if the pressure of overwhelming feeling and power and immensity squeezes the language into a tight wall of terror, thought, and devotion, dense in the sense of its own limits in the presence of the seemingly limitless mountains, sky, sun. After the overwhelming experience of the voidness and beauty of these mountains, this wind, which takes him beyond his own name, mind, beyond language itself, a ground squirrel brings him back, hardly able to stand but able to enact the simple ritual of honoring the Four Directions in a bow.

The key word in this last section is, strangely enough, "chlorophyll," from the Greek words for "green" and "leaf." Chlorophyll, the mother of photosynthesis, the quiet ability of plants to take hold of all this terrifying-beyond-voidness of beauty, wind, sky, mountains, unnamable light, and to earth it, make the food that makes the shit of the Great Bear, or the Ground Squirrel Buddha, or the poet. There is an intensity of engagement with the mountains here so deep as to represent an indigenous, populous Buddhist experience. And few white poets could get away with the "medicine man" self-reference, but Thomas does it perfectly, partly by virtue of his deep Montana roots, which of necessity include all sorts of life with Indian people, but also his poet's savvy in the line breaks here: "this wind / this wind! / keeps us / all alive / like a broken / down medicine / man I can hardly / stand / I must bow / to the Four Directions / and love / the wind(.)" This wind keeps us all alive. Like a broken down medicine. Man, I can hardly stand. I must bow to the Four Directions and love. The wind.

Dave Thomas writes about old Indian hippies like "Grandpa Adam Garadipe"; the demolition of the Orange Street Bridge; about Eddie's Club—the legendary Missoula bar of the 1960s and 1970s—now Charley B's; the burning down of the Roxy theater; the "Rough Morning" of a wicked hangover; the deep friendship of "Designing a Hole" with the artist Jay Rummel. "The Intermountain," his poem on the abandoned lumber mill yard just off the Orange Street Bridge, contains a certain affection for what is passing, has passed, for an older Montana, but also a sense of what continues.

There is a devotional quality to Dave's writing that goes beyond literature, that honors the dust that has "fed his bones" and contains the "inevitable sweat & the ache tools leave in your hands, whether they're a #2 shovel or a flat pick on Willie Nelson's guitar." These poems know the true names of things, weather, and pain in that coyote-way of a person who has found something worth doing and a place worth doing it in.

Poets are those responsible for the language itself; they are its most important "keepers." The echo of the old phrase "In the beginning was the word" is in them. These four poets of Montana, this place of continental collision and embattled refuge, Gibbons, Charlo, Lahey, and Thomas, are the poets of *here*, past, present, and future. None of them speaks from within the secure confines of the major institutions or recognitions of this culture, which is perhaps as it should be. They may be mad, impoverished, Indian, alcoholic, laborers, or they may be saints, teachers, chiefs, creators, sane, or all of these things together. Mostly they have been found by language, by the mute/muse, that dark/light daimon lady that sucks their throats and quickens their brains. They are the unlucky/lucky ones who cannot help themselves. They know the mines, the dams, the lumber mills, and moving vans, as well as the mountains and old ones, the Chinese herb doctors, butchers, and cold rivers. They know the Cabbage Patch and the railroads, too, and cold and heat and fast money and northern lights. They are the gandy dancers of the throat. The coyote skins of the fence. The booze bottles of Buddhism. The lookouts of the deaf. They keep the stories in the mind in the belly. Come join us, they say. Leave your fiberglass sailboats and moose antler chandeliers. Yes, you will have to get your hands, even your pretty souls, dirty, bloody, or perhaps broken (like Dave Thomas's broken hand swollen up like a hen's egg when a compacter slammed it against a ditch wall when they were too rushed on a job with a green crew) if you are to experience the best of the culture here. The innocence of the notion that we should or can separate the best from the worst is disastrous. It's in the blood, mountain blood, plains blood, mixed blood, Nez Perce blood, buffalo blood flowing like rivers on the steel rails, black Irish blood soaked into copper ore, snow geese poisoned in the bloody Berkeley pit, blood on the moon, the stars, the snow—the real Montana, lovely and fierce way out beyond the myth of the old or new West or the last best anything—this is the place, the backbone, the bloodline, these four poets continue to follow.

WORKS CITED

Charlo, Victor A. *Swift Current Time*. Dixon MT: Charlo Press, 2002.
Fiedler, Leslie. *A New Fiedler Reader*. Amherst NY: Prometheus Books, 1999.

Gibbons, Mark. *Connemara Moonshine.* Seattle: Camphorweed Press, 2002.
Haines, John. *Living Off the Country: Essays on Poetry and Place.* Ann Arbor: University of Michigan Press, 1981.
———. *Fables and Distances. New and Selected Essays.* St. Paul MN: Graywolf Press, 1996.
Lahey, Ed. *The Blind Horses and Still More Poems.* Missoula: The Bookstore at the University of Montana, 2001.
Thomas, David A. *Fossil Fuel.* Missoula: Montana Writer's Cooperative, 1977.
———. *Buck's Last Wreck.* Missoula MT: Wild Variety Books, 1996.
———. *The Hellgate Wind.* Seattle: Camphorweed Press, 2004.

CHAPTER THREE

West of Éire: Butte's Irish Ethos

MATTHEW L. JOCKERS

In 1891 a front-page article in the *Denver Sun* declared Butte, Montana, the liveliest town in the United States. By 1900 26 percent of Butte's "lively" and cosmopolitan residents were Irish. Most were miners drawn to the city by the promise of steady work and good pay in the mines of the Anaconda Company, a company owned by one of their own, native Irishman Marcus Daly.

For the Irish, Butte was unique among American cities. Butte historian David Emmons points out that in Butte the Irish did not "encounter . . . [a] hostile and entrenched society upon their arrival" (63). Unlike their countrymen in cities such as Boston and New York, Butte's Irish quickly established themselves in all levels of society. One byproduct of this relatively easy assimilation was the development of a body of Irish American writing remarkable for its singular and consistent emphasis on ethnic and community pride.

In terms of Irish American writing as a whole, Butte represents both a geographic and thematic point of difference. In the East, especially from 1914 to 1935, Irish American authors were tending to either avoid ethnic themes, as was the case with F. Scott Fitzgerald and John O'Hara, or to write what Charles Fanning has characterized as "green-tinged" Irish romances (*Voice* 241). Those writers who worked against these trends, writers such as Jim Tully from Ohio and James T. Farrell from Chicago, wrote a brand of "ethnic realism" that focused on the struggles of individuals growing up Irish in America. In the West, particularly in Butte and to some extent in San Francisco, the general sentiment is not lament but excitement. Rather than concealing Irishness, these western authors celebrate it. Throughout the early twentieth century, both in Butte and in San Francisco, Irish Americans were routinely writing of good fortune, ethnic tolerance, and the advantages of being Irish.[1] For Butte's Irish authors, this exuberance manifests itself in a body of literature that takes success for granted while largely ignoring the fact that the mining lifestyle was anything but easy.

Indeed, the consistency of the excitement and enthusiasm about Butte and its Irish community is downright paradoxical given the historical reality that "Butte's mines were arguably the most dangerous in the world" (Emmons 148). To better understand Butte's Irish American writing, we need to recognize that despite, or perhaps because of, dangerous working conditions and a high death rate, the Irish of Butte were socially and emotionally different from their counterparts elsewhere in the country. They were different not simply because they held steady, good-paying jobs, but because Butte's Irish were largely "in charge" of the city. Emmons points out that by the turn of the century the Irish in Butte had a greater proportion of the population than any other U.S. city, Boston and New York included. The great majority of Butte's Irish were miners, but when compared to other cities there were a disproportionate number of Irish and Irish American bankers, merchants, lawyers, politicians, and professionals as well.

Butte was and remains today a city of contrast, and the literature of the city reflects this; it is characterized by irony and contradiction. Here Irish writers yoke optimism with fatalism, treat death and danger in stride, and depict characters more likely to celebrate catastrophe than cry over it. In the early part of the twentieth century when Irish American authors elsewhere in the country were focused on the struggles of individual Irish characters, Butte's Irish were keen to explore and celebrate what it meant to be part of a collective Irish citizenry; there are no character studies but only community narratives. There are no stories of rugged individualism: no cowboys, no outlaws, no mountain men. There is no equivalent to *Shane* or *Huck Finn* in the Butte Irish canon. Instead there are works reflecting and illustrating a community, works with broad, macroscopic titles such as *The Glittering Hill*; *Mile High, Mile Deep*; *Butte Was Like That*; and *Copper Camp*. Joseph Duffy's book, *Butte Was Like That*, begins with the admonition that the reader should not expect to find stories about individuals: "real names," he writes, are "reserved for . . . obituaries" (Duffy 11).

And so the stories told are the stories of a people; of types, not of individuals. Many of these stories began life beneath the surface where the miners would "take five." Dinny Murphy, an Irish miner, recalled break time down in the mines: "Underground, you get together at lunchtime. You'd pick a spot that was well timbered and had good ventilation. . . . Everybody had a laggin, that's a three inch board, probably six feet long, and you'd stretch your laggin out and you'd sit on it to eat your lunch. That's when the fantastic stories would come out. You'd hear all about their wives' fights, all about their broken hearts, how tough they were, what good miners they were. Just some good stories" (D. Murphy 504–5).

Many of the "fantastic stories" surfaced and were reworked by Butte's Irish storytellers, poets, and serious writers of fiction. William Burke was a storyteller, a poet, and a writer. The preface to *Copper Camp*, a Works Project Administration (WPA) writer's project from 1943, notes that "If the regulations of the Montana Writers Project did not prevent, the cover of this book would bear the name of William A. Burke. . . . Through the years, Bill Burke . . . has garnered the anecdote and color of Butte" (v).

Copper Camp is a lively commentary on Butte and provides a useful foundation for understanding the city's literature and a less adequate, though entertaining, introduction to the city's history. Subtitled *The Lusty Story of the Richest Hill on Earth*, *Copper Camp* tells the history of Butte through a collection of fifty decades' worth of folklore, anecdote, testimony, and tradition; the text bears the mark of Burke's enthusiasm if not his name.

William Burke was a well-known storyteller and also a self-published poet of limited poetic talent. Some of Burke's poems are serious, some politically motivated, but the majority are lighthearted and informed by a sincere and overwhelming sense of ethnic and civic pride. The thirty-eight poems in Burke's collection *Rhymes of the Mines* all pertain to life in Butte. The poems mythologize the everyday and celebrate what it meant to be a citizen of "Butte, America," as it was affectionately known by the Irish who emigrated there.

His best known poem, locally at least, is simply titled "Butte." It is not uncommon to find lines from the poem reprinted on paper placemats in local diners or on kitschy mining-city postcards. The poem is a celebration of the city; it deals directly with Butte's ironic and antithetical character:

I'm a mile in the air
And five thousand feet deep
One half of me works
While the other half sleeps.
I'm the perch of the devil;
I'm the footstool of God.
Thrice those who are living
sleep under my sod.
I'm glitter—I'm glare;
I'm calm or hectic to suit;
I'm heartaches—I'm handshakes;
I'm lusty old BUTTE . . .

I'm a maelstrom of nations,
Of color, of creed
I'm Serb and I'm Irish
I'm Cornish—I'm Swede
I'm Russian and Polack
I'm English—I'm Finn
I'm Chinese—Jew—Syrian
I'm a Hun from Berlin.
I'm Mexican—Greek
And other countries to boot.
I mother them all; I'm cosmopolitan BUTTE.
(32–36)

Burke's homage captures Butte's antithetical character, and while not remarkable aesthetically, the poem exudes civic pride and local sentiment. Important to note is Burke's personification of the town. Unlike the many nameless or otherwise typified characters that populate Butte's Irish fiction, the city, and by extension the citizens, speak with a single, unified, identifiable voice. The emphasis in the final stanza underscores this point by drawing attention to the "maelstrom of nationalities" that form the singular voice of the city: the personal pronoun "I" that echoes throughout the poem is the voice of the many as one, not of the one among many.

Sentimentality in Burke's poetry is frequently over the top. "They've Moved Our Marcus Daly" is no exception. In this poem Burke laments the decision to move a statue of Daly from the post office to the campus of the Montana School of Mines. The poem opens,

Oh, Paddy, dear, and did you hear
Or has the news yet reached your ears?
They've moved our Marcus Daly
From where he stood so many years. (60)

The melody taken from "The Wearing of the Green" is awkward and ill fitted. It grates against the ear in what modern Irish readers might find a rather offensive repurposing of a familiar nationalist song. While accurate in emphasizing the close kinship that Daly had with his fellow Irish workers,[2] the poem is clumsy. Important though is Burke's use of the collective Irish voice. The poem is not about the moving of "a" statue; it is about moving "our" statue. Daly represented to Burke and to Butte's Irish the possibilities of Irish success in America, and in the poem the statue becomes an icon representing not a single man but the hopes and dreams of an ethnic population, a representation of what a race, a community, a people might achieve.

Daniel Liston is another Butte poet who understood that Butte's Irish identified as a collective, and Liston attempted to use this fact in promoting his socialist agenda. In "The Irish Scab," Liston plays on ethnic-Irish solidarity to criticize the "Irish Scabs" who "betrayed their Celtic blood" by working in the mines during the strike of 1917. The speaker argues that Irishmen in Butte owe it to their countrymen in Ireland not to work as scabs in this American mine, in this American city. Liston was born in Ireland in 1881; the details of how he came to Butte are uncertain. In Butte he was the "proprietor of Dublin Dan's Hobo Retreat," a pub where it is reported that he lured Sunday worshippers with banners reading "FOR A GOOD COLD SCOOP OF LAGER AFTER THE SERVICES OR A SHOT TO WARM YOUR INNARDS, GO TO DUBLIN DAN'S JUST AROUND THE CORNER" (*Copper Camp* 83,84). Liston's poems—most of which were written after 1914 and distributed in self-published pamphlets or in Industrial Workers of the World publications like the weekly newspaper *Solidarity*—explore the microcosm of Butte's Irish community within the macrocosm of Irish oppression back home.

It is unclear whether Liston was rejected or admired by his fellow Irishmen in Butte. Certainly there were serious labor concerns, and many of the locals would have appreciated Liston's proletariat leanings. However, Liston's passionate criticism of the Irish bosses, in particular of Marcus Daly, might not have found an equally appreciative audience. As Burke's poem about the Daly statue makes clear, Butte's Irish revered Daly. Liston was generally anti-English, antiestablishment, anti-"company" and, therefore, anti-Daly. In "The Pseudo Duke" Liston conflates the British aristocracy and the Anaconda Mining Company by comparing one "oppressor" to the other—the latter oppressor here is most certainly Marcus Daly. In "Poor Tim," Liston speaks of the power of the "Boss" (Daly or his associate) on "the hill" to sway votes on Election Day. He indicts the Irish miners who vote with the "Company" for Charlie Henderson, a man whom he describes as "A rank old A.P.A." Such a charge should not be taken lightly; the A.P.A., or American Protective Association, was a Protestant-minded organization with a singular focus on keeping Catholics out of public office. Linking Daly to the A.P.A. would be a dangerous sort of business. Though Liston saw himself, or his pseudonymous "Dublin Dan," as the mouthpiece and champion of the Butte workingman, he inadvertently criticized them in his denigration of the city's Irish. He saw, or at least characterized, Irish Butte's failure to embrace Marxism as a betrayal of ethnic blood. He was savvy enough to appeal to the Irish at the level of ethnic unity, hoping, one assumes, to conflate ethnic solidarity with worker's solidarity. But Liston failed to appreciate that being Irish in Butte was viewed as a ticket to success. It is not clear whether Liston had any tangible influence within Butte's tight-knit Irish community, but it is clear that he was aware of and sought to exploit the advantages of ethnic solidarity in order to push his socialist agenda. In a rather subtle but intentional fashion, Liston made use of Irish history in order to tap into deeper sources of Irish identity and ethnic consciousness, sources that reside outside of Butte. Such a technique was not uncommon among the big political machines of the East, but it seems unlikely that Liston's use of the tactic would have been successful in Butte. His Irish audience was not suffering under the thumb of Anglo-Protestant oppression but was making a decent wage under a boss with whom they identified.

Butte's Irish American novels are filled with the same strong sense of ethnic solidarity and civic pride found in Burke and Liston. Joe Duffy's 1941 novel *Butte Was Like That* consists of a series of fictionalized vignettes drawn from his days as a miner and laundry driver where he gathered "gossip with a ginger jar flavor." The book's central protagonists are Malone and Lanigan—men who represent typical Butte Irish. Duffy never gives them first names; they are simply "Malone" and "Lanigan." The men meet in the midst of a traffic accident in which Malone is injured while risking his life to save Lanigan from a runaway wagon. Later Lanigan helps Malone get a mining job through his friend McPhail, a man from the old sod who is the shift boss at the mine. McPhail becomes a central figure in the book. After years spent in the mines, he knows all the tales. The text becomes a chronicle of daily meetings between the three men as they lean on their shovels and take the customary "five."

McPhail's observations are reminiscent of Finley Peter Dunne's Dooley stories from Chicago. Both authors sought to capture a community ethos. Like Dunne's Mr. Dooley, Duffy's McPhail speaks in an Irish brogue and delivers practical, homespun philosophy. Dooley preached wisdom to Hennessey from behind a bar; McPhail preaches from behind a mucker's shovel deep within the mines. McPhail's stories, like Dooley's, sometimes have a serious message, as when he recounts political corruption in the Miner's Union, but most are more typically humorous. Prior to writing *Butte Was Like That*, Duffy had, like Dunne before him, worked as a journalist, and it was in that career that he developed his narrative technique and the characters that populate his fiction. Duffy's column "While the Boys Below Are Taking Five" was a regular feature in forty issues of *The Montana American*. Reminiscent of Dunne, Duffy used his column to bring a uniquely Irish perspective to local, national, and international events. Charles Fanning has argued that the "Chicago Dooley pieces constitute the most solidly realized ethnic neighborhood in nineteenth-century American literature" (*Exiles* 265). I would not argue this point; Dunne was a far more accomplished and sophisticated writer than Duffy. That said, Duffy certainly tried to capture the ethos of the city, and in some small ways he succeeded. Duffy, like those before him, stuck to the characterization of the Butte Irish as a collective, and he remained true to a focus on place over person. At the same time, his work fails to be introspective and lacks the self-consciousness of Finley Peter Dunne. *Butte Was Like That* is an entertaining portrait to be sure, but it ultimately fails to get beneath the surface.

Clyde Murphy's 1944 novel *The Glittering Hill*, published three years after Duffy's book, is significantly more refined, a novel that won E. P. Dutton's first Lewis and Clark prize. Montana literary historian Richard Roeder records how "a Hollywood group headed by Sam Jaffe bought up the movie rights [to the *Glittering Hill*], and rumors circulated that Humphrey Bogart would play the lead role" (158). Unfortunately for Butte and for Murphy nothing ever came of this.

Clyde Murphy was born in Great Falls and moved to Butte after World War I. He later earned a law degree from the University of Montana and in 1922 moved to Los Angles where he practiced law for seventeen years. In 1939 he gave up law to write. *The Glittering Hill* was his only novel. Critical reception was mixed, and rumors circulated that the book would be banned in heavily Catholic Boston where the mention of booze and whores in the context of Irish Catholicism might not be tolerated. But even those who reviewed it most unfavorably admitted to the novel's "realistic setting" and "convincing . . . picture of the times."[3]

Set in 1898 *The Glittering Hill* is largely historical. In creating the backdrop for his novel, Murphy is liberal in his reliance on actual figures from Butte history. The most obvious example is Murphy's fictional copper magnate Magnus Dunn, a character generously and obviously modeled after Butte's real copper king, Marcus Daly. Other characters, too, are clearly borrowed, as is the case with Nick Stryker whose fictional life mirrors the life of the litigious, would-be copper baron, F. Augustus Heinze. The historical subplot carefully follows actual events in Butte's history, especially the infamous "war of the copper kings" in which Daly and his rival, Williams Andrews Clark, fought for dominance of Butte's ore. While staying relatively true to historical events, Murphy delivers an entertaining portrait of Butte's Irish. The primary plot centers on the purely fictional Evelyn Shannon, Tom Gary, and Dennis Ignatius O'Shea. Evelyn, the child of lace curtain and shanty Irish parents, is trying to understand how to be Irish in America; Tom is the hardworking Catholic who finds his immigrant parents lack an enlightened sense of what it is to be in America; and Denny O'Shea is the archetypical comic Irishman: hard drinking, smooth talking, and not too responsible. As the historical plot unfolds in the background, Murphy provides, through his fictional characters, insight into the daily struggles and victories of the Irish working class. In the process, Murphy conducts a sort of sociological experiment in which he brings a variety of Irish characters into the Petri dish of Butte and then tackles such perennial Irish American conflicts as those between Irish and English, Catholic and Protestant, lace curtain and shanty, rich and poor, and the rather paradoxical conflicts that arose between Magnus Dunn (Marcus Daly) and his largely Irish workforce.

The later conflict is present early in the novel when Tom Gary and Denny O'Shea are on a train bound for Butte. After Tom and Denny announce their destination, the brakeman, a fellow Irishman named McGinty, scowls at the reference to Butte and says, "Each man to his own liking" (82). O'Shea, sensing McGinty's disapproval of Butte, asks, "What's wrong with Butte? . . . Butte's booming and the Irish have the inside track" (82). McGinty is unimpressed and goes on to separate himself from the Irish of Butte by whispering to O'Shea, "Them Butte Irish is the tricky-dicky kind" (82). It remains somewhat vague what McGinty means by this statement, but as the novel progresses we recognize that the close communal bond that kept Butte's Irish population together bothered McGinty. This bond, at least in McGinty's mind, was honored under even the most irrational of circumstances.

Communal unity manifests itself in a number of ways throughout the novel but is most evident in the relationship between Magnus Dunn and his Irish labor force. Even before arriving in Butte, Gary and O'Shea have heard of Dunn and are willing to side with him, sight unseen. In this sense, Murphy begins building on the theme of Irish solidarity in Butte even before his primary characters get there. Brakeman McGinty, not of the Butte Irish, refers to Dunn as "your tin god Magnus Dunn": "Your tin god Magnus Dunn . . . he brings shipfuls of Irish horses and Irish men from the old sod. And where do his cargoes end up? He drops the Irishmen into the mines to dig up money fur [*sic*] him. He puts the horses into pastures and they get sun and oats and mahogany stalls fur sleepin'" (84). The use of "your" here is ironic and speaks volumes: Gary and O'Shea do not know Dunn. Thus the use of "your" takes on a much more general meaning: "you Butte Irish." It is as if the two Irish travelers to Butte are in some sense repatriating themselves rather than simply immigrating. Not ironically, in the pages that follow, Tom and Denny are quickly accepted into Butte Irish community, and, on their first day in the city, they are invited to attend the wake of Toss O'Hara, a man neither of them knows. This wake proves to be the official and symbolic means by which they enter into the Butte Irish community—one Irish man is passing as two new ones arrive.[4]

When McGinty finishes his stories about the horrors of Butte and the greed of Magnus Dunn, Dennis O'Shea asks his friend, "What do you make of that talk?" (91). Tom replies, "Dunn's not that bad. . . . Most Irish like him" (91). Tom, it turns out, is right, but so is McGinty. The Irish miners of the novel persist in treating Dunn as a figure to emulate, despite the reality that many of them are suffering in the mines. Such was the case historically, and the Irish miners of Butte maintained a deep sense of loyalty to Marcus Daly. The story of Waterford immigrant Matt Kiely that is told in *Copper Camp* provides one example:

> He hit the town when it was a bleak, but wide-open, hell-roaring camp, and Matty was but a broth of a greenhorn straight off the boat. Marcus Daly, himself, gave Matty his first job, shoveling copper ore on the four-hundred-foot level in his big Anaconda Mine. And this Matty never forgot. To him Marcus Daly was both a saint and a guardian angel.
>
> Long after Daly had died and they had placed a statue of him on Main Street, Matty never passed the bronze memorial without reverently removing his hat and breathing a short prayer. (204)

Throughout Murphy's novel, the loyalty of the Irish is continually tested, and Dunn always comes out on top. We learn that the Irish miners saw Dunn as an example of what the Irish could achieve. Rather than dislike and disapprove of his opulent taste in horses, land, and architecture, they praised him and sacrificed themselves in the name of a vague ethnic bond. They saw him as a symbol of achievement and never lost hope in their own success, believing firmly in the conviction that though "Butte was a city where the poor stayed poor, . . . a fellow with a little money and a lot of guts had the world by the tail with a downhill pull" (C. Murphy 20).

In addition to elevating the image of the Irish in general, Murphy attacks those Irish who discriminated among themselves; he argued that internecine conflict had no place in Butte. Early in the novel, heroine Evelyn Shannon contemplates a trip to Butte and recalls some advice that "Dion Boucicault had given . . . to a young Irish friend who had been humiliated by a social slight. . . . 'Go west, my friend,' Boucicault had insisted grimly, 'and for God's sake, get rid of your Irish name.'" (48). Evelyn finds the idea of changing her name shameful and yet is bothered even more by how the reputation of the Irish has been marred by the stigma of the shanty Irish. She finally "settled into a comforting conclusion that as one of the Lace-Curtain Irish, she felt she might have been indifferent to the stigma cast by the Shanty Irish if all the others among the Lace-Curtain Irish had been brave enough to stand by their guns" (49).

For Evelyn's brother Jerry, the issue is not nearly so complicated, and he argues that "We're all Irish. . . . And we're all bog-trotters. We can claim that we're descended from the Irish Kings. We can insist that we're Lace-Curtain Irish or Brick-House Irish and we can sneer at what we call Shanty Irish but if the facts were revealed we'd find that we're all only a few years removed from the good old-fashioned pig-under-the-bed stock that has been the backbone of Ireland for centuries" (64). When their conversation turns to Butte, Uncle Pat, who has actually been there, argues that "Montana's more civilized than Chicago" (66). Jerry and Evelyn's mother, however, refuses to believe this and refers to the Irish who live there as a "bunch of peasant immigrants" (67). What Evelyn later finds in Butte hardly conforms to her mother's image of a peasant population. To the contrary, Evelyn finds a class of hardworking, congenial, intelligent Irish working men, and a place that she immediately christens "the glittering hill" (122).

When first introduced, Murphy's narrator describes Denny O'Shea as a "hard-bitten Irish-American" (109). When O'Shea introduces himself to the tenets of Mrs. Clancy's boarding house he calls himself "an upstanding, American-born, Irish Catholic gentleman"(127). Like Denny, Tom Gary is the son of Irish immigrant parents, but Tom is less comfortable with his identity as a second-generation son of immigrants; he is still struggling with what it means to be Irish American. Tom ponders this situation during a quiet moment at the wake of Toss O'Hara. Looking at those Irish around him, Tom thinks: "The Irish must change if they are ever to climb from the foot of the social and economic ladder. Maybe this rich new Montana country will offer enough work, enough opportunity to bring about a real change in the Irish" (175).

Tom, we learn, has left home and has both physically and emotionally distanced himself from his immigrant past: "He couldn't stand the bitter thinking, the narrowness, the prejudice, the rosaries every night" (131). He seeks for himself the very change that he wishes for the Irish in general. Surely Tom loves and respects his parents, but any time the subject of his parents comes up, he is quick to note that his father looked a lot like John Quincy Adams. After boasting about this point to Denny—who replies, "Whoever the hell Johnny Q. Adams was"—Tom asks himself "why it was that whenever his father came into his mind he first remembered that people said he looked like John Quincy Adams. . . . Why did he think it important that his father looked like Adams?" (129–30). Tom does not answer this question for readers, but we understand that Tom seeks to ground himself in an American identity. Butte's Irish will ultimately provide Tom with a workable identity model. He discovers that Butte's Irish are different: "These Butte Irish were his kind of people. He felt as if he had known them always" (176). Tom wonders to himself how it is that the Butte Irish can be unconcerned "about the cause of Irish freedom . . . the [so-called] evils of the English-Protestant world" (381). He resolves that "these Butte Irish are . . . different" (381), their loyalties are local, and he finds satisfaction in this separation from the past.

Murphy and his Butte Irish characters present a unique view of what it means to be Irish in America. In addition to an impressive sense of ethnic pride, they also possess a more local pride in their city and in its Irish patriarch. All of Murphy's Irish American characters have achieved something by going west, and most of them have profited in one way or another by moving to Butte. At its core, Murphy's *The Glittering Hill* is an insightful look at the diversified character of Butte's Irish. All of Butte's dimensions are contained within this book, from its thriving brothels and crowded bars to its Catholic churches and crowded wakes. Seen in the context of Irish American literature as a whole, *The Glittering Hill* is a groundbreaking work, a seminal study of one critical and otherwise missing piece in the story of Irish America.

Unlike Murphy's sometimes overzealous celebrations of Butte's rougher edges, Richard O'Malley, a writer of the next generation, provides a more objective perspective on Butte. Published in 1986 O'Malley's retrospective novel *Mile High, Mile Deep* successfully explores the antithetical aspects of Butte's Irish culture without getting caught up in the sort of Butte Irish euphoria we see elsewhere. Written late in his life, *Mile High, Mile Deep* is based on firsthand experience. O'Malley worked as a mucker and grew up among the Irish miners of Butte in the 1920s. Divided into two sections, "Summer" and "Winter," the novel juxtaposes the awe and innocence of youth with the understanding and experience of maturity: the intoxication of being part of Butte's Irish community and the sobriety that comes from seeing that community die.

Each of the two sections begins with a lyrical prose prologue in which O'Malley uses fragmented images to set the mood and scene. The prologue to "Summer" begins with a bucolic portrait of Butte prior to the discovery of copper when "deer moved shyly along Bell creek" and when "the Hill was pine-studded and fresh in the high mountain air" (1). Such description is reminiscent of the impressions registered by Evelyn Shannon in *The Glittering Hill.* But where Murphy's characters refuse to see with honest clarity the dark underside and underground world of Butte's mines, O'Malley shines the light of truth. His pastoral description abruptly shifts to a portrait of how Butte went from a mountain paradise to a metropolitan city: "Then men came. And one of them grubbed into The Hill and found copper. Others came and they ripped the guts out of The Hill" (1). The language here, "grubbed," "ripped," and "guts," is not the sort of language that we find in previous works and when we do see such language, it is typically couched in a context of heroism and strength, things of toughness to be admired as part and parcel of the masculine, romantic world of Butte. Here, however, they are negative, destructive words that predict the tragic conclusion of O'Malley's narrative.

Part one details in rather unconnected form the various boyhood adventures of Dick Maloney, the autobiographical narrator, and his friend Frank Lardner. The first of these adventures involves the wake of "Old Man Powers," an event, or rite of passage, that serves, as it does in Murphy's *Glittering Hill*, as an entry into Butte's Irish community: as one member passes, two new ones arrive. Old man Powers was an Irishman, a native of Killarney who came to America as a young man. He had been a miner and had worked in at least three of Butte's mines. Dick reports that "whenever anyone died out on The Flats that we knew, Frank and I went to the wake. You're supposed to pay your respects to the dead and then you can wait around for the lunch. There was always something to eat at a wake" (6).

After paying their respects, the boys head for the kitchen where the men were passing around a bottle of "moon." Among the men in the kitchen are five Irishmen and Mr. Trevithick, "a cousin jack from Cornwall and not Irish" (9). Trouble starts in the kitchen when Trevithick, rather than giving the customary toast to the dead man, remarks instead that "'E was a bleedin' fool for barring down like that. Hanybody barring down in a rill stope is asking for the worst" (9). Mr. Monahan warns, "That's no way to talk about the dead," but Trevithick replies, "Dead or not dead, it's true" (9). After this remark, Mr. Sullivan, from county Mayo, says, "It would take a cousin jack bastard like you to say so. . . . You Protestant clown I won't call you names, I'll just knock your head off" (10). Ethnic, religious, and national loyalties appear to trump local fidelities, but the reality here is that it is the breach of Butte-Irish wake etiquette that causes the problem. When Mr. O'Brien attempts to resolve the matter, a brawl between Sullivan (of county Mayo) and O'Brien (of county Cork) results.

The wake of "Old Man Powers" makes a useful introduction to the novel as a whole; we see both death and ethnic brotherhood on display. Powers's death in a mining accident foreshadows the death of Dick's friend at the end of the novel. Most of part two revolves around labor disputes and an eventual strike. There is violence, a great deal of drinking, and the continued omnipresence of death. When Dick's friend, Frank, is killed in a mining accident, readers are left with a pessimistic message about Butte. For O'Malley, even the tight-knit Irish community—with its network of support—fails to answer for the tragedy of his friend's death. O'Malley's retrospective portrait of Irish life has all the benefits of hindsight and offers an objectivity that is only possible with distance and time. Unlike Murphy's *The Glittering Hill*, which ends on a wholly positive note, O'Malley's Butte novel is an indictment of the inevitable end that came to many of the Irish miners. Death in O'Malley is not regenerative. Old man Powers is not replaced because Frank is dead and Dick leaves town.

O'Malley offers the voice of another generation, the generation that came of age in the era of the glittering hill but lived through the Depression and saw the hill reduced to a pit. In the final pages of the book, we are again at a wake, but this time it is not the wake of some unknown miner like those we have seen earlier. This time both readers and characters know the dead man. For the first time in Butte Irish fiction, we are lifted out of the world of the Butte-Irish collective where no one has first names and where one passing is marked by another entering. In this last Butte-Irish novel, we find rejection of the community ethos. As his friend Frank is lowered into his grave out on the Flats, Dick thinks about the Hill and about the community of miners and citizens who struggled to rip the ore out of the mountain; he says to himself, "You got him, you big dirty rock bastard . . . you got half of us alright. But you won't get me. Not ever" (304). At once this line registers Dick's connection to the collective—"you got half of us"—and, at the same time, his rejection of the "us" for the sake of "me"! In these words, we hear both a realization and a determination: a realization of the entropy in the system, and a determination to move beyond the system, to break away from the cycle that has become destructive.

Sixteen years after *Mile High, Mile Deep*, O'Malley produced a sequel titled *Hobo: A Depression Odyssey*. The book begins with Dick Maloney stealing away on a westbound train, leaving behind a Butte where there are no longer any jobs and not much in the way of optimism. Though this latest Butte novel lacks the sort of enthusiasm that we have come to expect from Butte's Irish American authors, there is no denying that O'Malley was moved and motivated by the spirit of community and ethnic solidarity that the city exudes. O'Malley's relationship to Butte reminds us a bit of James Joyce's uneasy association with Dublin. Joyce was a Dubliner whose life's work was devoted to the city, and yet he could not live there himself. He loved it and was its biggest critic. O'Malley ultimately left Butte. He traveled the world and then retired in the west of Ireland.[5]

Different from prominent Irish American writers such as James T. Farrell or William Kennedy, Butte's Irish American authors speak for an entire Irish population. Where others have focused on character—*Studs Lonigan*, *Quinns' Book*, *Bessy Conway*, *The Blakes and the Flanagans*, *The Dalys of Dalystown*, and *The Callahans and the Murphys*[6]—Butte's Irish have given us municipal narratives such as *The Glittering Hill*, *Butte Was Like That*, and *Mile High, Mile Deep*. Seen together, these works represents an enduring chronicle of one city's unique Irish American heritage. Though Butte has not produced a great American novel, or perhaps even a great Irish American novel, each of the texts explored here is worth a reader's time and consideration. These texts are historical chronicles and cultural artifacts. They provide contemporary readers with the opportunity to explore and understand a unique substratum of Irish American culture.

Thinking about how to place Butte's Irish American writing within the greater canon of Montana literature or within western American literature is, as Brakeman McGinty said, a "tricky-dicky" business. The city and its literature are enigmatic and are as atypical of the western experience as they are of the Irish American experience. Joseph Kinsey Howard once described Butte as the "black heart of Montana"; for Irish immigrants, at least, it was a black heart that could be mined and embraced.

NOTES

1. See Matthew L. Jockers, "A Literature of Good Fortune," *The Irish in the San Francisco Bay Area: Essays on Good Fortune*. Ed. Don Jordan and Timothy J. O'Keefe. (San Francisco: Irish Literary and Historical Society, 2005).
2. Daly was a great hero among the Butte Irish. He was the man to realize the potential for copper mining in Butte, and, as a result, he became one of the richest and most powerful men in the country. His beginnings were humble, however. He was born in Ballerooney, Ireland, and after coming to America, he worked as a miner in Nevada and Colorado. He had no formal education, and even after getting rich in Butte, he always maintained a close relationship with the Irish miners. When he died, a statue of him was erected in front of the post office.

3. This particular review, from *Kirkus* in 1944, also noted that the romance of the novel was "paper thin—the hero and heroine, two dimensional." A *Boston Globe* reviewer warned potential readers that the book was "Boisterous, turbulent, and lusty," and Jennings Rice of *The Weekly Book Review* noted that the book contained the "roughest, toughest, language [he had] yet come upon in print."
4. Butte's Irish population at this time, unlike Ireland's, was not only regenerating but growing.
5. After fifteen years in Ireland, O'Malley returned to the States, to Arizona, where he lived until his death.
6. *Studs Lonigan* by James T. Farrell takes place in Chicago; *Bessy Conway* and *The Blakes and the Flanagans* are by Mary Anne Sadlier and are both set in New York; *The Dalys of Dalystown* is by Dillon O'Brien and takes place in Canada, Michigan, and Ireland; *The Callahans and the Murphys* is by Kathleen Norris and is set in New York.

WORKS CITED

Burke, Bill. *Rhymes of the Mines*. Vancouver: Bill Burke and Son, 1964.

Duffy, Joe H. *Butte Was Like That*. Butte MT: Tom Greenfield, 1941.

Emmons, David M. *The Butte Irish*. Urbana: University of Illinois Press, 1989.

Fanning, Charles. *The Exiles of Erin: Nineteenth-Century Irish-American Fiction*. Chester Springs PA: Dufour Editions, 1997.

———. *The Irish Voice in America: 250 Years of Irish-American Fiction*. 2nd ed. Lexington: University Press of Kentucky, 2000.

Murphy, Clyde F. *The Glittering Hill*. New York: Dutton, 1944.

Murphy, Dinny. "I Found My Likings in the Mines." Comp. Theresa Jordan. *The Last Best Place: A Montana Anthology*. Ed. William Kittredge and Annick Smith. Helena: The Montana Historical Society, 1988.

O'Malley, Richard K. *Mile High, Mile Deep*. Missoula MT: Mountain Press Publishing, 1986.

O'Malley, Richard Kilroy. *Hobo: A Depression Odyssey*. Bloomington IN: AuthorHouse, 2002.

Roeder, Richard. "The Copper Pen: Butte in Fiction." *Montana and the West*. Ed. Rex C. Myers and Harry W. Fritz. Boulder CO: Pruett, 1984.

Works Project Administration. *Copper Camp: Lusty Story of the Richest Hill on Earth*. New York: Hastings House, 1943.

PART II Women Writing Montana

CHAPTER FOUR

Home on the Range: Montana Romances and Geographies of Hope

NANCY COOK

Go to any gathering of scholars in western American studies and watch what happens when someone begins a quotation that goes like this: "In the American West we are struggling to revise our dominant mythology, and to find a new story to inhabit. Laws control our lives, and they are designed to preserve a model of society based on values learned from mythology. Only after re-imagining our myths can we coherently remodel our laws, and hope to keep our society in a realistic relationship to what is actual" (Kittredge *Owning It All* 64). By the time the presenter gets to the word "struggling," lips move in unison, and the audience looks more like a Sunday school class reciting a familiar Bible quotation than a room full of academics. William Kittredge's words have become the mantra for "new Western" literary critics the world over and deservedly so. Many publishers have embraced this narrative "call to arms," and we now have dozens of revisionist studies of western American literature, as well as a distinguished crop of memoirs, short story collections, and novels, all positing "a new story to inhabit," or, at the very least, further critiques of the same old western story. Myth busters such as Mary Clearman Blew and Judy Blunt have insisted, quite eloquently, that we attend to the costs the old mythology has extracted from the women of the region. The books I discuss in this essay are, in many ways, unlikely companions to the work of such writers as Blew and Blunt, but they perform important cultural work for looking at the codes of the West from a gendered perspective.

Running along a parallel track, and seemingly unaware of either the new Western criticism or the revisionist memoirs and fiction in the marketplace, the popular culture industries keep churning out countless iterations of what looks a lot like the Old West mythology, and nowhere is this more evident than in the formula romance novel. Novels of frontier couplings, romantic captivity, and romantic renewal in both the old and the new West abound. My essay focuses on a group of these novels that takes Montana, past and present, as their setting. My interest in romance novels comes out of a larger interest in the relationship between genre and place, and so I resist many of the leading theories of romance that dismiss place as mere setting—absolutely interchangeable stages for the ritualized mating dance of the romance novel.[1]

Romance publishers seem conflicted in their emphasis on a novel's setting. On one hand, setting seems important enough for marketing teams to promote series set in particular regions ("Made in Montana," "Big Sky Brides," "Montana Mavericks," and "Code of the West," for example). In 1994, with the first appearance of Montana Mavericks, Silhouette sponsored a contest to promote the series, with the winner receiving a weekend getaway at Big Mountain Resort in Whitefish, Montana. "Fallen in love with Montana's Big Sky Country?" the insert asks. "MONTANA MAVERICKS has the answer to cure your yearning heart." By entering this contest, readers make the connection between the Montana of the romance series and Montana, the tourist destination. On the other hand, promotional materials, mailers, and blurbs rarely indicate where a novel is set. Harlequin's mailers and its website continue to list titles by subgenre, not by place-based series name. For example, the Harlequin mailer for April through June 1999 offers several titles set in the West, but they are not listed as such. Readers might recognize the names of authors who write western romances, but most of these authors set novels elsewhere as well. The titles and cover illustrations offer some idea of theme (*How to Catch a Cowboy* is one such title), but the principle of organization is the subgenre: "Harlequin Temptation," "Silhouette Desire," "Harlequin American Romance," for example. Given this conflicted marketing, how are we to evaluate whether or not place matters in these books?

Some places prove more popular as settings than others, and the ranching and cowboy West seem to have enduring popularity, judging from the consistency with which new titles with such characters appear every month. Silhouette chose to revive its Montana Mavericks series, and between 2000 and 2002 titles in the series regularly made the weekly "Top Ten" lists compiled by chain bookseller Waldenbooks/Brentanos.[2] Some authors who set books in a variety of places return to the West as a setting over and over again.[3]

While revisionist discourse has entered the disciplines of literary studies, history, and contemporary high-brow literature of the West (one thinks of Krista Comer's *Landscapes of the New West*, Cormac McCarthy's *Blood Meridian*, or William Kittredge's *Hole in the Sky*), the romance novels maintain and promote the West as a mythic and fantasy space, a pastoral world where intricate social constructs identified with urban culture have been sloughed away, revealing both an essential West and an essential character. It is a world that offers women liberation by means of the suppression of urban cultural markers and a stripping down to raw emotion and instinct. Many romance novelists have had great success with books set in western states, but Montana has become a particularly "hot" setting for romances. Dozens, even hundreds, have been published from the 1980s to the present, and since 1994, Silhouette has offered numerous titles in its Montana Mavericks series. Several other series or miniseries have appeared in which Montana serves an important role, even when it is not the only setting. Series such as Mustang, Montana and Made in Montana highlight the state on the cover, while more savvy readers will expect Montana or mostly Montana settings from series such as Home on the Ranch, Anne McAllister's Code of the West, and Janet Dailey's Calder family saga.

As fantasy space, apparently Montana has a lot going for it. It has been characterized by the media as a space where celebrities and other people of means can "drop out," and get back to nature. It remains uncluttered by big cities, and it is no longer associated with any major industry, so it is relatively free of negative connotations. Lightly populated, it remains "terra incognita" for many Americans. For romances, Montana offers many advantages. The region and the state have powerful mythic associations. As Janice Radway points out, the romance novels themselves "resemble the myths of oral cultures in the sense that they exist to relate a story already familiar to the people who choose to read them." She goes on to say that "romantic novels function for their reader, on one level at least, as the ritualistic repetition of a single, immutable cultural myth. However, one must also recognize that [readers] do not simply reencounter the story of a single heroine-hero pair because the romantic myth is itself disguised in the form of the realistic novel" (198).

When romance writers couple the powerful romantic myth with the mythologies of the West, they have a very efficient and compelling context within which they can create a new romance. These novels offer realistic settings, but their cowboy/rancher heroes come with many of the trappings of western mythology: they are independent, honorable, competent, protective, strong, quiet men who stand up for their land, their families, their employees, and their community against all opposition. They live in a place mythically identified as harsh but beautiful; spacious but lonely; where work is done the way it has been since the nineteenth century: on horseback. For the writer who has between 25,000 and 85,000 words to tell a story, mythic associations offer an effective shorthand.

If the hero is a Montana rancher, the reader already knows his values. If the heroine is a rancher, readers can be confident of her absolute strength and honor. Each will be a physically vigorous person at home in the great outdoors, but both women and men can easily be tested by the weather and the land. Their class status will be happily ambiguous—they own land, and sometimes lots of it (Dailey's Calder family ranches 60,000 acres), but they are manual laborers who never flaunt what wealth they have. This is not the world of the grizzled mountain man, for in the world of the romance, the male population consists of rodeo men and ranchers, all darkly handsome and twenty-five to thirty-five years old.[4] These are men who don't disappear to an office from nine to five. Men's domestic potential can be evaluated by means of their daily chores, how they run a ranch, how they care for employees and animals—in other words, their skills in husbandry. Novelist Anne McAllister puts it this way: "All *that* comes with Montana every time I use it as a setting. True or not in real life, all those things are invested in the literary landscape of Montana as it is used in romance. It also speaks a sort of 'back to basics' environment, where only things that *really* matter are important."[5] While romance novels aren't the only medium to appropriate and build on myths of the Old West—films such as *The Horse Whisperer* (1998),[6] the Montana Tourism Bureau, and the Philip Morris Company do so as well—they have used them to great effect.

In most of these books, Montana becomes an almost exclusively *pastoral* space, and many of that mode's features apply. The complexities of contemporary culture recede along with a daily grind. Ethical, political, and social questions appear mostly in relation to the land, which is always connected to a main character. In the world of Montana romances, only the weak and the bad see land as capital and try to make a killing. The hero or heroine may fight to save the ranch from foreclosure, she may suffer economic losses due to a weak cattle market, or rustlers, or both, but she *never* sells out to developers or movie stars. While questions of status or class may exist, the resolution of those differences is mediated by the relation to the land. A heroine or hero with money will almost always put that money into land. He'll bail out the family ranch, or occasionally he'll have to buy someone else's ranch, but money doesn't stay in the stock market; it always goes into the partnership. By the novel's end, both hero and heroine have contributed materially and the ranch is a partnership in more than name. But unlike the pastoral, where characters enter the green world, resolve conflicts that have been rendered in simpler terms by that space, and then *leave*, in these romances the characters settle down to life on the ranch. These books celebrate home making.

While nearly all of the romance novels in Montana rely heavily on myths of the Old West, they also offer elements of realism.[7] Writers and readers understand that each couple will face the challenges traditional to the genre, but they also understand "that character motivation [must] be realistic and convincing" (Radway 201). It is the mandate for realistic context, in character development, and in setting, or place, that allows romance novels to perform other kinds of cultural work and the kinds that can impact contemporary, actual Montana. Whether romance authors try to or not, they educate their readers in the geography, the social and economic fabric, and the political issues of a place. In *Reading the Romance* Janice Radway explored this phenomenon with a community of readers and came to the following conclusion:

> In fact, romantic authors often squander lavish amounts of space on the descriptions of foreign environments and historical customs that are very likely not already known except in the most skeletal way by the reader. Furthermore . . . the readers themselves "frame" or type these descriptive passages as valuable "information" and "instructional" material that can be stored as "knowledge" for use at a later date. . . . The success with which the ordinary is typically mimed in the romance thus seems to confer factual status on all of its other verbal assertions as well. . . . [E]ven if she has never seen the place it refers to or the object or custom it describes, she simply assumes that what it claims is true; she accepts it as fact. (195)

Romances create an inviting space for readers to learn new things. Writers often break the progress of the narrative in order to make the world intelligible to readers, and so, from the technical language of rodeo to conservation issues, writers explain things for their readers. Here's Janet Dailey: "One of the cowboys swung the gate open as Ty walked his speckle-faced sorrel out of the corral and finished coiling his rope after taking his turn in the breakaway roping competition. It differed from straight calf roping in that the cowboy was only required to rope the calf and let the loop snug up around its neck, then throw the rope away. The calf wasn't thrown and tied" (43). The educational agenda works well when one character is unfamiliar with the world of the other. When millions of readers the world over read about Montana in romance novels, they take the representation more or less at face value.[8] So what do they learn about life in Montana?

In *Montana Legacy*, for example, Minneapolis cop Kate Rawlins has inherited half of a Montana ranch from her grandfather. She left the ranch at the age of two with her unwed mother and did not return until she was informed of her legacy. Orphan Seth Hayward, taken in by Kate's grandfather, has inherited the other half interest in the ranch. He's worked there most of his life. Determined to learn about ranching, Kate tries to get Seth to teach her. In an early exchange, Kate reveals she has a lot to learn:

> "You've just met the lifeblood of this operation. Or part of it. We should have more than nine hundred calves this spring, if all goes well."
>
> "What can go wrong?" Kate gingerly stepped around a steaming plop of something the diameter of an extra-large pizza.
>
> "They were all checked in the fall, and the open cows were shipped—"
>
> "Open?"
>
> "The ones that weren't pregnant."
>
> Kate felt a twinge of sympathy for the cows. "Sort of extreme, isn't it?"
>
> "It's business. Ranchers can't afford to feed cattle that don't produce. We also have to deal with storms, drought, disease and coyotes. Even checking the cattle twenty-four hours a day during calving season, we can lose a lot of calves." The resignation in his voice hardened to steel as he turned to face her. "There's no financial security here. But this is a way of life and a legacy for the future. I won't let anything jeopardize this ranch." (29–30)

Not only does this passage teach readers a new vocabulary, as it defines an "open" cow, but also it sets up the contest between the hero and heroine, as it lays out both the challenges and the stakes. In the process, readers learn a little more about the difficulties of cattle ranching in Montana.

I have chosen to discuss a disparate group of novels set in Montana, with emphasis on Tami Hoag's 1994 novel *Dark Paradise.* These books represent a range of options available within the romance genre, from series romances, books of 185–250 pages that remain on the racks for one month, to mass-market major releases such as *Dark Paradise*, which clocks in at 528 pages. Whether set in Montana's past, as is the lesbian romance *Montana Feathers* (1990) by Penny Hayes, or set in contemporary Montana, as are Anne McAllister's *The Great Montana Cowboy Auction* (2002), Myrna Temte's *Sleeping with the Enemy* (1994), and Hoag's *Dark Paradise*, these novels offer their women empowerment in a mythic, rather than actual world. While this practice is shared by most current romances, it suggests particular ramifications for the American West as a region that exists very much within contemporary American culture.

Several critics of western American literature have written about the challenges gender has presented to writers and scholars alike. In light of the work of Melody Graulich and Krista Comer, these romance novels lie in an uneasy relation to claims that they are feminist revisionist stories of the new West. While Comer's project differs significantly from mine, her comments are instructive. On one hand, she points out that "many of the male writers of the new regionalism narrate their own stories through 'women's values' of community, relationships, social interdependence, and family, and in so doing, they reorient the geo-cultural imaginary away from masculinist and toward feminist social emplotments" (10). While the romance novels promote what Comer qualifies as "women's values," they remain problematic as thoroughly feminist texts, for reasons we will see. The romances also begin to address some of the same issues as the "new female regionalists" of Comer's study, for they, too, "deploy representations of western lands and nature to talk about . . . myriad *social and political* topics: the qualities and compromises of women's lives, racial history, the pain of racism, feminist political dreams and utopic societies, feminist erotics, postmodern economics, the relationships between human and nonhuman nature, the relationship of non-Europeans to nonhuman nature, . . . Anglo female stoicism . . . and the list goes on" (11). While it should be obvious that romance novels do not share the same agendas with western feminist writers such as Maxine Hong Kingston, nevertheless, they take up several of these issues, if only to make their heroine seem more realistic. Along the way, I think these novels allow, if not perform, a critique of the masculine West, even as they work toward a happy ending.[9]

In "'O Beautiful for Spacious Guys': An Essay of the 'Legitimate Inclinations of the Sexes,'" Graulich allows for a closer alignment between the works of Mary Austin or Jean Stafford and the romance writers I discuss, for as she observes, "most women writers attempt to merge 'the space, energy, and passion of the landscape' with 'the warmth of the hearth,' that they have always claimed the wider range of self-expression usually granted only to the male in our canonized literature (197).[10] While romance novels tend to be conservative, because, for the most part, they promote the heterosexual nuclear family, nevertheless, as I will argue later, the family ranch is an endangered species of a sort and, hence, not so easily aligned with patriarchal privilege.

The idea of empowerment for women within the romance genre is a controversial one. With the rise of feminist literary scholarship in the 1970s came critical attention to popular or mass forms of entertainment for women. Many of these early scholarly accounts of romance novels treated the books as an "opiate of the people," as critics struggled to account for the genre's increasing popularity. While generally sound in their scholarship, most of these analyses employed extremely simplistic ideas about reading, and readers.[11] Not until

Radway's 1984 breakthrough book, *Reading the Romance*, did readers become three dimensional and autonomous. In her study of "the Smithton women," a group of midwestern romance readers and their bookseller, Radway learns that these readers turn from their household worlds of never-ending responsibilities, physical exhaustion, and emotional depletion, to the privacy afforded by reading. Finding "it impossible to ignore their equally fervent insistence that romance reading creates a feeling of *hope* [emphasis mine], provides emotional sustenance, and produces a fully visceral sense of well-being," Radway searches for ways to explain such a response (12). Radway and others turned to the work of Nancy Chodorow to account for and theorize the way women readers of romance search for identification with characters who are nurtured, "mothered," if you will (13).[12] Radway's work, then, begins to see readers not as mindless victims of big publishers and mass media working to keep them anesthetized, but as discerning readers seeking to fulfill in fantasy what their lives don't afford them.

Subsequent work by other scholars in the history and sociology of reading has shown that readers rarely, if ever, occupy a single reading identity. Rather, more recent work shows that any given person occupies multiple readers' identities, as she moves from room to room, home to work, morning to evening, work to vacation. Furthermore, the other identities don't completely disappear when one dominates. That is, a reader reading the newspaper may retain some desire for elegant prose, and a reader of romances may still be attentive to "fact" and the "real," even as she seeks to escape those worlds. What I want to suggest here, before I turn to the novels, is that even though many of these narratives have what more critically engaged readers might classify as implausible, even silly bits, they perform important cultural work, and often in a fairly sophisticated way. The way they go about this work has implications for the way we think about Montana, its past, its myths, and its future.

As we have seen, publishers' promotional campaigns both reveal and conceal the precise setting of most novels. But they and their writers also seem to understand the importance of place in the "geography of hope" so important to readers. Several of the western romances, and all in the Montana Mavericks series, provide maps at the front of the book. These maps note major landmarks, national parks, the capital city, cities served by major airlines, interstate highways, mountain ranges, rivers, and Indian reservations, in addition to the fictional setting of the novel, which, in most cases is distinguished from the real locales. Several map legends note that "all underlined places are fictitious."[13] In other words, the text invites readers to orient themselves both to an actual geographic location, one they might wish to visit or where they live, and a fantasy space. Most authors take some care to get the landmarks right and to accurately place their characters in a landscape. Some make it a point to continue such orientation throughout the narrative. In *Staying the Distance*, Franci McMahon takes the time to orient the reader, for the two characters in the scene are Montanans, and presumably they already know where they are. Rachel owns a ranch from which one can see "The Crazy Woman Mountains," and her hired hand, Kate, is a Native American from the "Rocky Boys Reservation." Here's McMahon: "At twenty-one, Kate knew college was not in her future. Of course she could attend the tribal college in Harlem, up on the high line, that northernmost strip of highway and towns before the Canadian border" (7).

Place, these authors suggest, *is* important, as is their characters' response to it. It's almost a given that the insider, or local resident, whether hero or heroine, is deeply attached, even in love with his or her spot in Montana. The local hero or heroine worries that the newcomer won't respond appropriately to the place, hence many tests and declarations occur in relation to place. In *Sleeping with the Enemy*, Jackson Hawk, Cheyenne Indian and tribal administrator, takes city girl and assimilated Indian Maggie Schaeffer to a special place, testing her response: "Though he had few of the spiritual powers of his father, Jackson knew this ground was sacred. He silently offered prayers to *Maheo* and each of the four directions, then glanced at Maggie. Her eyes shone with the awed wonder of a child. When she spoke, her voice held a hushed reverence. 'Oh, Jackson, this is so . . . beautiful.' For once they were in complete accord" (106). Long before Monica Skye, the reclusive heroine of *Montana Bride*, realizes that she will marry Chicago commodities trader Austin Sinclair, her new next-ranch neighbor, the reader knows the outcome, for Austin truly loves Monica's place:

> "Coming here . . . to Montana. I'd always been so busy rushing to grab that next sale. . . . My life was passing by me so fast I was out of breath. That first trip out here, I had no idea places like this existed. I remember standing in my waders in the clearest, coldest damn water on planet earth, casting my fly, then casting again and again. I didn't particularly care if I caught anything, I just like the feel of the sun on my face, the sound of the water rushing over the rocks behind me. I remember spending hours inhaling the air. I guess you could say I got drunk on this place. But the oddest part was when I got back to Chicago. Everything there seemed unfamiliar to me as if I didn't fit in. I realized I didn't anymore."
>
> "You left your heart out here," she surmised. (Lanigan 78)

When Monica understands that Austin's heart belongs to Montana, readers know that it can then belong to her, for she has been represented as the very soul of Montana: a young, beautiful, virginal, cash-strapped orphan, running her grandfather's ranch on her own. Austin has responded to Montana in sensual terms, so readers know he will be a very good lover. Even more critically for the romance, it is Monica who has connected the sensual to the emotional in her response to Austin's story. In order to win his bride, Austin still has to prove that he is not like the "Hollywood boys" who have come to play in Montana's paradise (25). He has to prove that his makeover of the farmhouse he bought will still honor tradition, he has to learn how to be a good neighbor (as he does when he helps Monica deliver a breeched lamb, or when he rescues her from her burning barn), and he has to prove that he will be a partner, neither domineering nor weaker than the fiercely independent Monica.

In all of the novels, a person who responds inappropriately to the landscape is bad news. In *Montana Feathers*, Elizabeth Reynolds, a young and pampered easterner, learns to love the harsh landscape of nineteenth-century Montana *and* a widowed sheep rancher, Vivian Blake, but plans to return East with her fiancé, Jonathan Stanton. But it is Jonathan's patronizing and horrified response to the land and its people that finally determines Elizabeth's course of action. Jonathan crystallizes all that is limiting about the East (and men), and so when in exasperation, he shouts, "Damn Montana!" Elizabeth, at last, determines to stay on with her lover Vivian (245). In Janet Dailey's series saga of the Calders, a multigeneration ranching family, Tara Dyson sets her cap for the young Ty Calder. Tara has many marks against her: she's a Texan, her "daddy" is a rich oil man intent on cheating the Calders out of land, she's conniving; but worst of all, she hates Montana. Ty will run the ranch when his father is ready to turn over the reins. In *Calder Born, Calder Bred* Tara maneuvers her way into marriage with Ty, while Jesse, the daughter of a ranch hand, waits in the wings. Midway through the novel, readers know Tara won't last as Ty's wife, for she has the wrong relationship with the land. "There was nothing out here but endlessly stretching miles of more of the same. Its emptiness was almost oppressive, surrounding Tara until she felt like a minuscule object" (180). Montana is not a place for big egos. Characters must be humble before its powers, respect its challenges, and be appreciative of its beauty before they deserve a mate. We know that Tara is headed back to Texas, and that ranch-hand Jesse will prevail, because Tara dares to articulate what all the bad women in these novels feel: "I hate all of it. I hate this place and I hate this land," she says—100 pages before she heads out the door (303).

Set in present-day Montana, Tami Hoag's *Dark Paradise* charts the rejection and subsequent acceptance of California newcomer Marilee Jennings in New Eden, Montana. Jennings's role as outsider makes her acceptance by rancher J.D. Rafferty difficult, for J.D. has endured an upbringing with flighty women who weren't tied to the land. In many of these books, the hero mistrusts women because he was abandoned by his mother or stepmother, women like Tara Dyson Calder, who craved more attention than their husbands could give, women who sought the glamour of cities. J.D. had suffered under the reign of stepmother Sondra, mother of his irresponsible half-brother Will: "He had seen Sondra for what she was early on—a spoiled city girl who had fallen in love with the idea of loving a cowboy but had quickly fallen *out* of love with the realities of ranch life. She had taken out her unhappiness on her husband, punishing Tom Rafferty for her own failings and miseries, and punishing his eldest son for seeing past her pretty golden façade. Will had been too young to know the difference. J.D. had never been that young" (41). Not only does this passage set up the terms of Marilee's challenge—to prove that she's not Sondra—but it offers both Marilee and readers other challenges. The passage quoted above also warns its readers not to do precisely the thing the novel is designed and marketed to do: to "fall in love with the *idea* of loving a cowboy" (41, my emphasis). Implicit in this passage is the call for readers to understand "the realities of ranch life." Do these novels show such realities? Well, yes and no. Each offers some representation of the rancher at work. Most suggest financial hardship as a daily concern of the rancher. Each notes the isolation of ranch life and the simplicity of daily routine. Although modern technology enters the world of the ranch romance, it's only grudgingly. The heroine may teach her cowboy about computers, but for outside work, ranchers in these novels largely eschew four-wheelers and ATVs in favor of riding the range on horseback, no matter how slow or inconvenient.

For true to its pastoral and bucolic roots, ranch life in romance novels almost always centers on "husbandry" activities. Though readers learn that J.D. is a modern rancher who's "up on all the latest—electronic sales networks, computer tracking herd progress" and the like, those aren't the activities Marilee and readers see (171). When Marilee asks J.D., "Hard day at the office?" he replies, "the usual." And when prodded, the "usual" turns out to be: "Finished rounding up the breeding herd for branding and vaccinations. Colts needed riding. Bulls had to be moved" (155). In other words, ranch activity always reveals something about character or about theme. Here it returns us to procreation and the hero's physical domination over his "peaceable kingdom." Although the hero may not seem gentle to the heroine, his relationship to animals reveals a tender side and sends the appropriate messages. J.D. may seem hard and cold to Marilee, but with a "pretty little mare," the story changes:

> Her forelock hung in her eyes and she tossed her dainty head to fling it back. She belonged to the pharmacist in New Eden, who wanted her broke and safe for his twelve-year-old daughter to ride. . . . He enjoyed the work, and it brought in extra cash, something they never had enough of, ranching being what it was.
>
> "Nice mare, good mare," he murmured, letting the palomino rest again. *Mare . . . Mary . . . Marilee.* His mind drifted as he rubbed the horse's neck and slicked a gloved hand down her heaving side. (69)

Were Marilee to overhear this confused conversation between J.D. and a horse, rather than be offended, she, like any romance heroine, would see the hero's gentle side, would find his confusion heartening, and therefore strengthen her resolve. For the ranching activities in a romance novel don't build power or empire for power's sake; they don't speak primarily of sound business practice and land management; they speak of husbandry, of sensuality, of "Nature" as procreative force. The heroine reads ranching activity as an indicator of the hero's domestic potential.

Most of the novels set on ranches make the link between animal husbandry and human husbandry explicit, even the lesbian romances. In many cases, the characters establish a sensual and emotional bond during the delivery of babies—animal and human. In *Staying the Distance*, rancher Rachel calls the new vet, Margaret, recently arrived from the East, when one of her prized mares has trouble foaling. Margaret struggles to help the mare with the delivery and fears the foal will be stillborn. While Rachel looks on, Margaret works at the delivery: "Fighting to keep emotion off her face, she unbuttoned her coveralls and slid her right arm out of the sleeve, totally unmindful that her exposed breast was shining like a full moon" (23). The delivery is a difficult one, requiring teamwork, but ultimately, they are successful. As mare and foal get acquainted, "[b]oth women, sobered, looked at each other. There was a new respect in Rachel's eyes. She saw sitting beside her a tired, competent woman veterinarian. She also saw the bared Amazonian breast with the shucked sleeve of the coveralls wet and crumpled in the straw. A deep scarlet rose over Rachel's face" (25). Margaret picks up on Rachel's interest in her exposed breast and wonders to herself if Rachel could be a lesbian, too. Rachel doesn't know it yet, but by the end of the novel, she will take Margaret as her partner, sexual and domestic.

In *Montana Bride*, city boy Austin comes to the aid of rancher Monica as she helps deliver twin lambs. Austin helps, and as Monica delivers the second of the breeched twins, Austin exclaims:

> "One of each. A perfect family," and then goes to his SUV to extract clean towels for cleaning up themselves and the lambs. Austin sat back on his knees watching as the lambs sucked their mother and she licked their heads affectionately. "Nature is a curious thing. If I were this mother I'd be wondering where the heck the father was. Shouldn't he be here helping out? I should think pacing in the waiting room would be the very least he could do," he joked.
>
> Monica observed the sheep dourly, "She did just fine by herself. As most females do."
>
> "Especially you, right?" (100)

The scene centers on the confusion between the world of the human and the ovine. Austin insists on speaking of the ewe and her lamb in human terms, and while Monica resists some of his implications, she, too, links females of both species. But readers have just seen that the ewe did not do "just fine by herself," and needed Monica and Austin's help to deliver her lambs. Austin's success in the outdoor delivery room gets him sex with the virgin Monica within a page of the lambing scene.

This human-livestock connection can be taken to extremes. In a few of the novels, the hero helps deliver his heroine's baby in some isolated cabin far from doctors and hospitals. In *The Right Cowboy's Bed*, Ella, a twenty-eight-year-old virgin, gets pregnant during her first roll in the hay with Montana rancher Bryant. Ella convinces Bryant to marry her to make the baby legitimate, and they spend the novel working from a sham marriage toward one eternally bound by true love. Still struggling with their unexpressed feelings for each other, city girl Ella heads out to feed the cattle with Bryant during a severe winter storm. Their snowmobile dies just as Ella's water breaks, and their lives, and that of their unborn baby, are in danger. Bryant manages to get them to a remote line camp, where Ella's labor intensifies. When Ella realizes that she won't deliver the baby in the hospital, which is hours away, Bryant's independent and competent rancher persona kicks in. He assures her that "'we'll make do on our own.'" Ella is skeptical. "'You can't deliver the baby. You don't know anything about—' I've helped a fair number of cows give birth, honey. How different can it be?" (220–21). Readers who know anything about calving, or readers of Judy Blunt's *Breaking Clean*, might wince, hoping that Bryant doesn't drag Ella to her feet, lock her in a head catch, and get out the calving chains.[14] But romance readers recognize the scene as one crucial to Bryant's recognition of his love for Ella. And sure enough, as midwife, Bryant comes to understand the difference between his little heifer Ella and the ones standing in snow drifts outside:

> His stomach knotted when he saw the baby's head was crowning. The cabin was suddenly too hot and he felt drenched in sweat. *His son.* Not a calf. Not just anybody's child. . . . But his own son. . . .
>
> She gave him a weak smile. Her hair was damp and mussed, her cheeks pale, her eyes teary behind her glasses. "If you tell me he looks just like the last calf you delivered, I'm gonna kick you."
>
> "He'll be beautiful. Like his mom." (222–23)

Bryant and Ella manage a little humor as they playfully make and collapse distinctions between the bovine and the human. Readers know that after Bryant has looked at Ella's delivery and found beauty, it is certain that he'll eventually find the beauty and love in her heart and that they will be one happy family at home on the range.

The rancher's homeland is really no more than a "house of sky," a domestic space writ large. Unlike many contemporary ranches that operate with a minimum number of employees, romance-novel ranches often come with a whole bunkhouse full of ranch hands. These extras allow readers to see how those close to the characters perceive both the possibilities for and obstacles to the romance developing between hero and heroine. Often, one of the senior hands will stand in for the hero or heroine's deceased parents, as "the old retainer" figure. And in several cases, at least one of these supporting players is a Native American who reminds the hero or heroine not to get too possessive about the land, but always to care for it as one would a family member.[15] In this way, the ranch personnel simulate both a multigenerational family and a small community. Readers can see the hero or heroine's ethical sensibilities through the way he or she treats the ranch hands. In this matrix, protecting the employees, the livestock, and the land (and property values) becomes equated with protecting family values.

In the Montana of the romance novel, the kinds of conflict associated with modernity and urban culture are dismissed rather summarily, for neither character has to truly compromise values or sphere. They both operate in an enriched and enlarged domestic sphere; she often works in the house, he on the range—but for the most part, both work far from the complexities of contemporary business culture: accountants, inventory analysis, profit and loss statements, production efficiencies, vendors, markets, distribution networks. Careers that take the heroine (or hero) away from home are an inconvenient reminder of contemporary culture. Best for the ranch and best for the romance are those couples who learn to work together, as here, in *Renegade Father*:

> While she tied a loop, Joe moved aside to make room. He easily held the heifer in place while Annie reached into the birth canal and worked one-handed to slip the loop around the calf's tiny hind legs. They made a good team, she thought, not for the first time. Since he'd come to work for her, they'd had plenty of chances to work together. There was never a shortage of chores on a ranch the size of the Double C—repairing fenceline, going on roundup, putting up hay.... But the rhythm the two of them developed whenever they worked together on a ranch chore went back far longer than just the last eighteen months since he'd come to work for her, back to the time she had always thought of as Before. (10)

In romance novels the rhythm of work speaks to their compatibility—bodily and emotionally.

To return to *Dark Paradise*: Marilee has fled the life of a court reporter, and as for nearly all heroines who come to Montana, careers are taboo. While other romance settings allow for careers, in Montana ranch romances, the land demands all from its tenants. If the heroine can turn her work skills to the aid of the ranch as a bookkeeper, say, so much the better. While occasionally a heroine will juggle ranch and town life, it's only until the babies come. Marilee has potential for a career in music, but her promoters are the evil power brokers who oppose J.D. Her music soothes J.D., but not if she's paid for performing it. Moreover, Marilee has other work to do. She must help J.D. regain some of the qualities associated with childhood, for J.D. has been responsible for the ranch since youth and has never been nurtured. She must teach him how to smile again, and ultimately give him a child, so that he will correct the mistakes made in his own upbringing. And by the penultimate page (out of 528) she meets with some success. She's pregnant, though J.D. doesn't yet know, and he has returned to her. She challenges him to a dance, not a duel, and in an echo of *The Virginian*, finally it comes: "A smile played at the corners of his mouth. 'Come over here and say that, city girl'" (527).

Marilee has changed, too. As she has come to love the Montana landscape, so she has come to accept qualities in J.D. that she had earlier found abhorrent, uncivilized: "He was a man as hard and unyielding as the land that bred him, and she might spend the next fifty years tearing her hair out over his stubbornness, but she wouldn't trade a second of it for all the gold in California" (527). In attempting to "tame" J.D., Marilee has decided that she, too, will "stick." By the novel's end, California is no longer her home, for she has had the good sense to reject it, relegating it to a cliché. The land makes the people, this novel asserts; but once in a while, when an outsider can adapt, she's accepted, for she is a necessary component for invigorating the bloodlines. It's just good husbandry.

Dark Paradise offers a more clearly "environmental" angle as well. Bryce, a rich newcomer and part of the "Hollyweird bunch," has been buying up ranches, which he uses for the illegal hunting of imported endangered species (33). Marilee's efforts first to discover these crimes, then to stop them, further demonstrates her transformation from careless newcomer and outsider to environmentally responsible local. In depicting the challenges her heroine Marilee faces, Hoag lays out thumbnail sketches of some of the debates that have engaged Montanans (and other westerners) for years. She characterizes the poles of the debate:

> When one person pointed out that development would bring jobs to the valley, another countered that the jobs would be low-paying service occupations. When one charged that the influx of tourists was a disruption to a way of life, another argued that the town would die without those tourist dollars. Cattlemen spoke out angrily about the political clout wielded by radical left-wing environmentalists who owned second homes here and were fighting to stop everything from grazing on federal land to eating red meat. Environmentalists fought back, slamming the cattle industry for overgrazing and destroying wildlife habitat. (79)

Both Marilee and J.D. engage in these debates to some degree, but for the most part Marilee doesn't so much evaluate the oppositional arguments as she assesses the people who make the arguments. The issue for her is with whom she will align herself, and how her choices will bring her closer to or farther away from J.D. In going after Bryce and his crimes, Marilee distinguishes herself from the careless, even rapacious outsiders, and positions herself for the move to insider, responsible landowner, and eventually, to a place as J.D.'s partner on the ranch. Her efforts also help protect J.D.'s land and legacy. By the novel's end, she has earned both her place on the land and her place at J.D.'s side, for she has vanquished the "darkness" in this paradise. Through romantic assimilation, the urbanite heroine finds the essential meaning of life, a powerful connection to a place, true love, and full recuperation from the negative effects of modernity. As long as the marriage holds, so will the environmental ethic. In the Montana of the romance novel, one can save the forest, or the spotted owl, with the right roll in the hay.

The education of the outsider and his or her move, first to the insider's bed, then to becoming an insider, is a plot device common to a great many of the romances set in Montana. And although the "native" hero or heroine, the landowner who encounters and falls for the outsider, often misreads his or her lover as immutably a "city girl" or "city boy," it is often because the lover has been read through the lens of the past, rather than through the lover's own behavior. J.D. reads Marilee first through her conniving friend Lucy, then through his flighty stepmother Sondra, so he must learn to be discerning about the past. He must preserve his legacy, ranching traditions, and he must relinquish his assumptions about city girls and their ability to adapt to ranch life. The insider/outsider problem is usually a greater obstacle for the characters to overcome than it is for readers, and for a couple of reasons. First, as discussed earlier, romance writers generally create texts that welcome readers into their world. They explain the terrain and the local practices, and they rarely, if ever, keep readers at a distance by using coded language readers are unlikely to understand. And second, readers themselves often have had the experiences associated with both insider and outsider status. As novelist Anne McAllister notes: "However palpable the tensions are that exist in Montana, the issue of insiders and outsiders is not unique to the state. In fact, it is part of the very subject I'm addressing in my Caribbean island book at the moment. It has to do with progress and change and opportunities. It has to do with haves and have-nots. It has to do with money and lack thereof. It has to do with differing sets of values and world views in collision with each other."[16] In each of the romance novels set in Montana, if the tension between insiders and outsiders is a plot point, and it usually is, the characters must find some sort of resolution. Change must occur so that while distinctions can still be made between good outsiders and bad ones, some outsiders can be integrated into the community.

And *here* is one of the places where these novels can perform cultural work for Montanans. We have seen how these novels represent Montana and its ranching community, and I have suggested some ways in which Montana offers a rich location for the cultural work of the romance as a genre. But now I would like to turn to what these novels might do *for* Montana and Montanans. In nearly every one of the romances set in Montana, both the hero and the heroine must learn to reject past patterns of behavior, especially past patterns regarding relationships, in order to claim their one true love. In other words, these novels thrive on appropriate compromise. Some things must never be compromised: love of and respect for the land, livestock, neighbors, community, or the commitment to honor, integrity, and responsibility. All must attend to ranching traditions and land stewardship as their legacy. But these characters must learn to trust each other, to respect each other as equal partners, and they all must learn to communicate.

In *Breaking Clean*, Judy Blunt describes a ranching culture where silence is golden, where assumptions fester unarticulated, where seldom is heard those encouraging words "I love you" (10). In nearly every romance novel, the bodies of the hero and heroine know that they are destined for each other early on in the narrative. It takes the length of the novel, however, for the hero and heroine to learn how to articulate their emotions in language, and the language is *always* absolutely clear. Hints and approximations don't count in romance novels—each must say "I love you." The assumption is that once the hero and heroine can say these most difficult words aloud to each other, they can talk about other things honestly. The strong, silent type may be attractive initially, but for the fantasy to outlast the sexual couplings, the characters must learn to talk. In this insistence, romance novels have something to teach closed-mouth ranching communities. And ranchers throughout the West recognize that open and effective communication is a cornerstone for their survival. At recent meetings of an organization that helps teach ranchers the skills necessary to keep their ranches and reach profitability, lack of communication was cited repeatedly as a profound obstacle to success. The legacy issues that are resolved so tidily in romance novels account for an increasing number of ranch sales. Generational strife is heightened in lean economic times, women feel disenfranchised, families share ownership but not goals: it has reached crisis proportions in the "new West."[17]

Montana romances combine elements found individually in other types of romance novels, but Montana serves as a place conducive to the seemingly "natural" linkage between finding love and finding a place to love, meaningful and remunerative work, a commitment to a cohesive and supportive community, partnership with one's spouse, and a stable and safe home. In an era when many Montanans struggle to stay on the ranch, or to stay employed while staying at home, the romance resolution is a hopeful one. And although these novels clearly represent fantasy and not reality, they offer models for partnerships between men and women, as well as reassurance that the values held by many ranchers are values shared by a world-wide readership. In an era where organizations such as the Forest Guardians have targeted financially vulnerable ranchers in an effort to drive them into bankruptcy, and therefore to lose their leases on federal land, good PR, no matter the source, is welcomed. And for all their idealism and conservatism, romance novels reach millions of readers the world over. The version of ranching these readers see is one where ranchers are stewards of the land, not rapists; preservers of open space, not subdividers; partners with their spouses not master/slave; manual laborers not spendthrift tycoons; and community-oriented, not isolationist "Freemen."

These books encourage tourism, it's true. But the romance reader as tourist just might be looking to meet a ranching family and learn about the business (and lifestyle) on the way to Glacier or Yellowstone Park. Ranchers have begun to seek such tourists out, for it's both an opportunity to educate and to supplement uncertain income from livestock production.[18] These idealized versions might linger with readers as they move from romance reading to newspaper reading, to voting. Romance critic Carol Thurston offers the comments of a romance reader from Louisiana: "'Reading makes me think, makes me explore how I feel about relationships, prejudices, wars, personal tragedy, life itself. It builds my confidence to think out how I would handle certain situations—gives you a good feeling to conclude that you could cope with this or change that, and also helps explore your own morals and beliefs'" (132). When legislation appears, romance readers just might make a connection and understand that battles over public lands, over commodity prices, over farm subsidies—all involve the lives of real people, ones they have come to respect through the portraits found in romances. Of course such representations tell only part of the story, but it is a part that isn't often told in urban newspapers or on the nightly news.

And what of Montanans? Are these books to be scoffed at, dismissed as more instantiations of the crippling old myths? These books are read in Montana. Go to any used book store with romance titles, go to any drugstore, any grocery store, any Wal-Mart or Pamida in the state and you will find these books. Left on the night stand or in the bunkhouse, these formulaic offerings of an idealized world just might feel at home within "a geography of hope."

NOTES

I wish to dedicate this essay to the memory of Leslie Fiedler, the first professor I met who read and wrote about popular romances. Thanks to Melody Graulich for coaxing me into rethinking my stance on these books, and thanks to Lynne Derbyshire, Valerie Karno, Karen Markin, Libby Miles, Andrea Rusnock, Cat Sama, Marie Schwartz, and Eve Sterne for their support and cheerful dispensation of criticism.

1. In *Love's $weet Return: The Harlequin Story*, Margaret Ann Jensen goes as far as to claim: "[S]etting is one of the most flexible elements in the formula. It is also one of the least important elements, because the setting is ultimately reduced to providing the background for the real focus of the story, which is the romance. After all, one can fall desperately in love anywhere in the world, whether it be under an apple tree in North America or a palm tree in Africa" (80).

   Although several of the many studies of romance novels mention setting in passing, I have not found any that take location to be an important aspect of romances, nor have I found any treatments that look at the ethics of representation of place. Kay Mussell briefly discusses the use of "exotic" locales, but simply categorizes them by type (64–65, 85–86). While a close analysis of the scholarship is beyond the scope of this essay, let me suggest, briefly, why critics might dismiss place as an important category in the study of romances. Critics may be reluctant to take on place as an important category because they have a great deal at stake in representing romance reading practices within a feminist discourse. In defending the genre, they tend to universalize women readers rather than analyze differences among them. While some critics offer a cursory mention of racialized readers, most work to rehabilitate the genre through an emphasis on worldwide sales figures and foreign translations, a kind of "we are the world" approach.
2. Waldenbooks/Brentanos lists appear on the website for Romance Writers of America (www.rwanational.org).
3. See titles by Lisa Tawn Bergren, Carla Cassidy, Janet Dailey, Charlotte Douglas, Lois Dyer, Sally Garrett, Jennifer Greene, Lisa Jackson, Anne McAllister, Jackie Merritt, Laurie Paige, Cheryl St. John, and Pat Warren.
4. The demographics of ranchers in romance novels has everything to do with readers' demographics and very little to do with actual demographics. According to the 1997 Census of Agriculture, the average age of a farm/ranch operator in Montana was fifty-four, with the number of men under age thirty-four about 0.5 percent of that population. According to a state census analyst, most of the small numbers of women ranchers are widows, with fewer than 150 women producers under age thirty-four. These figures cover any agricultural operation that produces or anticipates $1,000.00 or more in sales. Only 29 percent of operations in 1997 farmed or ranched 2,000 acres or more, so the young, single rancher of these novels is very much a mythical figure. Nevertheless, stories abound concerning the invasion of single women looking for a Robert Redford–style cowboy after the 1998 release of *The Horse Whisperer*.
5. From e-mail correspondence with Anne McAllister, November 6, 2002.
6. The film was adapted from the hugely successful novel, published in 1995 under the same title by Nicholas Evans.
7. Readers may find that my reading of romance novels offers a critique of Leslie Fiedler's infamous essay, "The Montana Face." My work certainly stands in relation to that essay, but the relationship is complex, involves both Fiedler's "Montana:

P.S." and "Montana: P.P.S.," and warrants a detailed discussion that is beyond the scope and aims of this essay. I'm working on it.

8. Harlequin has been reluctant to release actual sales figures, and I have been unable to get any current sales figures, but even using statistics from the early 1980s, the numbers are staggering. Using Harlequin Enterprises as her source in the early 1990s, Cathie Linz claims that romances comprised "35 to 40 percent of all mass market paperback sales," and that Harlequin reported "annual sales of over 190 million books worldwide." Writers in the Harlequin stable routinely see their books translated into at least twenty languages, and Anne McAllister reports fans from Zimbabwe to Korea to the Orkney Islands. If we surmise from the easy availability of these romances in Montana, and their popularity in used-book stores across the state, we can assert Montana romances are popular in Montana, too.
9. While several of the romances in Montana feature Native American characters, they do not promote diversity. Native characters generally speak for the past and for a land ethic, with only a cursory attempt by authors to represent social issues for Native characters in a contemporary context. Of course, these writers don't emphasize real social issues for *any* characters, especially issues of poverty. In novels such as *Sleeping with the Enemy* and *Dark Paradise* racial tensions, like class and gender ones, exist only to be neutralized by romantic coupling.
10. Interior quotations from Dawn Lander and Mary Austin. See Graulich 197.
11. For a good overview of scholarship on the formula romance, see Merja Makinen's *Feminist Popular Fiction*.
12. See, for example, *Reading from the Heart: Women, Literature, and the Search for True Love* by Suzanne Juhasz.
13. All of the books in Silhouette's Montana Mavericks series begin with a map, and in the newer part of the series, the map is followed by a genealogical chart.
14. Blunt's description of the usual rancher's way of calving versus her own thoughts on the subject offer a biting commentary on these romance-novel scenes. See Blunt 276–91.
15. Tami Hoag has a few of these characters in *Dark Paradise*. Samantha is a beautiful young Native American woman married to J.D.'s half-brother Will. She will have to overcome both a crippling lack of self-esteem and the effects of a particularly gruesome attempted murder before things work out for her. Hoag has two "old retainers," one white and one Indian. In addition to helping with the livestock, Chaske, the Indian, dispenses wisdom. To J.D.'s obsession with keeping his ranch intact, and keeping his neighbors from selling out, Chaske reminds: "Man can't own the land, you know. . . . Man comes and goes; the land will always be here. White men never figure that out. All we own are our lives" (366).
16. Personal e-mail correspondence with Anne McAllister, November 6, 2002.
17. Communications issues have been considered paramount by participants at schools and conferences operated by Ranch Management Consultants, as well as by Holistic Resource Management consultants. For literary treatments of this issue, see work by Blew, Blunt, Jordan, Kittredge, and others.

18. The Montana Board of Tourism lists both "dude" ranches and ranch home stay options for tourists. A collaborative based in Bozeman, Montana, seeks to use such farm and ranch vacations to promote the viability of family-owned farms and ranches. Some readers who have logged on to romance writer Anne McAllister's website (*www.annemcallister.com)* and posted in her "Guest Book" have indicated that they seek vacations in Montana where they can experience ranch life.

WORKS CITED

Blew, Mary Clearman. *All but the Waltz: Essays on a Montana Family*. New York: Viking, 1991.

———. *Bone Deep in Landscape: Writing, Reading, Place*. Norman: University of Oklahoma Press, 1999.

Blunt, Judy. *Breaking Clean*. New York: Alfred A. Knopf, 2002.

Comer, Krista. *Landscapes of the New West*. Chapel Hill: University of North Carolina Press, 1999.

Dailey, Janet. *Calder Born, Calder Bred*. 1983. Reprint, New York: Pocket Books, 1984.

Evans, Nicholas. *The Horse Whisperer*. New York: Delacorte, 1995.

Fiedler, Leslie A. "The Montana Face." 1949. Reprinted in *The Last Best Place: A Montana Anthology* (744–52). Ed. William Kittredge and Annick Smith. Seattle: University of Washington Press, 1991.

———. "Montana: P.S." *Unfinished Business*. New York: Stein and Day, 1972. 139–44.

———. "Montana: P.P.S." *Unfinished Business*. New York: Stein and Day, 1972. 145–50.

Graulich, Melody. "'Oh Beautiful for Spacious Guys': An Essay on the 'Legitimate Inclinations of the Sexes.'" *The Frontier Experience and the American Dream*. Ed. David Mogen, Mark Busby, and Paul Bryant. College Station: Texas A&M Press, 1989. 186–201.

Hayes, Penny. *Montana Feathers*. Tallahassee: The Naiad Press, 1990.

Hoag, Tami. *Dark Paradise*. New York: Bantam, 1994.

The Horse Whisperer (film). Director: Robert Redford, 1998.

Jensen, Margaret Ann. *Love's $weet Return: The Harlequin Story*. Bowling Green OH: Bowling Green State University Popular Press, 1984.

Juhasz, Suzanne. *Reading from the Heart: Women, Literature, and the Search for True Love*. New York: Penguin, 1994.

Kittredge, William. *Hole in the Sky*. New York: Knopf, 1992.

———. *Owning It All*. St. Paul MN: Graywolf Press, 1987.

———, ed. *The Portable Western Reader*. New York: Penguin, 1997.

Krentz, Jayne Ann, ed. *Dangerous Men and Adventurous Women*. Philadelphia: University of Pennsylvania Press, 1992.

Lanigan, Catherine. *Montana Bride*. Silhouette Desire series. New York: Silhouette, 1998.

Linz, Cathie. "Setting the Stage: Facts and Figures." *Dangerous Men and Adventurous*

Women. Ed. Jayne Ann Krentz. Philadelphia: University of Pennsylvania Press, 1992. 11–14.

Maclay, Charlotte. *The Right Cowboy's Bed*. Toronto: Harlequin, 2000.

Makinen, Merja. *Feminist Popular Fiction*. Basingstoke, Hampshire UK: Palgrave, 2001.

McAllister, Anne. *A Cowboy's Promise*. Silhouette Desire series. New York: Silhouette, 2001.

———. *The Great Montana Cowboy Auction*. New York: Silhouette, 2002.

McCarthy, Cormac. *Blood Meridian*. New York: Random House, 1985.

McMahon, Franci. *Staying the Distance*. Ithaca NY: Firebrand Books, 1994.

Mogen, David, Mark Busby, and Paul Bryant, eds. *The Frontier Experience and the American Dream: Essays on American Literature*. College Station: Texas A&M University Press, 1989.

Mussel, Kay. *Fantasy and Reconciliation: Contemporary Formulas of Women's Romance Fiction*. Westport CT: Greenwood Press, 1984.

Radway, Janice. *Reading the Romance: Women, Patriarchy, and Popular Culture*. 1984. Revised ed. Chapel Hill: University of North Carolina Press, 1991.

Rustand, Roxanne. *Montana Legacy*. Harlequin Superromance, Home on the Ranch series. Toronto: Harlequin, 2000.

Stegner, Wallace. *Where the Bluebird Sings to the Lemonade Springs: Living and Writing in the West*. New York: Penguin, 1993.

Temte, Myrna. *Sleeping with the Enemy*. Montana Mavericks series. New York: Silhouette, 1994.

Thayne, Raeanne. *Renegade Father*. Silhouette Intimate Moments series. New York: Silhouette, 2001.

Thurston, Carol. *Romance Revolution: Erotic Novels for Women and the Quest for a New Sexual Identity*. Chicago: University of Illinois Press, 1987.

CHAPTER FIVE

Feminism and Postmodernism in the New West: Mary Blew and Montana Women's Writing since 1990

WILLIAM W. BEVIS

Montana literature since 1990 has been distinguished by women writing about women, including work by Dee McNamer, Annick Smith, and Teresa Jordan, a new biography of Mildred Walker by Ripley Hugo, and two recent award-winning books, *Perma Red* by Debra Earling and *Breaking Clean* by Judy Blunt. Among the many fine new works of the past fifteen to twenty years, however, Mary Blew's *All but the Waltz* (1991) begs discussion because it employs an extraordinary relation of voice to text, raising crucial issues of feminism and postmodernism in the new West.

In the 1970s and 1980s, the issues surrounding pioneer women's memoirs included debates on why women came west (e.g., dragged by men or for opportunity), and whether the landscape tradition was itself masculinist, excluding women. Much of that feminist scholarship focused on the overland trail diaries and the homesteading experience. By contrast, however, we now have accounts by women who were born to old ranches—notably Blew and Blunt in Montana—and who had absorbed feminist issues before they wrote. In the 1990s, we entered a new phase of western women's writing, well beyond pioneering memories: books by fourth-generation ranch women and second (and third) generation feminists.

MARY BLEW'S VOICE

In their introduction to the anthology *A Circle of Women*, Mary Blew and Kim Barnes discussed being western women writers in 1994, beginning with the idea of giving audience to silent, suppressed voices: "As children, we could easily have believed that our mothers had no stories. What we discovered as we grew older was that the women had kept their stories secret. Sometimes they were whispered between generations, sometimes not even that" (x).

Interestingly, Blew and Barnes accepted some of the "cowboy" virtues that earlier feminist writers (many from back East, or France) had resisted: "The end of the myth of the West is where we began. And we are still drawn to the values of that myth: the courage, the self-reliance, the toughness" (x). As we shall see, those traits remain in Blew's style, of mind as well as of writing: a flint-hard eye, Clint Eastwood staring down a memory. As *The New York Times* said of *All but the Waltz*, Blew "writes with fierce pride and unforgettable clarity."

Both Barnes and Blew also value the primacy of landscape in their experience, in contrast to 1970s feminists (such as Annette Kolodny, in *The Lay of the Land*), for whom the "virgin land" of the West was an exclusively male fantasy. Blew, however, while acknowledging that "I have been imprinted from birth by that landscape," and "I am bone-deep in landscape," also feels "a kind of aversion" to the "displacement and loneliness" that that hard land surrounds (*Circle* 376). This cowboy toughness and complex love/hate relation to Montana space are also dramatically shared by Judy Blunt in *Breaking Clean*, the title itself—among many possibilities—describing rejection of marriage and ranch by means of a boxing or a rodeo metaphor: breaking clean in the ring or out of the chute on a bronc or a bull. The bronc is their attitude, and the bull is their prose. As second-generation feminists, women of the West no longer have to accept all of that masculinist cowboy tradition, and no longer have to reject it all. As we shall see, this blunt bull can carry us in new directions, complicated, contradictory, and more indeterminate than Clint Eastwood in *Unforgiven*.

What *are* the women's stories, so long suppressed? How are they different from the men's? Quite apart from the subject matter (as we shall see, Blunt is eloquent on gender roles), Blew and Barnes offer two traits: communal stories and "quilted" or fragmented narrative.

The communal theme is both simple to grasp and historically complex. Blew has grown up not only with the new feminism since the '60s, but also with the new western revisionism, which in some ways was symbiotic with both feminist and postmodern theory. When Annick Smith, at an early meeting of the editorial board of *The Last Best Place* around 1985 (Blew was there), said that the primary Montana story had changed from killing the bear (from Lewis and Clark onward) to pulling the calf (in Doig and the end of her own film, *Heartland*), she was proposing that the Montana story had changed from the self-reliant individual battling against nature to issues of family, society, community, context. Her remark was in concert with the new social history and the reinterpretation of the West that would emerge in Patricia Limerick's and Richard White's histories a decade later. White, particularly, documented the myriad ways in which the West was settled by kinship, organizations, the state. In this case, the suppressed women's stories of which Blew writes, stories of endless, lonely work for others (There are those who make a mess and those who clean it up, as Blunt's mother said), stories of children, relationship, nurturing, abuse, family disaster, seem to be part of suppressed western stories of community—whether supportive or self-destructive—which are only now coming to light.

The second characteristic of women's stories, "quilted," is more subtle and takes us to the heart of Blew's technique. Naturally, when editing an anthology one stitches together the scraps available, so "quilting" was a convenient metaphor for Blew and Barnes. But the theme of a patchwork or inadequate or antinarrative narrative, a story that does not easily or exactly fit together, also runs throughout Blew's memoir *Balsamroot*, published the same year as *A Circle of Women*. Blew's aunt Imogene "has no narrative that will contain her parents" (3); Blew writes pages of free association, quilting fragments of family memories as did Faulkner's Benjy (22–23); she is writing a "communal novel" (114). And perhaps most telling, Blew says: "One story can be narrated only by denying another" (149). In *Balsamroot*, Blew is intrigued by the resistance to storytelling she had explored three years before in *All but the Waltz*. In Blew, "quilted" is a homespun metaphor for an "écriture feminine," a postmodern destruction of consistent narrative and coherent voice. These antilinear, antinarrative themes are certainly part of the decade (see the recycling structures of Maclean's *Young Men and Fire* and of Welch's *Killing Custer*), but more than most Blew takes them to heart as a woman and as an intellectual: because of her finely honed skepticism, the fragmented, revised, contradictory form works very well for her.

An excellent example of Blew using skepticism to disrupt narrative, to assert indeterminacy and yet gain new sympathy and understanding, occurs in *All but the Waltz* in the section titled "The Unwanted Child." She sets up the story as follows:

> But my mother had another, darker reason to be angry with me, and I knew it. The reason had broken over me suddenly the summer I was seven and had been playing, on warm afternoons, in a rain barrel full of water. Splashing around, elbows and knees knocking against the side of the barrel, I enjoyed the rare sensation of being wet all over. My little sister, four, came and stood on tiptoe to watch. It occurred to me to boost her into the barrel with me.

My mother burst out of the kitchen door and snatched her back.

"What are you trying to do, kill her?" she shouted.

I stared back at her, dumbfounded.

Her eyes blazed over me, her brows knotted at their worst.

"And after you'd drowned her, I suppose you'd have slunk off to hide somewhere until it was all over!"

It had never crossed my mind to kill my sister, or that my mother might think I wanted to. (172)

At this point the story might well end, or move on to other examples of parental madness. Blew, however, turns in quite a different direction, for what "crossed my mind" or did not, the process of association and reflection, is always the heart of her story: "or that my mother might think I wanted to. (Although I had, once, drowned a setting of baby chicks in a wheelbarrow.) But that afternoon, dripping in my underpants, goose-bumped and ashamed, I watched her carry my sister into the house and then I *did* go off to hide until it was, somehow, all over, for she never mentioned it at dinner." The emphasis is mine, and of course the "did" and the exact repetition of her mother's words ("off to hide") suggest some validation of her mother's point of view, a validation that began, however parenthetically, with the memory of the chicks. And what will come next? We can see Blew's mind at work as she begins to question her own assumptions: her absolute certainty—"It had never crossed my mind"—is generating a reaction, a reconsideration of "never." The very next paragraph: "The chicks had been balls of yellow fuzz, and I had been three. I wanted them to swim. I can just remember catching a chick and holding it in the water until it stopped squirming and then laying it down to catch a fresh one. I didn't stop until I had drowned the whole dozen and laid them out in a sodden yellow row" (173).

Wow. But surely she doesn't think that bathing with her sister. . . . Next:

"What the mind refuses to allow to surface is characterized by a suspicious absence. Of detail, of associations. Memories skirt the edge of nothing. There is for me about this incident that suspicious absence. What is being withheld?" (173).

Almost everyone who has read *Waltz* says that Blew is tough on herself, painfully honest. Here the honesty shines a white light of self-interrogation on the way she remembers or suppresses, and why: "Had I, for instance, given my mother cause to believe I might harm my sister? Children have done such harm, and worse. What can be submerged deeper, denied more vehemently, than the murderous impulse? At four, my sister was a tender, trusting little girl with my mother's wide gray eyes and brows. A younger sister of an older sister. A good girl. Mommy's girl" (173). We notice that her sister had "my mother's wide gray eyes" and watch the thought develop immediately into full sibling rivalry: "Mommy's girl." Perhaps she had indeed given her mother "cause to believe," in a glance, a look. . . . Then just as suddenly Blew moves out of herself, generously, into her mother's psyche: "What do I really know about my mother's feelings toward her own dead sister? Kathryn's dolls had been put away; my mother was never allowed to touch them" (173). And now hanging in the indeterminacy of a fragmented narrative, quilted scraps of three-line paragraphs that cannot quite be combined, that are stitched next to each other in suggestive juxtapositions, Blew recalls one more shred of sibling war and rage: "'I'll never, never love one of my kids more than another!' she screamed at my father in one of her afternoons of white rage. The context is missing." The context is the ultimate suspicious absence. I have quoted every word in the one-page section; there are no elided transitions; it ends with "The context is missing." From the cubists to the postmodernists, the shape of what we know is not visionary but pastiche, quilted, pieces juxtaposed. In another sudden change of voice, we are back to ranch business: "During the good years, when cattle prices were high . . ." (173).

This book is a "woman's story" in more than content, more than a story of washing in tubs, or hard work, or loneliness, or men trying to deny her an education or liberty. This is a new voice, a way to conceive of a woman as speaking against, in contra-diction to the dominant western male voice of terse certainty, common sense, natural authority. Blew's self-consciousness, self-criticism, hesitancy, second thoughts, giving way to a generous entertaining of others' thoughts and feelings, admitting all the while that memory cannot be trusted, that one story erases another, that all stories impose order on chaos, which in this memory of her sister she plainly refuses to do . . . these habits of the mind and heart are the deliberate antithesis of certainty, patriarchy, control.

In calling this voice postmodern I am invoking a broad and historical understanding of postmodernism, which was born with Stein and Picasso, the cubists, atonal and polyrhythmic music, and jazz, which produced the Joyce that Derrida took as his foundation, was buried by T. S. Eliot and new criticism, and arose again in the 1960s when the implications of radical modernism finally seeped down to academic departments of literature and philosophy. The characteristics of radical modernism/postmodernism in art are fragmentation, improvisation (or the imitation of improvisation), indeterminacy, and a questioning of voice (the voice changes, or is contradicted, or is untrustworthy).

By the '70s this questioning of voice, especially in Derrida, had taken a more Buddhist turn (following Nietzsche's lead) toward a deconstruction of the idea of self. The heart of this postmodernism is skepticism about claims to coherence and authority in knowledge and perception.

Just as serene Buddhist traditions are filled with wild masters indulging a theater of ego, postmodernism from Stein and Breton onward has always hung in the paradox between radical indeterminacy on one hand (at the extreme, nonsense), and grand new claims to ideological certainty on the other (at the extreme, manifestos of nonsense). At times, in the 1970s and 1980s, ideological certainty seemed to pass from master to pupil more easily than indeterminacy; nevertheless, in spite of the excesses of some disciples, and in spite of the theater of proclamation from Nietzsche and Stein to Derrida, in seminal texts indeterminacy has always been at the heart of postmodernism. Blew, who came to her position with a keen irony in the context of this zeitgeist (yes, zeitgeist), has very little ideology and a great deal of skepticism, as we shall see in the next section when her postmodernism becomes a western feminism.

With her undeniably western ranch credentials, Blew has the authority to speak in a new, anti-authoritarian woman's voice(s) and to say "This, too, is now western." A flint-hard indeterminacy. Sharp words, sharp reversals, no easy answers. We know her at a distance by that style, by the way she sits her horse . . . then another, and another, and then dismounts.

READING ABRAHAM

Is the section on drowning her sister only one page, a technical tour de force of indeterminacy, or does it point to a major theme in Blew's work? In chapters one and two of *Waltz*, Blew makes clear that for her, to write as a western and Montana woman in the 1980s is to write differently from the men (especially from Doig, trusting his memory, and Maclean, trusting narrative control), and the difference is that she's uncertain. Her memory cannot be trusted—the pigs were on the island, yet the pigs could not have been on the island—and in the Abraham chapter she shows that her opinions cannot be trusted either. It's certainty itself that she distrusts, the "patriarchy" of certainty and the way in which certainty controls and directs its stories by denying others. She will define herself by allowing second thoughts, contradictions, an openness that loses control of narrative, by writing a story in which the narrator is not the boss but a character changing, changing stories, learning, being wrong. "No story is ever the whole story," as Blew says in *Balsamroot* (151). Maybe a patchwork of evolving stories is what a woman can contribute. This strain of feminism has assigned to gender (or to marginalization) the skeptical modernism/postmodernism of Nietzsche and the late Wallace Stevens, who realized the exfoliation of voice when the gods had fled: "If nothing was the truth then all things were the truth."

Mary Blew is sly. Uncertainty is her organizing principle, but this is not easy to believe as you read sentence by sentence. She is so clear and so analytically exact that the reader, having seen the subtitle "Essays on a Montana Family," may well expect a linear consistency. Uncertainty in Blew is never vagueness or waffling; it is an epistemological principle, a deep skepticism about how we remember, how we feel, how we know. Objective accuracy is impossible; a story can only be true to a narrator's fancies and foibles. This is the philosophical uncertainty of a mind too keen to deceive itself, reminding us of Eliot's comment on Henry James, that he had a mind too fine to be violated by an idea. Entertaining many ideas, however, watching them react to each other—that's another matter.

This chapter is about Blew's great-grandfather, Abraham, but it's really about her father and she knows it, or rather we watch her come to realize it in a chapter that *seems* structured by improvisation. At the bottom of the opening page of the chapter, opposite a photograph of great-grandparents Abraham and Mary, she writes that they, "so adult that their faces were dressed in stone" (curious, since in the picture both have the trace of a sly smile), "receded into a single dimension of authority to be plotted against and outwitted" (15). Why does she see "a single dimension" (authority) in these adults, rather relaxed in a casual pose, and why "to be plotted against"? This seems a pretty strong response to a man she had never met, the wry man in the picture. They "were never flesh and blood" (16), she goes on. Really. Then whence the passion?

Sure enough, the very next paragraph tells us, "Later I came to disapprove of Abraham," setting up the last three pages of the chapter, "and to believe that he would have disapproved of me" (16). On what grounds does she believe that? She answers right away: "Abraham was a paterfamilias, an oppressor, a traditionalist like my father" (16). Aha. Perhaps it was her father who disapproved. The facing page completes the theme: "Sometimes at night I . . . heard my father's words, like an unwanted legacy, censorious, deluded, deaf to any answer: *Somewhere you got the idea in your head that you know something, but you don't know a goddamned thing*" (17).

Her father—the source of her passion, anger, and revolution ("to be plotted against")—is revealed.

Two observations: the words "paterfamilias, an oppressor" are formal jargon, signs of a mind being violated by a fairly predictable idea, indeed by an entire paradigm of certainty. Certainty is not sly; certainty is masculinist; it is itself the oppressor. Her certainty will come back to haunt her, and she will reject it. Second, the direct and shocking memory of her father's disdain is introduced as an "unwanted legacy." There's the real subject of the chapter. How do we deal with an unwanted legacy? You can't give it back—but maybe you can change your relation to it.

Twenty pages follow before the passage we will consider begins, pages exploring the nearly indecipherable papers and personal notes that Abraham left behind and that have come down to Blew through the family, never read. In those pages a rhythm is set up, alternating between resentment and admiration of her father and a more nuanced, varied, but parallel set of responses to Abraham as she attempts to rescue him from the legacy of her father's disdain and suicide: "I felt rising anger and resolve. By God Abraham, *he* may have left without saying goodbye, but *you*, Abraham! I know how to make you talk to me! . . . I went to my chest and lifted out the bundle of Abraham's papers." (18–19). But all the way through, the reader is wondering if perhaps the father will be rescued too, if reconciliation to the great-grandfather surveyor will also teach a rapproachement with the real paterfamilias, the unfamiliar familiar dad. She looks again at the same picture and does not see stone but "a man whose handsome arched brows and eyes . . . were my father's to the life." So her father was handsome, while "to the life" suggests such family/blood intimacy. In the following pages, fresh attacks on the surveyor's geometry/patriarchy alternate with an intimacy and intensity comparable to love: "Just what Abraham saw was, for me, an insistent unknown . . . I pored over the minuscule script . . . searching . . . I stole time . . . I huddled . . . absorbed, guessing, pausing . . . promising myself . . . I began to feel an intimacy like the first unspoiled stages of a love affair" (22–23). As always in Blew, the vacillating voice and alternating structure calls into question narrative design: "And where was Abraham's starting point on the envelope in front of me? Where was his ending?" (19).

Blew's three-page ending to the chapter is a carefully controlled "improvisation," a series of reversals and revisions and unexpected revelations concerning her patriarchal legacy:

> I felt stale and saddened as I came to the end of Abraham's papers. His vision, like my father's, was linear; it ruled out the faces on the margins or at the shrunken end of his perspective, and one of those faces was mine.

> Where could I find certain footing or even air to breathe in his world of right angles? Seen through Abraham's tunnel vision, I was a runaway daughter [wait a minute, he never knew her], a failed "little wife," an uppity woman who *somehow got the idea into her head she knows something, but by God she don't know a goddamned thing.* Within the terms of Abraham's conversion of place from habitat to real estate, with all its concurrent assumptions about patriarchy and patrimony [but the terms in italics were her father's terms], I was left with no more integrity of self than the Jockos [Salish Indians whom Abraham had met]. (36)

On first reading, not knowing where Blew was going, I found in this paragraph far too many neatly packaged "concurrent assumptions" of her own. I wrote in my margin, "Does the dogmatic feminism hurt the narrative?" In fact it will explode it. But notice that the formulaic language of patriarchal theory again accompanies surfacing resentment of the father, a resentment clearly projected onto the great-grandfather. In the next paragraph, she follows this ideological certainty to an appropriately extreme, black-and-white conclusion: "As I had expected at the beginning [of the chapter as well as in reading Abraham's papers], Abraham and I had nothing to say to one another and no way to say it if we did." We are back to square one: Abraham is stone, not flesh and blood. He is the Other. But think: the emphasis on "say," and "way to say," might remind us that both Abraham and Blew are writers, indeed have met as writers, as people who "say."

Then, having come to a dead end of theoretical certainty and complete alienation from Abraham, Blew makes a sudden, wonderful, and most characteristic move, a move that seems improvisatory, a move that relinquishes her own control: she gives the narrative over to a friend. The next paragraph of the quilt begins with a different fabric: "In the spring of 1990 I went . . . to Great Falls" to speak about Abraham and his papers. There a friend (unnamed; it was Bill Thackeray of Northern Montana College) was fascinated by Abraham's careful preservation of apparently ephemeral notes: the scrap paper was wrapped in bundles with string. Blew quotes a full paragraph of Thackeray's long letter to her; Thackeray surmises that Abraham had some audience in mind, probably "descendants unknown." He goes on to say, "I think perhaps Abraham had you specifically in mind as audience, and what a touching and lonely act his writing then becomes" (37) Blew offers no comment. A break follows. Then, Blew has totally changed her tone: "Abraham, in my imagination your buggy rolls over the prairie swells . . ." (37).

Now consider what has happened. After an all-out attack on patriarchs, using aggressive 1970s feminist rhetoric, she admits—tacitly—to being brought up short by a friend. That friend is given the narrative, literally: he has the page, quoted at length without reply from Blew. That friend is male. He is suggesting a "touching and lonely" relation of Abraham and Blew. Wonderfully, Blew dives right in to try out this new possibility. The generosity of this move, immediately replacing the programmatic certainty of patriarchal theory with empathetic reconciliation, is impressive. Gender roles have been reversed. She has allowed a male friend to teach her a more subtle and familial view—and she has recorded the influence in print. Her woman's strength is in not feeling the need to defend a position. With one page left we have no idea where this story might go.

The long, lyrical, Doig-like paragraph rolls on, following Abraham's buggy "over the prairie swells toward the bristling fringe of pines along the river breaks" (37). In Blew's imagination the country is now Charlie Russell country, beautiful and vast. "But you, Abraham, in your suit and vest and watch chain, you hold the reins" (37). Suddenly, control is beautiful too. "Your horses break into a trot, and you brace yourself on the footboard and lean into the wind, still zestful, still as lean and limber as a young man, although your shreds of hair are white now" (37). Flesh and blood, no longer stone, and looking good. And what of Blew's father, will he receive these unlooked-for blessings, share in this grace?

> The towheaded boy in the back seat, your grandson [Ah, that would be Blew's father, and now she does indeed see her father in new light] bumps against your folded transit and chains and the fishing tackle you carry everywhere you go. . . . He is a good boy, careful and accurate like you. . . . He learns quickly, but he has inherited your talent without your opportunities; there will be no Lafayette College for this boy growing up in the West. And he has grown up with your love for the Judith Basin without your long vision; only three times in his life will he venture far from the shadow of that blue Butte. (37–38)

So reading and considering Abraham, who came to the Judith from Pennsylvania, has given Blew new understanding of her father, a third-generation local rancher through and through. Is that why he so resented Blew's education, and her leaving? This would not be the first ranching family that has devolved from globetrotting grandparents and Harvard educations to isolated lives in an isolated county, full of resentful fantasies about the dark world beyond. Some of them get no farther than the legislature.

Having purged resentment from her memory of Abraham, and having forgiven her father (for the moment), Blew turns back to address her ancestor directly: "Abraham, your photograph hangs over my desk" (38), and she thinks how far she is from home (although "over my desk" brings Abraham closer). She chides Abraham a bit for his blindness to the Indians, her last flash of political correctness, then she turns in the final paragraph to his writing. "Your papers rest on my desk" (38). Writing is how they have met, and Blew now admits that she too is writing as well as reading Abraham. In this beautiful paragraph, Abraham's ephemeral papers—"I am afraid they are disintegrating"—lead her to conclude the chapter with an awareness of her connection to Abraham through words, and through what words do: "Words, words, words, more words, the shapes for what we otherwise would never know, the stuff by which we reduce the terror of endlessness, as you, Abraham, understood so well" (38).

In three pages, Blew has gone from "nothing to say to one another and no way to say it if we did," to a reciprocal saying and listening made not just of words, but of disintegrating words, "stuff," shared "shapes," shared "terror," and in the final verb, shared understanding.

The nature of that final understanding is interesting and, again, generous. For while Blew has come to this revelation by vacillating between respect and resentment of authority, by giving the narrative to Bill Thackeray, and then by losing control, she joins Abraham, "paterfamilias, oppressor," "linear . . . in his world of right angles," in appreciating the rage for order that lies in language, in "words, the shapes for what we otherwise would never know" (38). She admits that without language's imposition of order, the geometry of words laid on the land, we would be in chaos. Words "*by which* we reduce the terror of endlessness" (38, emphasis added), suggests purpose. She has identified with the enemy, the surveyor, the father: he who imposes order. But she has also subverted that order. Abraham, too, spoke *because* he lived with "the terror of endlessness." Order is a necessary illusion, as Nietzsche said, a vital lie.

Another paterfamilias surely helped to shape these words. Dick Hugo had died in 1982, just before Margaret Kingsland gathered a group to plan *The Last Best Place* and Blew began writing the piece on her father's death. Blew had read Hugo's last poems, including "The Standing Stones of Callannish." As the ancient Celts are erecting the strange stones (picture Stonehenge), purpose unknown, Hugo imagines a woman "urging them on and muttering hard at the sky / a word we've lost. It sounded like 'shape.' It meant 'world.'" Stonehenge, like language, is an imposition of shape, of order; it creates our world. And both Hugo and Blew knew the famous and beautiful end of Maclean's *A River Runs Through It* of 1978: "Under the rocks are the words, and some of the words are theirs." So she has reconciled to Abraham, originally a figure of oppression, by their shared need for "logos," the imposition of order by words: "In the beginning was the word, and the word was with God, and the word was God." That's what John's gospel told Maclean's father, and what Maclean's father told him, and that's what Hugo and Blew's great-grandfather told her. An entire pantheon of Montana pater(s) familias.

But of course Blew's logos/order is not quite Hugo's or Maclean's, for she has already deconstructed her own memory and voice, and she has undermined the notion of a single overarching logos, Hugo's one "world," or a single underlying logos, Maclean's word beneath all rivers and rocks. It is clear that she and Abraham share an *attempt* to establish order through words, they share a provisional "understanding." What they understand is that words "make shapes for what we otherwise would never know." But "make shapes for" does not equal "tell," and "what we otherwise would never know" implies but does not equal "what we do know." It's a marvelous sentence: we make shapes for the unknowable—a visionary kind of not knowing. Were the pigs on the island? How did her father die? We are joined together by making up these stories to "reduce the terror of endlessness." We are joined by using a word that "*sounded* like shape. It *meant* world." Maybe Hugo was a bit sly himself.

Such a shifty technique answers patriarchal, rational, imperial control with open-ended, irrational, contradictory, and indeterminate forms.

Blew's affirmation of a provisional unity through words puts her in Irigaray's paradox, in which an écriture feminine, based on a deconstruction of logos, cannot be écriture. Blew has joined Abraham through words that are not really logos; they are "stuff." Her "understanding" is not of an ultimate order but of a process, that we make words in order to reduce the terror of endlessness. And in Blew this postmodern understanding, understanding of a shared confusion, is feminist: it is a woman who has been able to give her narrative to a friend, even to a man, to change her voice, her attitude, her prose, and finally, to embrace the patriarchal Other by subverting his certainty as well as her own.

"I will say: today, writing is woman's. . . . It is much harder for man to let the other come through him. Writing is the passageway, the entrance, the exit, the dwelling place of the other in me . . . and for men this permeability, this non-exclusion is a threat, something intolerable" (*Newly Born Woman* 85–86).

The speaker is not Blew but Hélène Cixous.

In feminism too there have been poles of certainty (gender stereotypes, fixed roles, exclusive ideologies) on the one hand, and uncertainty (women as capable of contradiction, emotion, irrationality, permeability, indeterminacy) on the other. In the first three-fourths of the chapter Blew plays with the terms of ideological certainty ("paterfamilias, an oppressor") to analyze her situation, define patriarchal issues, and sharpen her awareness of resentment of her father. Then she complicates this paradigm with increasingly contradictory views of Abraham, and in the conclusion she embraces the other pole, that her strength as a woman writer is in losing control, losing certainty, embracing contradiction, and allowing the Other to become part of her: "for men this permeability, this non-exclusion is a threat, something intolerable." And because she redefines Abraham's logos as well as her own, dragging him with her into the room without walls, this feminism becomes a ground, or shifting sand, on which she and Abraham, daughter and patriarch, the other and the other, can meet in one condition: "words . . . by which we reduce [but not erase] the terror of endlessness, as you, Abraham, understood so well."

Blew is also, of course, privileging family over theory. Montanans are like that.

Blew's father loved A. B. Guthrie Jr.'s *The Big Sky*, which she partly blamed for "the mythic Montana of the past" that shaped the way her father died. Guthrie's Boone embodied the western male myth of a natural man: "A man's body acted for him" (*The Big Sky* 340). In her work, Blew has flat left Boone behind. She argues for examining our motives, considering consequences, questioning ourselves.

In *Ten Tough Trips* (1990) I argued: "What Boone embodies is a European fantasy of escape from civilization, from complication, from responsibility. We will set out for a more simple, empty space, and arrive there with a more simple, empty psyche. 'Get away from it all.'" (19). Blew and I were working on our two books (her *Waltz*, my *Ten Tough Trips*) in the 1980s, as we also worked together on the editorial board of *The Last Best Place*. In my analysis of Guthrie, and in Blew's technique, one can see a common response of that time to western myths. Blew is not interested in a primitivist fantasy of escape from the evils of civilization to a natural (and antisocial) paradise. Blew doesn't run away from the responsibilities of the psyche. Her feminism and new western communitarianism are symbiotic. She remains to do the hard work, the woman's work she seems to say, of understanding.

I first taught *All but the Waltz* in 1993. Students, especially Montana female students, loved it right away and saw its difference, its tough originality. "She doesn't want her child!" the young man said in class. "It happens a lot," an older woman replied. "Thank goodness someone has finally said it."

Blew's book always came at the end of the course, right after Maclean, and the contrast was obvious. One student, Rachel Smith, quoted Blew's "What the mind refuses to allow to surface is characterized by a suspicious absence," and said the quotation expressed exactly what she had disliked in Maclean: in that beautiful story, too much was being withheld, avoided, controlled. She also came to appreciate Blew's antinarrative storytelling versus Maclean's seamless design: "*All but the Waltz* is cohesive without chronology. It does not travel from A to B. . . . It is more like rain when it first starts splattering on the ground. All over the place, but eventually everything is covered."[1]

BLUNT SPEECH

For twenty-two years the final papers in the Montana Writers course included, if students wished, up to four pages of personal testimony. One of those four-page essays from an unknown student, which I read out loud to a stunned class, is now the first chapter of Judy Blunt's *Breaking Clean*. Blunt won a Whiting Award in 2001 for the book, the clear successor to Mary Blew's *All but the Waltz*. Together, these two books bring remarkable strength, analysis, and eloquence to the subject of growing up female on, and beyond, a Montana ranch:

> Like my parents and grandparents, I was born and trained to live there. I could rope and ride and jockey a John Deere as well as my brothers, but being female, I also learned to bake bread and can vegetables and reserve my opinion when the men were talking. When a bachelor neighbor began courting me when I was fifteen, my parents were proud and hopeful. Though he was twelve years older than I was, his other numbers were very promising. He and his father ran five hundred cow-calf pairs and five hundred head of yearlings on 36,000 acres of range.
>
> After supper one spring evening, my mother and I stood in the kitchen. She held her back stiff as her hands shot like pistons into the mound of bread dough on the counter. I stood tough beside her. On the porch, John had presented my father with a bottle of whiskey and was asking Dad's permission to marry me. I wanted her to grab my cold hand and tell me how to run. I wanted her to smooth the crumpled letter from the garbage can and read the praise of my high school principal. I wanted her to tell me what I could be.

> She rounded the bread neatly and efficiently and began smoothing lard over the top, intent on her fingers as they tidied the loaves.
>
> "He's a good man," she said finally. (4–5)

Blunt's story is remarkably similar to Blew's: "My options were as frightening as they were simple. I could marry, or I could leave" (204). For both, as women, there was no way they would take over a ranch. Blew didn't want to stay. Blunt had a brother to inherit her father's ranch, and after she married the neighbor, "He turned, pointing the hat straight at me. 'Don't think you're going to run this ranch,' he said" (279). However, both women (probably most men and women who wind up writing books) are unusually bright, strong willed, and independent, and Blunt would be the first to say that her story is not her sister's story.

On women's issues there is remarkable continuity from Nannie Alderson's memoir of the 1880s through Blew to Blunt, covering a century of ranching experience. Still in that first chapter she wrote for class, Blunt tells us there were indeed other options:

> I stuck with the bargain sealed on my parents' porch for more than twelve years, although my faith in martyrdom as a way of life dwindled. I collected children and nervous ticks the way some of the women collected dress patterns and ceramic owls. It was hard to shine when all the good things had already been done. Dorothy crocheted tissue covers and made lampshades from Styrofoam egg cartons. Pearl looped thick, horrible rugs from rags and denim scraps. Helen gardened a half acre of land and raised two hundred turkeys in her spare time. And everyone attended the monthly meetings of the Near and Far Club to answer the roll call with her favorite new recipe. (8)

All three women would have preferred to be at the corrals, on a horse. Blunt's story replays almost exactly Nannie Alderson's: "As my family grew, my activities outside the house shrank in equal measure. . . . For the first two years, I had reveled in the freedom and status of outside work, getting to know the expanse of prairie and badlands that was my new home. The spring before Jeannette's birth, I rode in the branding roundup . . . but the neighbors were aghast, especially the men" (Blunt 255). A week later she is thrown and a bit trampled, and a few months on she is kicked in her pregnant stomach by a cow. She quits, "finally convinced I couldn't have it all."

It had been the same for Blunt's mother:

> My mother despised the repetitious and thankless nature of housework and was an expert horsewoman. . . . I was a daughter, and must be penned to my seat with threats until I learned to cook and sew. . . . But it was also Mom who hazed for me the first time I left the corral on my green-broke bronc, Sunny, riding up to turn him from the barbed wire fence as we bolted across the pasture. "Stay with him," she cheered, and I did, until the front cinch broke and Sunny bucked straight through the reservoir with her good saddle hanging upside down on his belly. I dusted off my pride while Mom rode after the colt, leaning sideways at a full gallop to jerk the buckle on the flank cinch and snub the hackamore rein to her saddle horn. Womanly arts be damned. I wanted the ease, the power, of my mother, horseback. I wanted the real myth, and I set out to get it. (96)

But that life was closed to these women. "The roles went like this: Every rancher who stepped out the door scratching a full belly through a clean shirt had a partner who was willing to stay indoors and wash another load. 'Someone to make the mess, and someone to clean it up,' as my mother put it" (95).

Like most things, gender roles can be various and contradictory. In the 1950s, for instance, New England girls in private schools were expected to compete and develop themselves in athletics, scholarship, everything, from grade school through college—nothing like the cheerleading mentality in middle America—and then, after graduating from Vassar, they were supposed to marry a Yale boy and stay at home in the suburbs. That was a sucker punch. Blunt describes a similar paradox out West, where many of us think women had more active roles, and where many progressive policies originated:

> Most of the women in my community were like my mother—strong, capable women whose names were listed on the ranch deeds alongside their husbands' but who accepted second say in the business of it. On the fringe of their wifely example lay . . . the Calamity Jane type of mythology that held just enough truth to be dangerous. In these stories, landowning women were admired for their staunch independence and toughness—the sort of women who hired cooks and ran their own ranches. They were in books. And every ranch wife I knew crossed over just enough to make the stories seem possible, if not practical. (95)

Like the men, the women also were caught in a western mythology that romanticized their roles. Blunt continues, as usual bringing us back to reality: "I knew women savvy to the working of cattle and horses, women who rode the hay rake in June and took to the field to harvest. But without exception, they picked up a thank-you and walked back to tackle the work that was theirs alone. Woman's work. If I learned nothing else in my early years, I learned the scorn that twisted those words into insults" (96). Like Blew, Blunt sees most of these habits of subordination and domination as embedded in the culture. They do not necessarily blame individual men; or more precisely, both are harder on fathers and fathers-in-law than on husbands. When Judy's husband points his hat at her and says, "Don't think you're going to run this ranch," he's not a personal tyrant, but a decent man born to a tyrant's role. Blunt and Blew, because of their habits of analysis, tend to find people trapped in a culture, unable to see out. Other writers who also should know, notably Bill Kittredge, are eloquent on the way the isolated fiefdoms we call ranches breed a man, however humble in speech, who expects his authority to be unchallenged.

For both Blew and Blunt, control is the issue, as it is for Debra Earling's character Perma Red, and for Aunt Imogene in Blew's recent *Writing Her Own Life*, and for Margaret Bell in her memoir recently edited by Mary Blew and Lee Rostad, and as it was for Grace Stone Coates, Bell's mentor in the 1930s. Since male control is embedded in culture, the problem is not just men controlling; it is also women acceding to that control. As Blew might, Blunt considers her own state of mind at marriage, with considerable sympathy for the groom's situation as well as her own:

> If I tell these stories now, I do so because so much of what I learned circles back—*Shut up, pay attention, do what you're told.* I was eighteen when I walked down the aisle on my father's arm. The groom was almost thirty, a man of simple tastes and few passions, staunch honor and little experience. I joined him at the altar, bristling with independence yet eager to please, desperate for attention yet filled with the fierce energy born of old anger—a riddle behind my homemade veil. From my parents to the unwitting hands of my husband I passed the terrible power of judgment and reward, the absolute authority I connected with love. (35)

"The absolute authority *I* connected with love." If Blew and Blunt are rescuing the woman's voice from western stereotypes, they are also continually rescuing feminism from ideological stereotypes. While politically and culturally severe, both books are also rich with sympathy, vision, and a nuanced understanding. Shapes for what we do not know. Communal shapes for communal unknowns.

One community, or at least stretch of land that comes to mind reading these books is the Hi-Line, that long northern half of Montana from Glacier Park to North Dakota. Blunt and Blew, and Dee McNamer, are from the Hi-Line or close to it; they are the first major Hi-Line authors since Welch. ("It's not the end of the world, but you can see it from there.")

From this eco-critical perspective, in Hi-Line books the wind never stops, speech is short, and illusion is short-lived. Realism springs not from gender, but from place. While I am admiring how these women appropriate a terse, western male voice to their own purposes, the voice also reflects bioregional realities. As Blunt says: "Wind was dependable. Government agencies were not" (28). "It was common sense to expect the worst. No rancher made his reputation on how he handled good fortune" (29). And at the end of "Salvage," the mother of all blizzards story in western memoir since Granville Stuart in 1887, Blunt comes to spring in the country that is bone-deep in her and Mary Blew:

> At roundup and branding, we rode in the dust of survivors, cows with healed stumps for ears and tails, cows that grew old grazing lush grass over the graves of their sisters. The most lasting reminders were felt in the absence of things we had come to expect, the silence of summers without hearing the rusty-hinge sound of a cock pheasant, years without the harmony of pronghorns, the way they swerve and dodge over the cured grass like a school of fish. . . . Every generation relearns the rules the fathers have forgotten. One rule is awareness, the need to see past the power of human hands on the land, to the power beneath it. Those who forget have the wind to jog their memory, wind slipping evenly through the sage, dusting evenly across the fields. Watch your back, it's whispering. *This land owes you nothing.* (60)

After the blizzard of 1887 Granville Stuart said, "I never again wanted to own an animal I could not feed and shelter."

On the one hand, the traditional Montanan's appeal to a threatening nature beyond us and superior is obsolete, as our heated cars and air-conditioned tractor cabs suggest. The whole state could be astrodomed for the cost of a war or two. On the other hand, the new biosphere research suggests that we must indeed recover humility, that our conquest of nature is illusory. The empire of nature may strike back. Traditional humility—watch your back—is in vogue again.

Blew and Blunt's work is clearly looking back to a lost past, however. There's no way around it. As Blunt says, "My story would not happen in this age of VCRs and satellite dishes, computers and CD-ROMs. Self-contained ranch communities still exist out here . . . but today the world comes to them" (158). Just as *The Last Best Place* chronicled a phase of Montana literature, a flowering of sophisticated modern literature out of classic western roots, so Blew and Blunt's books, distinguished by the application of the best minds and pens to bygone days, tell of an agricultural past that is already legend.

That cannot be the future of Montana writing. The circle will be broken, because the pressure of necessity that has shaped their lives has changed. Already, one could argue, the pressure of necessity in Montana has shifted, for most people, from space—wind, distance, heat, drought, winter—to time: a Bozeman mother juggling a job, daycare, driving the kids to soccer. We are modern. Dee McNamer particularly has turned her attention to this new world, the town world. Annie Proulx in Wyoming is writing boldly of the new West, and Rick Newby's anthology *The New Montana Story* and Ken Egan's recent criticism in *Hope and Dread in Montana Literature* address these issues.

Blunt ends her book with the extended calf pulling that Annick Smith envisioned in the 1980s. And perhaps these books spell the end—there are other people alive who have similar memories, but it's hard to imagine they can write any better—the end of the second phase of Montana writings. We have killed the bear, and we have pulled the calf. What's next? It will have to include, at some point, the stockbroker's trophy cabin on the Blackfoot River, or over half the state living off a service economy or a government paycheck (in 2000, those income sources together were twenty-four times greater than net farm income in Montana). Or a Big Sandy organic rancher (Senator Tester) fighting Cargill and Monsanto and corporate control of seed banks, now genetically altered. There's a wind that blows everywhere, equally. McNamer's *My Russian* is set, pointedly, in a placeless university town (Missoula?). In so many ways, parts of Montana will become anywhere. However, the new stories, and new mythologies, will have to reflect the new realities. But just as Mildred Walker and Bud Guthrie and Dick Hugo were inspirations for craftsmanship, for a honed style and fidelity to words, words, words, the women of the 1990s have set new standards for honesty, for subtlety of voice, for subtlety of narrative, and for blunt speech.

NOTE

1. Quoted from Rachel Smith's essay from my Montana Writers course.

WORKS CITED

Bevis, William W. *Ten Tough Trips: Montana Writers and the West.* Seattle: University of Washington Press, 1990; reprint, Norman: University of Oklahoma Press, 2004.

Bell, Margaret. *When Montana and I Were Young: A Frontier Childhood.* Ed. Mary Clearman Blew and Lee Rostad. Lincoln: University of Nebraska Press, 2002.
Blew, Mary Clearman. *All but the Waltz: Essays on a Montana Family.* New York: Viking. 1991; reprint, Norman: University of Oklahoma Press, 2001.
———. *Balsamroot: A Memoir.* New York: Viking, 1994; reprint, Norman: University of Oklahoma Press, 2001.
———. *Sister Coyote: Montana Stories.* New York: Lyons Press, 2000.
———. *Writing Her Own Life.* Norman: University of Oklahoma Press, 2004.
Blew, Mary Clearman, and Kim Barnes, eds. *Circle of Women: An Anthology of Contemporary Western Women Writers.* New York, Penguin, 1994; reprint, Norman: University of Oklahoma Press, 2001.
Blunt, Judy. *Breaking Clean.* New York: Alfred A. Knopf, 2002.
Cixous, Hélène, and Catherine Clément. *The Newly Born Woman.* 1975. Trans. Betsy Wing. Reprint, Minneapolis: University of Minnesota Press, 1986.
Earling, Debra Magpie. *Perma Red.* New York: Putnam, 2002.
Egan, Ken, Jr. *Hope and Dread in Montana Literature.* Reno: University of Nevada Press, 2003.
Guthrie, A. B., Jr. *The Big Sky.* 1947. Reprint, New York: Houghton Mifflin, 1965.
Hugo, Richard. *Making Certain It Goes On: The Collected Poems of Richard Hugo.* New York: Norton, 1984.
Jordan, Teresa. *Cowgirls: Women of the American West.* New York: Doubleday, 1982.
———. *Riding the White Horse Home: A Western Family Album.* New York: Pantheon, 1993.
Kittredge, William, and Annick Smith, eds. *The Last Best Place: A Montana Anthology.* Helena: Montana Historical Society Press, 1988.
Kolodny, Annette. *The Lay of the Land.* Chapel Hill: University of North Carolina Press, 2005.
Maclean, Norman. *A River Runs Through It.* Chicago: University of Chicago Press, 1977.
McNamer, Deirdre. *Rima in the Weeds.* New York: HarperCollins, 1991.
———. *One Sweet Quarrel.* New York: HarperCollins, 1994.
———. *My Russian.* Boston: Houghton Mifflin, 1999.
Newby, Rick, ed. *The New Montana Story: An Anthology.* Helena: Riverbend Publishing, 2003.
Proulx, E. Annie. *Close Range: Wyoming Stories.* New York: Scribner, 1999.
Smith, Annick. *Homestead.* Minneapolis: Milkweed, 1995.
———. *In This We Are Native: Memoirs and Journeys.* New York: Lyons Press, 2001.
Welch, James P., and Paul Stekler. *Killing Custer: The Battle of Little Big Horn and the Fate of the Plains Indians.* New York: Penguin, 1994.

PART III Gay and Lesbian Literature Under a Big Sky

CHAPTER SIX

West of Desire: Queer Ambivalence in Montana Literature

KARL OLSON

> Before we were a nation, long before, a Spanish explorer of the continent, bravely lost in the wilderness, wrote, "We always held it certain that, going towards the sunset, we should find what we desired."
> —A. B. Guthrie Jr., "West Is Another Word for Magic"

> [B]efore they were even quite out of sight of the city they had turned their tragic mounts to the west and they rode infatuate and half fond toward the red demise of that day, toward the evening lands and the distant pandemonium of the sun.
> —Cormac McCarthy, *Blood Meridian*

A dam is built in Montana. Its construction is the central event in two Montana novels, set on opposite sides of the Continental Divide and in juxtaposed ethnic communities. In D'Arcy McNickle's *Wind from an Enemy Sky* the dam cuts off the water supply of the Little Elk tribe, a culture that is itself being methodically diverted by white infiltration. Developer Adam Pell is baffled by the shockwaves set off by his project. His nephew is murdered while working on the dam; a sacred bundle entrusted to his care ends up misplaced, "tattered and profaned"; and the tribe Pell professes to admire in the West is thrown into turmoil by the anti-Indian policies Pell supports in boardrooms back East. A Little Elk elder, not unaware of the tribe's role in its troubles, notifies his people: "That man from the East took the water from the mountains and spread it over the land, and some of our people will say it was a good thing. Maybe he is a good man—I watched him, and that is what I think—and yet he will destroy us" (187).

In the fiction of A. B. Guthrie Jr., the dam finally breaks, wiping out a town and scarring the valley. Guthrie's dam is the culmination of westward expansion efforts that stretch back nearly a hundred years to the period of his first novel, *The Big Sky*. *The Big Sky*'s mountain man Boone Caudill plunders his way across the territory, blazing a wide trail for the nation building that will eventually pave over his Edenic dream. "It's all sp'iled," he finally acknowledges to fellow trader Dick Summers. "The whole caboodle. . . . This here finger pulled the trigger. I reckon I sp'iled it all." Dick concurs: "[E]verything we done it looks like we done against ourselves" (385). In *The Last Valley* Mort Ewing, an early homesteader, watches his fellow settlers transform the Teton Valley by "overgrazing and overcropping and timber up on the headwaters that never should have been cut." Surveying the aftermath of the dam's breach, he declares: "At every turn, sometimes it seems to me, man fucks himself" (265).

Providing too little or too much, the dam illustrates Americans' struggle to control a geography that fluctuates between the "savage, competitive world and the gentle cooperative world" (Bass 80). While nature appears to set the ambivalent terms of our contract with the West—"The camas with the blue flower will save you from starvation; the one with the white flower will poison you" (DeVoto "Foreword" xi), Bernard DeVoto cautions—colonialism hauls its own carpet baggage into this environment. Guthrie perceived Montanans to be "on both sides of the fence . . . margins on one hand, masses on the other" ("Preface" xviii). Today, Jared Diamond asserts in *Collapse*, Montanans are confronted by the fact that "long-standing and continuing opposition to government regulation is responsible for degradation of the beautiful natural environment" (64–65). This is, DeVoto claims, a "simple ambivalence" (*Western Paradox* 348), and—as it relates to the land—the most obvious. "You could love such a country but you were bound to hate it, too—and the splits in the Western soul begin right here" (DeVoto "Foreword" xi).

It follows then that Montana writing is "dialectical to the core, representing competing responses to common concerns" (Egan xxvii).[1] Guthrie's and McNickle's novels are essential chapters of this canon and provide a natural introduction to this discussion. Guthrie's interlinked historical novels are "obsess[ed] with the disintegration of landscape" and characterized by "a voice of romantic despair" (Blew 205). "Each man kills the thing he loves," Guthrie lamented in 1954. "We kill the thing we love because we don't have clean choices and, lacking them, destroy our loves by a sort of attrition until at last, numbed and sullied by necessity, we may wonder what it was we ever loved, or how it was that once we loved it. That is one of the tragedies of the lives we have to lead" ("Historical" 3).

In *The Surrounded* and *Wind* McNickle reveals another side, and an indigenous perspective, of colonialism's botched relationships to the region. "The Indians were robbed," he reminds us in *Wind*. "The real loser was the country itself. . . . The land was the loser, but of course the Indians were part of the land" (230). McNickle's Montana novels, like Guthrie's, chart "the crossroads, that legendary tragic setting, where many options and opportunities converge, but where disaster lurks. McNickle writes in the tragic mode of the impossibility of choice, the failure of hope, the loss of innocence" (Welch 182).

It is here, on the love/hate equipoise westerners maintain with the West, that I detect a queer edge.[2] Mort Ewing's salty verdict is a common denominator of Montana literature, with the idiom reinterpreted from writer to writer. In commentary packed with allusion, DeVoto describes white westerners as "just hired hands, principals in a gaudy drama that might be called 'The Rapers Raped.' . . . Already aware that he had missed the moon, the Westerner now understood that the cartridges he had been shooting with were blanks" ("Foreword" xi). Stephen Graham Jones takes metaphor to the hilt, in his hallucinogenic novel *The Fast Red Road*. Blackfeet protagonist Pidgin consents to star in a porn flick where he is told Indians will remain "unviolated, [in] an alternate future, as yet unwritten"—only to discover the five-hundred-year-old script unchanged: "the Indian always gets it up the ass" (115). "What recourse has a doubly self-exposed sucker got?" DeVoto asks. "He can make himself the butt of his own sardonic joke, and he can seek compensation in splendid dramas that confer the hero's role on him" ("Foreword" xi).

While Guthrie diagnosed ambivalence as "beyond the guiles of psychiatry," an attitude that boomerangs between political and environmental concerns through an "evil accident of existence" ("Historical" 3), he must have known the queerer intent behind the epigram he pegged as "universal." "Each man kills the thing he loves," the line Guthrie conscripted from Oscar Wilde's poem "Reading Gaol," has no connection to debates over land use. The poem is grounded in the suppression of homoeroticism.[3] While Wilde blamed his reckless lover Alfred Douglas for precipitating his notorious downfall, he also conceded, "I ruined myself. . . . Nobody great or small can be ruined except by his own hand" (150). Wilde would forever be associated with sodomy and its prohibition, and his seven-word stanza summed up not only his own liability but also a subtle indictment of a society blinded by ambivalence.

That queer ambivalence would insinuate its way across oceans, mountains, and decades to address environmental concerns in Montana literature is no accident. In *American Sympathy*, Caleb Crain sees American literature as the repository for a homoeroticism that was once openly valued in daily life. As same-sex affection became more "difficult for society," it also was made "imperative in literature." This tension, says Crain, gives "much of early American literature its distinctive color." As a rule, the canonical works are based on homoerotic themes—"a rule that literary history would accentuate . . . [as] the canon was refined" (151–52).

Crain echoes Leslie Fiedler's earlier, and still controversial, premise that "homosexuality glorified" permeates all fiction. The male fleeing civilization for the intimacy of other males is "a fundamental American archetype" (*Love and Death* 341)—and forever linked to the notion, found "everywhere in our classic fiction," that paradise is "in the process of being destroyed" (351). Our homoerotic Eden is invariably "associated, for historical reasons, with the 'West,'" leading Fiedler to suspect that the western genre is particularly "informed" by homosexuality (355).

While queer Eros has its place, carefully folded, sometimes encoded, in western narrative, I am interested here in what has become the other side of the literary coin: the tragic consequence of homoerotic desire—homo*thanatic*ism, if you will—in the western imagination. By imbuing Thanatos and the instinct for destruction with queer connotations, writers achieve two ends: they perpetuate the notion that homosexuality inevitability leads to disaster, and they bestow a distinct but subtle queerness—Thomas Mann's "voluptuousness of doom"—on more universal forms of tragedy.

QUEER COUNTRY

What of the early Montanan who *really* "fucked himself," or (to give the phrase a more precise turn) who submitted to the sexual desires of other men? In the framework of pioneer pragmatism and indigenous tradition, homosexuality not only existed—in some cases it must have flourished. While the early European attack on Native acceptance of sexual diversity was brutal and permanent, later sexual refugees managed to find a territory less influenced by eastern opprobrium, and westering individuals of all persuasions enjoyed situational sexuality in remote settings. Historical queer space, like wilderness, dwindled, of course, as more and more Euro-Americans migrated, intent on hammering the jagged edges of the West into the right angles of home. But the region has remained a destination, if only in the imagination, for all manner of social nonconformity.

Two lesser-known contemporaries of Guthrie and McNickle—Myron Brinig and Thomas Savage—make explicit the connection between the degradation of the West and the deprivation of the queer.[4] Through the novels *Singermann* (1929), *This Man Is My Brother* (1932), *The Sun Sets in the West* (1935), and *Footsteps on the Stair* (1950), Brinig follows "the giants of men . . . murders, strikes, [and] loves" in a mining boomtown (*Footsteps* 307). Like Brinig, Savage constantly returned to Montana settings and queer themes. *The Pass*, his first novel, was published in 1944; *The Power of the Dog* (1967) garnered national notice for its "diabolical plot"; and *The Corner of Rife and Pacific* (1988) reworks the rural territory of Savage's earlier books.[5]

In 1863 Thomas Savage's ancestors struck it rich in southwest Montana mining districts, developed the area, and launched a ranching dynasty that straddled the border of two states. His grandmother Elizabeth Yearian was Idaho's "sheep queen" and first woman legislator, and his stepfather came from a Montana political family. In 1920, when Thomas was five years old, his mother remarried and mother and son moved to the Brenner ranch in Horse Prairie. Wrote Savage:

> The region was barred from the world, even from the rest of Montana, by the continental divide. In the summer the divide rose high, jagged and blue, its front scarred by the deep gashlike canyons that even during the hottest summers withheld some snow. . . . In the winter the divide loomed as a grim white wall. Gone was the road, buried beneath the snow. Those on the prairie shut the rest of the world from their minds; from November till June the prairie was their world, their world a broad valley hemmed in by mountains. (*The Pass* 17)

On the surface Savage's Montana is full of "the usual and the expected, the appearance of the sun, the chilling voice of wild geese wedging south, the breakup of the ice, the shy green grass on the slopes, the heady breezes that disturb the purple camas. Sun, geese, and waving camas all point to the knowable future, and the world was well" (*Power* 265–66). Characters build rural infrastructure and preside over sprawling ranches, generally hoping the valley can be "beaten, roped, and hog-tied" (*The Pass* 78). But beneath the cycle of seasons and work, Savage stirs darker currents. Nature does some wrangling of her own. Sometimes a man loses his land, or a lover. In this West sexually ambiguous ranch hands find their voices and an effeminate boy saves the day. This is "queer country," a grizzled prospector warns newcomers in *The Pass* (3).

A daydreaming child on a wagon train learns early "that to be a man was the most important thing in the world, and a man kept his mouth shut" (*Pass*

21). That child may dutifully join the campaign to defend American manhood, "tak[ing] a new gun to bed, but only because his father had given it to him" (*Corner* 64), only to find in adulthood that his own son has "a lot of sympathy for girls and no interest in them" (166)—and no interest in taking over the ranch. Land—where "damp soil exuded seminal odors and the air was rich with the promise of growth" (30)—is identity. "Such aristocracy as existed in the West was based squarely on ownership of the land," Savage explains (102). But a rancher knows "that if you trusted anything too much it turned on you. He watched the land, loving it, expecting it to betray him" (*The Pass* 25). When a ranch is repossessed, the emasculated former owner is forced to rethink the "hidden contours" of his life.

While Savage knew firsthand the ups and downs of western aristocrats, he also spent time in bunkhouses, shipyards, and rail yards, observing the dispossessed West. He reserves a place in each novel for the westerner who does not write checks, claim family, or seek medical attention. He may be a foreman and a prized worker, like Slim Edwards in *The Pass*, but his most valuable possession is a cigar box of memories. He lies in a bunkhouse, in a snowstorm, haunted by the ranch hands that have "drifted, like tumbleweeds" in and out of his life. He ticks off a litany of men. The Mexican. The one with the harelip. One used to work in a circus.

> There was the red-haired fellow with the scar on his right cheek. . . . And the fellow with the battleship Maine tattooed on his back in red and blue. . . . All these men drifted on and left nothing behind but a whisky bottle or an old pair of overalls hung on a nail. When you looked at the overalls gathering dust over the faded blue, you remembered a fellow. . . . Sometimes a man left his name on things. . . . A few of them had their names on the wall of the toilet out back, and when you sat there you thought about the men. Maybe that's why they wrote them. (*Pass* 251–53)

Inside Slim's cigar box is a letter from another ranch hand, "Pete—poor old Pete," who "had written from Butte when he was drunk." Slim revels in the secret inscribed on his queer heart, safe in the knowledge that the bank cannot repossess his nostalgia for "poor old Pete"—"like they could take a man's land and his cattle."

In *The Power of the Dog* Savage takes us deeper into this landscape. From the conflicted lives of three gay men on a ranch, he unfolds a lyrical triptych of desire and tragedy that crosses class lines and generations. Middle-aged bachelor brothers George and Phil Burbank run the family ranch south of Dillon in the 1920s. George marries a widow from a nearby railroad town and adopts her teenage son, Peter. George's defection to women brings out an animosity in Phil that leads to a series of showdowns with those whom he believes are encroaching on his all-male idyll. Critics point out Phil's villainy: he is boorish, a misogynist, a racist, and he takes pleasure in belittling intellectual inferiors.

But Phil also has a capacity for passion that, given its transgression, is nothing short of heroic. And his uncanny ability to detect the secret lives of men fosters in him a measure of empathy for the nameless, ubiquitous itinerant workers kicking around the valley. Phil's great love was Bronco Henry, "that best of cowboys" who, even when running a high fever, "made one of the prettiest rides a fellow ever saw" (17). Henry taught Phil how to look at their environment and "arrange the facts of Nature into patterns that would stir the senses" (137).

Encoded in the patterns of sage and rock on the hillside above the ranch is Phil's memory of an older cowboy pursuing—and catching—the boss's son. Henry broke from "the usual tribe of men," both by "learn[ing] a scorn of Death" (223) in the corral and by daring to love another man. Phil returned Henry's affections, while Death reciprocated Henry's scorn: in *Power*'s haunting backstory, Phil watches helplessly from the top rail as Henry is trampled to death.

Peter, meanwhile, transplanted to a strange, new environment, seeks not only "companionship in his own image" (32) but also vengeance for losses already experienced in his young life. When Phil discovers Peter shares Bronco Henry's intuitive gift, he begins to resurrect his dream of a remote, homoerotic utopia. "Phil, at that moment in that place that smelled of years felt in his throat what he'd felt once before and dear God knows never expected nor wanted to feel again, for the loss of it breaks your heart. . . . The boy wanted to become him, to merge with him as Phil had only once before wanted to become one with someone" (262–63).

By training his desire on Peter, Phil flirts with disaster. In the end Phil's lust is no match for Peter's. Peter expertly manipulates Phil in a way that "few human beings" would understand. They share "a kind of bond—a bond of hatred, maybe, but Peter felt that one kind of bond could be just as useful as the other" (188). In a final misstep, Phil takes the weapon he fashioned out of Peter and inadvertently pulls it on himself.

Phil's memories of Henry, and his dream of a life with Peter, are entangled with apprehension of regional change and technological advances. He disparages dry-land farmers who divvy up and fence off the range; for Phil they represent feminized domesticity of the land, and their new barbed-wire fences inhibit his freedom. More at home with the ambiance of the bunkhouse, he resents his brother's wife and regards the lingerie she hangs to dry as a shot over the bow. Phil's West is under heterosexual siege. "Progress" is flooding his homotopian fantasy. "[Y]oungsters who had yearned to be cowpunchers now wanted to be engineers" (*Pass* 77).

"The Old West was dead," Myron Brinig wrote of Savage's Montana, "and not all the dude ranches dotting the plains and the slopes of the Rockies could resurrect it" (*Footsteps* 301). Ironically Phil Burbank's own livelihood factored in the death of his dream: Americans, nourished by the meat raised by western livestock companies, would grow prolific enough to challenge the cattle rancher's dominance of the range.

SUBTERRANEAN PASSAGEWAYS

Upon arriving in Butte, Savage's cowhand Pete would have found plenty to write home about. In fact, he might have found this new chapter of his life dropped into the middle of a Myron Brinig novel. If in Savage's world "the thing unsaid [was] more important than the thing said" (*Power* 243), Pete would quickly learn that Brinig's world was wide open—a carnival atmosphere of easy money, round-the-clock diversions, all-male saloons, industrial-strength prostitution, shameless political corruption, and melodramatic labor strife. The itinerant laborer knew he could get his queer needs met here.

There's the saloon with a bar half a block long and sawdust on the floor, for example, in Brinig's novel *Footsteps on the Stair*. An effete rich kid, slumming, meets a lanky miner at the bar. The miner boasts, "I can tell by a man's face what's under his pants." He unbuttons his trousers, exposes his penis, and closes in on his companion with a "leering sliding motion." "It belongs to the whole wide world," he announces to the younger man. "It belongs to whoever wants it bad enough" (182–83).

Butte—"the look of the town, the streets galloping up to the sky and down again, the hum of the mines on the hill, the high heady air that made the mind light, the body light as a feather, the imagination shining bright as a star" (*Footsteps* 306)—left an indelible mark on Brinig. He was three years old when his family of Jewish Romanian immigrants moved to Butte in 1900. The city was 65,000 strong. One-fifth of the population worked the mines and smelters, producing nearly one-quarter of the world's supply of copper. The chamber of commerce announced, "Butte is not one, but really two cities, one above and one below ground, both worth crossing the nation to see" (Writers Project 19).

Observers described "a raw town, a hard-fighting, hard-living, hard-drinking town, but also a gay, careless and tonic town" (Howard 85), a "stridently male, profane" city reeking of the "men-ness of men" (Writers Project 76). Long after he had left, Brinig could not stop writing about Montana's urban center.

Brinig used Butte's cityscape to map the emotional life of young queer men in the early twentieth century. Brinig's recurring protagonist is a "boy in a Northwestern mining town, full of inexpressible, unutterable dreams" who "[does] not know how profoundly he [is] a part of this North, this West, this magical atmosphere" (*Sun Sets in the West* 5, 23). As incongruous as his setting, he knows he is different, but not "how sad and lovely that difference [is]."

The city brightens when a precocious youth dons his first long pants, drinks his first beer, and contemplates his sexual awakening. "The sun had a strong, mature warmth in it. There was a proportion, a symmetry to the buildings, the streets" (*Singermann* 292). "[W]alk[ing] above the half-naked miners with their sweating arms and chests" (358), Brinig's boys long to be introduced to the "subterranean passageways of life" (293). But for all the "beauty about these Montana twilights" there is also "sadness in the air" (336). Characters are "cursed from childhood with a perverse love for the unattainable" (*This Man Is My Brother* 76); the city is "composed of the blood and agony of men" (*Singermann* 357).

Brinig fully develops queer—and regional—despair in his last Butte novel, *Footsteps on the Stair*, and in the story of Irish American rich boy, Jimmie Joyce. Jimmie is "not like other men, but something by himself, his spirit grappling with his flesh, his soul and desire interlocked in continuous struggle" (183). Frightened of his sexuality, he "feign[s] a lack of interest in other men, a purely defensive measure to save himself from unhappiness and ridicule" (173). When a prostitute encourages Jimmie to take on his own clients in the Red Light district—"Once in a while she had a visitor who asked where he might find a nice-looking boy"—Jimmie demurs. His inner battle characteristically flares up as he observes a brother-in-law in bed: "He felt the undeniable sexual quality of the man, the temperature of sex and even the smell, the imprint, the stale, sickening, odoriferous sweat of sex all over his body, clinging to the hairs of his chest, deep in the tangled mass of his black hair. . . . Jimmie was attracted and repelled" (272). Jimmie's only apparent consummated relationship begins with a note of promise on a trip to San Francisco. It is brief and ends badly. The lover—who at first appears to Jimmie to be his "exact counterpart. My reflection. My shadow. My twin" (279)—is transformed by a night of booze and sex into a monster:

> He lifted himself slightly to look at his companion. . . . The other was lying on his back breathing heavily through his open mouth. The face was very pale and thin, the skull of a man just before it becomes poor Yorick, still unclean from living, a narrow, damp, chinless face. It was a head that looked as if it should be attached to a small disease-bearing animal. . . . The hands were a peculiar gray shade, long and thin, crab-fingers turned green from slow decay. . . . Jimmie looked at this figure with a feeling of mixed horror and revulsion. His body felt thinned out of any stamina or decency, in a state of sickness, beside another body that had already rotted away and stank of death. (284)

Jimmie retreats to his first and loyal lover and "counterpart," Butte. He becomes a fixture in Depression-era saloons, particularly those where "there were no women to spoil the sanctity of male exclusiveness. There were only miners, unshaven, dressed in their overalls and work shirts, loud, obscene, their breath stinking of beer and whiskey" (314). In one saloon drunk miners cheer: "Gimme a kiss, Jimmie. Amour!" In another, where patrons knot around the piano, Jimmie calls out song requests. "'Show Me the Way to Go Home' . . . Play that" (312). Jimmie is "looking for his lost soul" and townspeople are tolerant, for in Jimmie "they sensed . . . tragedy" (305).

As the town queer and wide-open city decline together, Brinig weaves a two-tiered allegory of regional despair and sexual confusion. While Jimmie views his environment contentedly through the amber of whiskey and beer, a visitor provides a reality check: "It's like living in a cemetery to stay here. . . . This is a ghost town (302)." Butte has become "[b]ones and dust . . . fading brick and wood, old dates on buildings—1876, 1892, 1901, stillness and dust and the everlasting mountains" (301). For some, "the mystery of Jimmie Joyce's life was never made completely clear" (303): why does the heir to a modest fortune choose to "[grow] old with the town," live in a deteriorating house, wandering the streets at all hours? What is not fully comprehended is that Jimmie is "inhabited by ghosts in the same way as the town" (307). Jimmie *is* Butte.

While Brinig was one of the first Americans to publish sympathetic gay themes in the mainstream (and the first Jewish writer to do so), he was unable to completely break with "the rule of concessiveness . . . in which the price of greater access was the confirming of homosexual stereotypes" (Cady 30). His Butte novels operate an endlessly revolving door of taboo, tradition, self-disclosure, and self-censorship. Nevertheless, Brinig could telescope beyond ambivalence and visualize a more optimistic future for gays and lesbians, as he did in his assessment of his first gay character, Harry Singermann: "He had simply revealed his love of beauty in a person of the same sex. Was it such a sin? . . . Perhaps this future race . . . will solve Harry's peculiar problems of conduct, of desire and anguish? They used to throw men like Harry into prison. We have made some headway in this regard. We are beginning to study the problems of men and women like Harry, and there is certain tolerance manifested nowadays" (*This Man* 305).

Brinig was less generous with the fate of the city that fostered his queerness. "Mining camps do not last forever," he predicted in 1932. "They have a way of giving up unexpectedly; the people vanish, the streets and houses crumble slowly, inhabited by invisible ghosts" (*This Man* 4). Brinig's West, like Savage's, disintegrates under the improbable weight of Manifest Destiny. While Savage intimated that homoeroticism might have preserved the land, and Brinig expected time would save homosexuality, both writers obligated their queer captains to go down with the regional ship.

THE LAST BEST AMBIVALENCE

"Guilt and Frontier are coupled," Fiedler wrote in his treatise on the Montana character ("Montana Face" 745). "'The Frontier' has always been the edge of . . . colonialist expansion," Montana-based critic William Bevis elaborates: "'We kill what we love' is the story of that frontier, because the narrative of expanding capitalist production and consumption is the opposite of a sustainable narrative" (260). McNickle tactfully reminds us that Manifest Destiny failed to sustain indigenous people; it was their "misfortune to have been 'discovered' at a time when . . . competition for raw materials . . . allowed no latitude for concessions to humane principles" (*Native American* 46). The Montana of the "New West" is "filled . . . with Indian remains" and overrun with "Cowboys for Christ" (Morris 183); "a played out landscape, inhabited by played out characters. These characters come expecting . . . the Old West, and find instead a New West, one that cannot, *will* not sustain their . . . worn-out beliefs" (181).

Homothanaticism thrives in this system. And the act of killing what we love, when the object of desire and disdain is of the same gender, has become a permanent staple, if not standard, of western literature. Owen Wister's 1902 progenitor of the form, the homoerotically charged *The Virginian*, anguishes over the sacrifices made to "heterosexual imperative" (Handley 51); having risen in the ranks of his ranching community, the Virginian lynches his former companion turned cattle rustler. Updating the Virginian's century-old dilemma, Montana writer Kim Zupan takes us to the dark heart of the Rocky Mountain front, in "The Mourning of Ignacio Rosa," where a taciturn rancher murders to prevent revelations of his relationship with a Mexican wrangler. The staunchly closeted Ennis Del Mar in Annie Proulx's now iconic "Brokeback Mountain" warns his sexually adventurous lover Jack Twist, "all them things I don't know could get you killed if I should come to know them" (275). In each case the gay-basher and man-loving man is interchangeable, lending credence to James Baldwin's observation that "[t]he object of one's hatred is never, alas, conveniently outside but is seated in one's lap, stirring in one's bowels and dictating the beat of one's heart" (686).

Bevis challenges us to rethink such dichotomies. "Are we sure that killing what you love is a universal human fate," he asks, "or is it a pattern that our first world culture is perfecting?" (257–58). He criticizes the concept of catholicized tragedy for its tendency to destroy "our will for social, political and environmental reform." If the classic western theme is ambivalent, Bevis concludes, it is one "we must rewrite" ("Nature" 254). Crain agrees with Bevis's assessment, if not his prescription: "'Each man kills the thing he loves' . . . dissolves particular, conflicting emotions into a general idea. It is also quietist" (246). While such sentimentality is excusable in light of Wilde's unjust treatment—"Nevertheless, the line is untrue. . . . [T]he destruction of love is not inevitable" (238–39).

Marilynne Robinson hypothesizes, however, that it is "the function of myth to encode ambivalence, to allow a culture to maintain . . . incompatible ideas in some sort of stable relation with each other" (58). Literature is precisely the place to express and explore ambivalence, whether or not it leads to social or political change. If it is mere device to portray the queer and antiqueer, or nature lover and the consumer of natural resources, as living in one skin—few literary devices have proven so expedient or effective. One need not defend the practice of "killing off the queer"—either in art or in life—to appreciate that each act of homothanaticism in our literary tradition, while difficult to ignore, illuminates homoerotic impulses that would otherwise go overlooked.

I contend that queerness is more than a convenient device; it is essential to the equation. Representations of anal sex "dramatize . . . the ambivalence of relations between men" (Simpson 133). Sexual penetration requires the "scary ability to imagine ourselves and everything we hold dear, at least for a moment, as relatively valueless" (Warner 213). Queerness elevates loss, for "[o]nly in the transgressive moment do we solitary humans relinquish the social identities that individuate us and distinguish us" (Browning 88). If homosexuality "rob[s] the normal—who are simply the many—of their very necessary sense of security and order," it also challenges the conviction that "the race is and should be devoted to outwitting oblivion" (Baldwin 102). Postmodern theorist Lee Edelman observes that, by removing himself from the "narrative movement toward a viable political future, the queer comes to figure the bar to every realization of futurity, the resistance . . . to every social structure or form" (4).

By staging queerness as a metaphor for Montana's dichotomies and dilemmas, novelists like Brinig and Savage create a mirror through which the westerner can examine his desire for and penetration of place. Neither westerner nor queer is a stranger to alienation. Both know that attempts to manipulate nature are ultimately futile; that boom is invariably followed by bust, and desire by nostalgia. "If you can't fix it you got a stand it," Ennis instructs Jack with a characteristic pragmatism that could apply to homosexuality or Rocky Mountain winters (Proulx 269).

The West is "the last theater of the oldest ambivalence in American culture, the historic doubt as to the compatibility of freedom and civilization" (Robinson 50). Indeed, Gregory Morris suggests in an analysis of new West fiction, ambivalence won the West. Queerness pushes ambivalence to its most extreme—and, perhaps, its most useful. "[W]hat is queerest about us," says Edelman, is a "willingness to insist . . . that the future stop here" (31). What is queerest about the West (to paraphrase Edelman) is the potential for Manifest Destiny to unravel here. To the extent that queerness throws a wrench in the works, its pragmatism offers a lighter footprint. As counterintuitive as it seems, the region's salvation may hinge on queer ambivalence.

NOTES

The author wishes to thank the following individuals for their assistance in shaping this essay: Melissa Kwasny, Pamela Savage, Rick Newby, Earl Ganz, Alan Weltzien, Mark Medvetz, Jim Rogers, Sherry Jones, and David Moomey, as well as PRIDE Inc., under the leadership of Diana Longdon, for a generous research sabbatical.

1. For an extensive study of the tragic/comic dialectic in Montana literature, see Ken Egan's *Hope and Dread in Montana Literature.*
2. I use the terms *queer*, *gay*, *homoerotic*, and *homosexual* somewhat interchangeably. Typically we delineate the individual as gay, his orientation and specific sex acts as homosexual, his desire as homoerotic, and the social and political ramifications of his behavior or desire as queer. If there are exceptions to these guidelines, I've probably found, and exploited, them.
3. For more on the erotic subtext of Wilde's poem "Reading Gaol," see Caleb Crain's *American Sympathy: Men, Friendship, and Literature in the New Nation.*

4. It is entirely possible that Brinig and Savage are lesser known *because* of their sensitive handling of gay issues. Their work, especially their queer-themed work, is missing from nearly every discussion of the Montana canon. (A passage from Brinig's fiction, one that does not involve homosexuality, is included in the anthology of Montana literature *The Last Best Place*.)

   Furthermore, sympathetic portrayals of homosexuality, written in the 1920s to the 1960s, could have raised suspicions of an author's own fitness for literary acclaim in the West. Though Savage appeared to live a conventional heterosexual life, rumors of his "San Francisco lifestyle" circulated in publishing circles and among some relatives. There seems to be minor confusion over Brinig, who was more open about queer sexuality. Ludger Brinker in *The Gay and Lesbian Literary Heritage* labels Brinig as "not gay" (409), while Ron Fischer describes Brinig as "a gay writer" (1), and Lois Palken Rudnick identifies him as "one of several homosexual artists" in Mabel Dodge Luhan's orbit (302). In his unpublished memoir and in interviews Brinig identified himself as bisexual. The evidence points to male partners and long-term homosexual relationships. Pamela Tollefson reports that Brinig is buried in Shelter Island, New York, where he had resided with "his male companion of many years" (169).
5. I have purposefully limited the scope of this essay to writers who began writing in the first half of the twentieth century and whose focus in fiction is on roughly the same historical period—the turn of the twentieth century and years preceding WWII. I suppose it's no coincidence that these were white men writing, within the constraints of their time, about the queerness of other white men. With little exception, I have not had the latitude to include post-Stonewall gay fiction (the Stonewall riots of 1969 being the rather arbitrary and political start of the "modern" gay movement); Montana-based lesbian fiction; or stories of indigenous Two Spirit traditions. Of the latter, there is a rich heritage that has been analyzed, compiled, and promoted by historians such as Will Roscoe and Walter Williams and others. Unfortunately, fiction involving the queerness of women in early Montana is virtually nonexistent and warrants (in my opinion) deft and passionate research.

WORKS CITED

Baldwin, James. *Collected Essays*. New York: Literary Classics of the United States, 1998.

Bass, Rick. "A Fitting Desire." *Orion*. (May/June 2005): 80.

Blew, Mary Clearman. "Shane Rides into the Millennium." *Fifty Years After the Big Sky: New Perspectives on the Fiction and Films of A.B. Guthrie, Jr.* Ed. William E. Farr and William W. Bevis. Helena: Montana Historical Society Press, 2001. 201–9.

Bevis, William. "Nature and Other Nonsense: *The Big Sky* at Fifty." *Fifty Years After the Big Sky: New Perspectives on the Fiction and Films of A.B. Guthrie, Jr.* Ed. William E. Farr and William W. Bevis. Helena: Montana Historical Society Press, 2001. 247–63.

Brinig, Myron. *Footsteps on the Stair*. New York: Rinehart, 1950.
———. *Singermann*. New York: Farrar & Rinehart, 1929.
———. *The Sun Sets in the West*. New York: Farrar & Rinehart, 1935.
———. *This Man Is My Brother*. New York: Farrar & Rinehart, 1932.
Brinker, Ludger. "Jewish-American Literature." *The Gay and Lesbian Literary Heritage*. Ed. Claude J. Summers. New York: Henry Holt, 1995. 408–10.
Browning, Frank. *The Culture of Desire: Paradox and Perversity in Gay Lives Today*. New York: Crown Publishers, 1993.
Cady, Joseph. "American Literature: Gay Male, 1900–1969." *The Gay and Lesbian Literary Heritage*. Ed. Claude J. Summers. New York: Henry Holt, 1995. 29–32.
Crain, Caleb. *American Sympathy: Men, Friendship, and Literature in the New Nation*. New Haven CT: Yale University Press, 2001.
DeVoto, Bernard. "Foreword." *A Treasury of Western Folklore*. Ed. B. A. Botkin. New York: Crown Publishers, 1951.
———. *The Western Paradox: A Conservation Reader*. Ed. Douglas Brinkley and Patricia Nelson Limerick. New Haven CT: Yale University Press, 2000.
Edelman, Lee. *No Future: Queer Theory and the Death Drive*. Durham NC: Duke University Press, 2004.
Egan, Ken, Jr. *Hope and Dread in Montana Literature*. Reno: University of Nevada Press, 2003.
Fiedler, Leslie. *Love and Death in the American Novel*. 1960, 1966. Normal IL: Dalkey Archive Press, 2003.
———. "The Montana Face." *The Last Best Place: A Montana Anthology*. Ed. William Kittredge and Annick Smith. Helena: Montana Historical Society, 1988.
Fischer, Ron. "Introduction to *Singermann*." Unpublished, 1995. Montana Historical Society.
Guthrie, A. B., Jr. *The Big Sky*. Boston: Houghton Mifflin, 1947.
———. "The Historical Novel: Tramp or Teacher?" *Montana Magazine of History* (Fall 1954): 1–8.
———. *The Last Valley*. Boston: Houghton Mifflin, 1975.
———. "Preface." *Montana, High, Wide, and Handsome*. By Joseph Kinsey Howard. New Haven CT: Yale University Press, 1959; reprint, Lincoln: University of Nebraska, 1983.
———. "West Is Another Word for Magic." *Big Sky, Fair Land*. Ed. David Petersen. Flagstaff AZ: Northland Press, 1983.
Handley, William R. "Wister's Omniscience and Omissions." *Reading "The Virginian" in the New West*. Ed. Melody Graulich and Stephen Tatum. Lincoln: University of Nebraska, 2003.
Jones, Stephen Graham. *The Fast Red Road: A Plainsong*. Tallahassee FL: FC2, 2000.
McCarthy, Cormac. *Blood Meridian*. New York: Vintage International, 1985.
McNickle, D'Arcy. *Native American Tribalism: Indian Survivals and Renewals*. 1973. Reprint, New York: Oxford University Press, 1993.
———. *The Surrounded*. New York: Quality Paperback Book Club, 1998.

———. *Wind from an Enemy Sky*. New York: Harper & Row, 1978.

Morris, Gregory L. "How Ambivalence Won the West: Thomas McGuane and the Fiction of the New West." *Critique* 32, 3 (Spring 1991): 180–89.

Proulx, Annie. "Brokeback Mountain." *Close Range: Wyoming Stories*. New York: Scribner, 1999.

Robinson, Marilynne. "Hearing Silence: Western Myth Reconsidered." *Northern Lights: A Selection of New Writing from the American West*. Ed. Deborah Clow and Donald Snow. New York: Vintage Books, 1994.

Rudnick, Lois Palken. *Mabel Dodge Luhan: New Woman, New Worlds*. Albuquerque: University of New Mexico, 1984.

Savage, Thomas. *The Pass*. Garden City NY: Doubleday, Doran, 1944.

———. *The Corner of Rife and Pacific*. New York: William Morrow, 1988.

———. *The Power of the Dog*. Boston: Little Brown, 1967.

Simpson, Mark. *Sex Terror: Erotic Misadventures in Pop Culture*. Binghamton NY: Harrington Park Press, 2002.

Tollefson, Pamela Wilson. *Myron Brinig's Butte: Jews in the Wide Open Town*. Master's thesis, University of Montana, 1994.

Warner, Michael. *The Trouble with Normal: Sex, Politics, and the Ethics of Queer Life*. New York: The Free Press, 1999.

Welch, James. "The West from Two Perspectives." *Fifty Years After the Big Sky: New Perspectives on the Fiction and Films of A.B. Guthrie, Jr.* Ed. William E. Farr and William W. Bevis. Helena: Montana Historical Society Press, 2001. 175–85.

Wilde, Oscar. *De Profundis and Other Writings*. 1954. Reprint, New York: Penguin Putnam, 1986 .

Wister, Owen. *The Virginian: A Horseman of the Plains*. New York: Macmillan, 1902.

Writers Project of Montana. *Copper Camp*. Helena MT: Riverbend, 2002.

Zupan, Kim. "The Mourning of Ignacio Rosa." *The Best of Montana's Short Fiction*. GuilfordCT: The Lyons Press, 2004. 309–32.

CHAPTER SEVEN

"Just Regular Guys": Homophobia, the Code of the West, and Constructions of Male Identity in Thomas Savage and Annie Proulx

O. ALAN WELTZIEN

"I think what a man needs is odds against him."
—Phil Burbank, *The Power of the Dog*

"But if you can't fix it you got a stand it."
—Ennis Del Mar, "Brokeback Mountain"

I

In her 1992 essay, "Engendering the West," Katherine G. Morrissey reminds us that "in popular culture as well as scholarship the American West is most often associated with masculine images. . . . Imbued with these masculine images, the ideology of the West celebrates a particular, and gendered, form of American identity" (Morrissey 133). Since then, scholarship, particularly postmodernism, has taught us to revision racial, ethnic, and gender borders as fluid and malleable, creating a more complex and accurate regional ideology and portrait; unsurprisingly, though, popular culture sustains its traditional biases and resists the more sophisticated understanding provided by scholarship. A few years after Morrissey's essay, Julia Watson concluded her excellent survey of Montana women's autobiographical writing—her title, "Engendering Montana Lives," echoing Morrissey's—declaring that "Montana writing can no longer be cast exclusively in the image of the white male adventurer's 'tough trip.' Being of an 'other' gender and/or ethnicity and/or sexuality makes for adventurous living even when people don't leave home, above all in a West that remains judgmental about those who transgress its myths" (Watson 154). At the twentieth-first century's dawn, the many regional inhabitants "remain" seriously "judgmental about those who transgress its myths." Circumstantial evidence reveals a tough residual climate of homophobia, for example, which inhibits an expanded and expansive definition of masculinity.

I tell a tale of the dark side of "adventurous living" involving gay men who "don't leave home." The tale involves two writers, the older one recently emerging from a period of obscurity and the younger, a friend at the top of her form. From it I speculate about the politics of literary reputation, the abiding presence of homophobia in the Northern Rockies, and the possible role of literature in weakening that presence. The latter issue is endlessly problematic, of course. The relevant texts of Thomas Savage and Annie Proulx do not offer much hope for gay men except to the extent that they courageously insist on the need for change: for a more inclusive masculinity that embraces, rather than shuns and despises, gay men. It is no accident that Savage's *The Power of the Dog* (1967), long out of print, was republished by Little, Brown in June 2001—in part because of (then) Little, Brown editor Emily Salkin Takoudes's personal mission and Annie Proulx's interest—after the decade that saw the emergence of queer studies in literary criticism. Sexual minorities and our ideological constructions of them have become big academic business. Analyzing the phenomenon of the "Queer Moment" in the 1990s, the collection, *Regarding Sedgwick: Essays on Queer Culture and Critical Theory* (2002), salutes the pivotal role of critic Eve Koslovsky Sedgwick, called by Simon Watney the "*primum mobile* of queer theory" (*Regarding* 1).[1] Critics such as Michael Warner and Eve Koslovsky Sedgwick have overturned psychoanalysis's legacy equating gayness with deviance or etiology. On the first page of *Epistemology of the Closet* (1990), Sedgwick throws down the gauntlet: "An understanding of virtually any aspect of modern Western culture must be, not merely incomplete, but damaged in its central substance to the degree that it does not incorporate a critical analysis of modern homo/heterosexual definition" (Quoted in *Regarding* 243). As will be seen, in their drastic revisions of Freud and Lacan we can read a sea change between Savage and Proulx, one that no longer relegates sexual minorities to the dustbin of "abnormality."

Many, myself included, judge *Power* to be Savage's best novel, and its story of a homophobic, repressed gay rancher, Phil Burbank, has apparently reached its proper time of release, like an aged cabernet. Occasionally, such a happy story emerges from the depressing vagaries of literary reputation. A column appearing in the *Great Falls Tribune* (11 December 2001) devoted to Proulx's role in the reprinting of Savage's novel concludes, "For a writer, it's important to be a little ahead of the curve. But three decades is exceptional." This particular curve, which traces "repressed homosexuality displayed as homophobia" (Proulx "Afterward" 277) and our general discomfort with and intolerance of sexual minorities, "transgress[es]" the masculinist "myths" Watson cites. Savage's *Power* and *The Sheep Queen* (originally *I Heard My Sister Speak My Name*, 1977), republished in October 2001, and Proulx's "Brokeback Mountain," the concluding story in *Close Range* (1999), together begin to crack that code of the West that marginalizes rather than welcomes gay men.

I live in southwest Montana, and on both the old and new state literary maps, Thomas Savage's name is the most prominent in our corner, yet I knew next to nothing about him until the late 1990s. Ironically, both Savage and his wife, Elizabeth Savage, enjoyed big careers as novelists, as traced by their friend, Montana State University–Billings professor Sue Hart, in her *Western Writers Series* monograph (1995) devoted to them. Savage's *Power* stayed on the *New York Times*' "New and Recommended" list for nearly two months and garnered excellent reviews, according to Proulx's "Afterward" in the reprinted paper edition (277), yet it sold poorly, and although it was optioned as a film six times, according to Hart (33), remarkably, no film has emerged. *The Sheep Queen* received similar glowing reviews, particularly one from Jonathan Yardley, but it, too, disappeared off the screen. Savage's final novel, *The Corner of Rife and Pacific* (1988), received several literary nominations or awards, yet Montana's grand literary centennial project, *The Last Best Place*, published the same year, contains no excerpts or mention of Savage in its 1,100-plus pages. The first significant work of criticism devoted to Montana literature, *Ten Tough Trips* (1990), excludes Savage as well. More remarkably, *Writing Montana: Literature Under the Big Sky* (1996), which includes Julia Watson's essay, contains no mention or discussion of Savage. Nor is he cited or discussed in the more recent *Hope and Dread in Montana Literature* (2003). These omissions are inexplicable.

In her monograph, however, Hart concludes her discussion of Savage suggesting one possible reason for his temporary eclipse if not exclusion from these three primary Montana literature texts: "It is perhaps his insistence on portraying this darker side of both the Western landscape and the people who live there that has denied him full recognition as a writer, even in his home territory" (Hart 46). The particular "darker side" embodied in Phil Burbank, however, did not strike Hart (personal communication) as forcefully as it has Proulx, myself, and others. Hart calls Burbank "one of the true villains of Western American literature" (32), which Proulx echoes in her "Afterward" published six years later. For Proulx, Burbank is "one of the most compelling and vicious characters in American literature," "a vicious bitch" who "spews hatred and scorn" (287–88, 293). In this Burbank brother, Savage has created a protagonist who fascinates with his sustained, calculated cruelty toward Rose, his new sister-in-law, general corrosive contempt, and fierce self-hatred. Burbank invites armchair psychoanalysts to plot his case history, and Proulx reads him thus, irresistibly concluding, "in wanting to touch and have Bronco Henry [a crucial, minor character dead long before the novel], he was forced to recognize and confront the enormous fact of his own homosexuality. His private obstacle became this thing that he knew about himself, something that in the cowboy world he inhabited was terrible and unspeakably vile. Following the code of the west, he remade himself as a manly, homophobic rancher" (288–89).

Proulx and others cite implicit regional "codes"; Watson cites "Western" "myths" clearest in their "transgress[ions]." Burbank faces odds heavily against himself, more than he understands (260). Savage set *Power* in 1924 and wrote it midway through the sexually liberated 1960s, yet during both periods "the code of the west" remained tightly sealed; how closed is it at the beginning of the twenty-first century?

Proulx reminds us in her "Afterward" that, among those many laudatory reviews, only one—significantly, an anonymous review in *Publisher's Weekly*—accurately named its subject in Phil, "a repressed homosexual" who "is plotting a homosexual involvement with the boy [Peter Gordon]" ("Afterward" 278). Such a slight glance at the novel's subject in 1967 indicates that those sexually liberated years were not consistently so. This is not the only subject of *Power*, but it is its primary one. I cannot dispute Proulx's evocation of Beaverhead County, Montana's "powerful work ethic," "rough and masculine in ethos," which she deems "long gone" (280). While much has changed in my giant county and the Northern Rockies, the gender code of the West is not "long gone": gay men remain marginalized, although, at least in intellectual circles, queer studies dulls the edge of stigmatization. The tangible effects of urban queer studies in the rural Northern Rockies remain limited, I suspect. In his seminal (pun intended), midcentury essay, "Come Back to the Raft Ag'in, Huck Honey!" (1948), Leslie Fiedler defined the code in terms of an archetypal repression: "The existence of overt homosexuality threatens to compromise an essential aspect of American sentimental life . . . a kind of passionless passion, at once gross and delicate, homoerotic in the boy's sense, possessing an innocence above suspicion" (143). Both Savage and Proulx, for different reasons and with different effects, endorse and extend Fiedler's reductive formula of American literary history to "boy's books" that "proffer a chaste male love as the ultimate emotional experience," "a conventionally abhorrent doctrine of ideal love" (144, 147).

Tracing the wellsprings of regional homophobia lies beyond the scope of this essay; explaining the engines of sexual repression and resulting self-hatred in Phil Burbank, however, leads easily to an analysis of Proulx's treatment of two gay men, Ennis Del Mar and Jack Twist, in her short story that closes *Close Range*. Together, Savage and Proulx probe the potent endurance of homophobia even as their stories implicitly recommend breaking the code by proclaiming the legitimacy of sexual minorities. Enduring regional homophobia comprises a main theme in Beth Lofreda's haunting book of investigative journalism, *Losing Matt Shepard: Life and Politics in the Aftermath of Anti-Gay Murder*. Lofreda reminds us in the preface, "Homophobia works not just through the viciousness of physical violence but also through the daily erosion of selfhood by the friction of widespread, casually expressed hatred" (x).[2]

II

The question of why most reviewers and readers of *Power* misread or at least downplayed its primary subject until recently is central to my inquiry. Academic interest in gay and lesbian studies has broadened the ways we understand sexuality even if it has not yet eroded older gender stereotypes sustained by popular culture. Yet I don't think the emergence of queer studies, for example, is a necessary precondition for reading Phil Burbank as a repressed homosexual turned homophobic misogynist and even misanthrope. It is hard to ignore the textual evidence. Consider, for example, the psychoanalytical implications of the novel's harrowing opening—what that long-ago anonymous *Publisher's Weekly* reviewer deemed "unnecessarily graphic brutality in its opening paragraph" that would repel many readers (Proulx "Afterward" 278):

> Phil always did the castrating; first he sliced off the cup of the scrotum and tossed it aside; next he forced down first one and then the other testicle, slit the rainbow membrane that enclosed it, tore it out, and tossed it into the fire where the branding irons glowed. There was surprisingly little blood. In a few moments the testicles exploded like huge popcorn. Some men, it was said, ate them with a little salt and pepper. "Mountain oysters," Phil called them with that sly grin of his, and suggested to young ranch hands that if they were fooling around with the girls they'd do well to eat them, themselves. (3)

This precise, painfully violent rendering prompts our squeamishness, which does not dissipate amidst the sexual jokes and lore surrounding Rocky Mountain oysters. Phil's sure hand in the annual castration scene replays and confirms his own self-emasculation as the reader senses, with increasing conviction, his buried attraction to yet distance from those "young ranch hands" and revulsion from heterosexuality. Phil regards the surprising marriage of his stolid brother, George, to Rose Gordon, an attractive widow, as an act of gender betrayal. In the opulent ranch house, a bathroom filled with the "Old Lady's" toiletries connects the parental bedroom with the bedroom Phil shared—until now—with George. Phil always avoids this bathroom with its "offensive odor of women" and the occasional washed undergarments, the sight of which repulses him (101). In the past, the parents would unlock the intervening door when done with their ablutions, and now Phil, hearing the door locked and seeing a thin band of light, pruriently imagines the newlyweds coupling in the parents' bedroom, his gorge rising (102). The misogynist son has no interest in usurping and replacing his father. News of George's imminent marriage forces the parents, living in luxury in a Salt Lake City hotel, to fleetingly ask the question they cannot face: "'Do I think there might be something—something wrong—with Phil?' The Old Gent felt hollow in his stomach, but it was a relief to get the thing out in the open. 'If there is, it's not your fault.' 'Nor is it yours,' she said, and looked at her watch" (92).

That "code of the west" echoed by Proulx renders Phil's homosexuality unmentionable, and the parents' desperate search for explanation, sense of failure, and silence resonate from 1924 through the present. That resonance is the burden of Freud's linkage of homosexuality with narcissism, as Michael Warner summarizes Freud in his key essay, "Homo-Narcissism; or, Heterosexuality" (1990): "[H]omosexual desire *reduces* to narcissism with significant remainder and hence is a developmental misdirection. . . . The theoretical tradition continues to reveal [homosexuality] in the light of pathology" (553). Savage underlines, with increasingly broad strokes, his protagonist's homosexuality and repression. The occasional, wistful references to Bronco Henry, Phil's idealized lover, a slightly older ranch hand who died in the corral in front of Phil's eyes when Phil was twenty years old (263), are matched by the description of Phil's secret bathing hole, a willow copse planted by him and George as young teenagers along a bend in the creek. "A sacred grove," "a place of ablutions," it becomes a site for sexual narcissism in which the man—who never lets anyone see him naked—becomes again a virginal adolescent "strangely moved by his own naked reflection," and possibly one who touched Bronco Henry there (263). The scene conflates Freud's formulations of primary and secondary (i.e., mediated) narcissism in his explanation of gayness as pathology.

If the bathing scene implies his gayness, the castration scene implies his chronic repression of it. But Savage writes the former only to depict its violation, at least according to Phil, since Peter Gordon—his future idealized partner, but at this point the chief object of his contempt, a "sissy" he calls "Miss Nancy"—has spied on him, interrupting his masturbatory reverie (170–71). The bathing hole scene implies that the engines of repression are never wholly successful, and that gayness remains a condition to be ferreted out by the sexual majority; it exists not in its own right but to be uncovered, if not ridiculed and punished. The subtext prescribes ongoing marginalization, condemnation, and worse. In Phil Burbank, Savage could be seen as accepting Lacan's "evident connection between the narcissistic libido and the alienating function of the *I*, the aggressivity it releases in any relation to the other": "[T]he formation of the *I* is symbolized in dreams by a fortress, or a stadium—its inner arena and enclosure . . . two opposed fields of contest where the subject flounders in quest of the lofty, remote inner castle whose form . . . symbolizes the id. . . . Similarly, on the mental plane, we find realized the structures of fortified works, the metaphor of which arises spontaneously, as if issuing from the symptoms themselves, to designate the mechanisms of obsessional neuroses" (384–85).

In this view, denial of sexual identity leads to its unpredictable expression, masked or otherwise. For Savage, Phil's exposure measures the extent of judgment against transgressed regional gender myths mentioned by Watson. For queer studies, the bathing scene should be read as a source not of endless stigma, but of endless opening for identity formation and articulation. Regarding the term *queer*, Eve Koslovsky Sedgwick defines the opening and revises Lacan: "If queer is a politically potent term . . . that's because, far from being capable of being detached from the childhood scene of shame, it cleaves to that scene as a near-inexhaustible source of transformational energy" (*Regarding* 5).

The final third of *Power* strips away Phil's homophobia and affirms his gayness at the price of his life. His conscious plot, to drive a permanent wedge between Rose and Peter by replacing the mother with himself and fatally sabotaging the marriage (226–27), disappears inside Peter's ferocious plot to avenge his mother and kill Phil, and that in turn depends on the unconscious plot, the resurgence of Phil's erotic desire (257). For Phil, Peter, a booksmart teenager who studies his father's medical books and understands far more than Phil imagines, has come to replace Bronco Henry—or, given their respective ages, Phil has become Bronco Henry and Peter, a projection of his adolescent self. Independently of Phil, there is more than a little evidence to suggest that Peter is himself a closeted gay. His personal habits, dress, and feelings about his best friend (an attractive fellow chess player) all suggest his effeminate nature, and he does look prissy in his stiff jeans as he walks past the bunkhouse. Neither high school athlete nor ranch hand, he is a momma's boy—but, a precocious student, he absorbs his late father's medical textbooks without difficulty. Given these tendencies, *Power*'s climax could also be read as a younger gay man's revenge on the older gay man's conscious refusal to acknowledge and accept his own sexuality. Peter will kill Phil because Phil will not out himself.

In Lacan's famed metaphor, Phil's *I* has breached the castle keep of his id. Peter has found him out at his bathing hole, perhaps drawn by some innate desire, and read him correctly since then, knowing that a touch will awaken Phil's buried sexuality. Peter has just wrung a rabbit's neck as deftly as Phil castrates steers and admitted he immediately saw the large running dog on the hillside that only Phil sees—Savage again intoning his title drawn from Psalms 22:20 (259–60). Phil no doubt construes them as a natural pair yet for all his superior intelligence, he cannot fathom the engines of repression or his vulnerability—his own tilt from predator to prey: "The boy wanted to *become* him, to merge with him as Phil had only once before wanted to become one with someone, and that one was gone. . . . Ah God, but Phil had almost forgot what the touch of a hand will do, and his heart counted the seconds that Peter's was on him and rejoiced at the quality of the pressure. It told him what his heart required to know"(263). Savage metaphorically hints Phil's idealized union, a conjoining of bodies, through their shared project, the braiding of a rawhide rope, though the fact that, in *Power*'s final paragraph, the reader learns Peter, agent of death, had given Phil rawhide tainted with anthrax (275–76), suggests again the problematic status of a sexual minority. In this light, gayness exists to be sublimated or discovered and killed. Savage ironically addresses both reader and Phil in the passage immediately following the one quoted above, the climax of this novel's case study:

> Please, was it not Fate (because a man must believe in something), was it not Fate that the boy had looked on him in his nakedness in that hidden place known only to George and to himself—and to Bronco Henry? Just so, he had looked upon the boy's nakedness in that eternity when the boy had walked proud and unprotected past the open tents, jeered at, scorned—a pariah. But Phil knew, God knows he knew, what it was to be a pariah, and he had loathed the world, should it loath him first.
>
> His voice was husky, "That's damned kind of you, Pete," and he slid his long arm about the boy's shoulders. Once before that day, he'd been tempted,

> and desisted, because he'd always sworn out of that old loyalty never again to make that move. (263)

This laying on of hands propels Phil out of his idealized monogamous relationship with long dead Bronco Henry as he fatally misreads Peter's motives. Because Phil "must believe in something," he assumes Peter, a stranger to the ranch world, to be as much a "pariah" as himself. And to some extent, Peter is also sexual outcast. Savage's narrator concludes the case study inviting our agreement, summarized by Proulx's verdict quoted earlier. By adolescence Phil had internalized the judgment voiced much later by his parents, that there is "something wrong" with him, and the resulting self-hatred fuels his misanthropy, which shields his sexual repression as an ego defense mechanism. Before Peter awakens Phil's desire, Phil has counseled him, "'I think what a man needs is odds against him'" (260), and *Power* defines those "odds" as more powerful than Phil understands, for he cannot predict the consequences of sexual repression. That's a fierce, emblematic running dog on the hillside above the ranch, after all—the ranching world's judgment forever hounding him. While he registers the effects of his venomous contempt on others, above all his new sister-in-law, it lies beyond him to know or control the psychic energy consumed by his deep self-contempt. The state of siege in Lacan's metaphoric definition of the *I* is apt. Phil Burbank, a house divided against itself, fascinates us because of the severity of his cruelty fueled by self-hatred, and there is no more cogent an explanation for it than that provided by the novel, which endorses the psychoanalytic account of homosexuality overthrown by queer studies.

The Sheep Queen, published a decade after *Power*, explains Phil Burbank's origins in Ed Brewer, older brother to Charlie Brewer, the protagonist's, Thomas Burton's, stepfather. Critics have long recognized *Sheep Queen* as Savage's most autobiographical novel, and while we must grant a novelist the usual imaginative license, we can interweave details between Savage's biography—until 1942 he was known as Tom Brenner, as he'd assumed his stepfather's surname (Hart 9)—and the story of Tom Burton/Brewer, Savage's protagonist and surrogate, without distorting either (e.g., the family resemblance of B—— or Br—— surnames). *The Sheep Queen*, after all, begins, "So I will call myself Tom Burton, or Thomas Burton, as the name would appear on the novels I write. I am too difficult for some readers and my sentences are sometimes more than statements" (3). And both Burton/Brewer and Savage/Brenner were born in 1915. The later novel, dominated by Burton's first-person narration, provides a briefer but more pungent view of Phil Burbank, as many of Ed Brewer's calculated cruelties and physically repellent details belong to Phil. As we say in Montana, he's one disgusting son of a bitch—the real savage—who "never bathed," reeks of urine, and examines at the dining table "those strong, hard hands for traces of escaped mucus" when he blows his nose "into a filthy blue bandanna" (226). With Ed Brewer, we read backward and forward into *Power*'s terminally lacerated Phil and plot the emergence of a repressed gay protagonist. Savage, for example, stresses Brewer's "bizarre modesty" and "strong, naked hands" (227). In *Sheep Queen*, Ed Brewer tries to "woo" Tom's half-sister, rather than himself, "away from [their] mother" (227), object of his torture. In the first mention of Ed/Phil, the act of marriage becomes gender betrayal since, during an awkward social scene, he "rudely remained in his bedroom at the back of the first floor, lying (I knew) with his hands laced behind his head, lying on the brass bed whose twin had been abandoned by my stepfather at his marriage to my mother" (159).

Savage begins with misogyny: "Ed was a bachelor by profession, a woman-hater" (223)—as though these respective conditions can only be identical—whose "purpose was to destroy my mother, and that is what he did" (228). This writer's conflation grants no space between bachelorhood and misogyny, nor any between the latter and homosexuality. In *Power* Phil drives Rose Gordon Burbank to drink; in *Sheep Queen* Ed tortures Tom's mother into quiet alcoholism for "almost twenty years" until he dies from a haystack pole splinter infected with anthrax, those "clever naked hands" (227) ultimately destroying him (229). Ed concentrates his venom on beautiful Beth, Tom's idealized mother, though his contempt, like Phil's, is pervasive: "Part of Ed's secret knowledge is that he knew that almost everyone is vulnerable, that almost everyone can be destroyed" (225). What animates such Iagos? What conditions best explain their emergence? It is easy to read Burton's/Savage's hatred in Oedipal fashion, as the younger man, in the form of *Power*'s Peter Gordon, repeatedly kills the older figure who shattered his mother's health. I am less interested in the act of literary revenge—Savage eternally savaging Ed/Phil—however, than the conceptual transition from the later Ed Brewer to the earlier Phil Burbank. Unsurprisingly, Burton, an established novelist autobiographically reviewing his earlier life, admits his own impotence and desire to destroy the man destroying his mother: "I often wished Ed dead. How I wished I had been older and ready to pit my intellect against his, to find the clue to his own weakness and destroy him. But when I was old enough, sure enough to speak out, he was dead, but too late for my mother's good" (227).

The Power of the Dog precisely realizes Tom's desire. Ed's "own weakness" is his misogyny, and Savage conflates several conditions—bachelorhood, misogyny, and gayness—to create his homophobic, repressed gay rancher. He puts the final hex on Ed by transforming him into gay Phil. These conflations are, of course, as arbitrary as they are erroneous: most bachelors don't inherently hate women or are covert or overt gay men. Savage's reductionism implies the Freudian, punitive judgment against gays, one consistent with *Power*'s Burbank parents and its treatment of one: exposure and eventual death. His implied attitude, hardly a liberal one, undercuts the courage of his (character) creation. After his closely argued rebuttal of Freud and Lacan, Michael Warner (1990) calls for a new theory of sexuality that rejects psychoanalysis's "allegory of gender" and undoes its lasting damage: "the central premises and vocabulary of psychoanalysis have been designed for a heterosexist self-understanding"; and "the theorization of homosexuality as narcissism is itself a form of narcissism peculiar to modern heterosexuality" (560).

If Ed Brewer in *Sheep Queen* explains Phil Burbank in *Power*, he does not explain entirely our sense that the world should have afforded this tortured man a better shake—our idealistic sense that he should have had some chance, rather than none, to become himself. To construe Phil as a product of his environment, as Proulx does, faults the environment for disallowing space for sexual minorities. In a rural culture famous for letting each other alone, we fall short to the extent that we disavow and castigate gayness or lesbianism or bisexuality as "weakness" and oppress the approximately 10 percent of us who aren't heterosexual. There is nothing new here, yet homophobia, particularly among young people not yet settled into their own sexuality—witness the semantic histories of "homosexual" and "queer" and the range of antigay jokes—bespeaks severe limitations in our sexual tolerance. Fiction such as *Power* instructs us in our limitations just as it implicitly asks more of us.

III

Continuing my tale of gay men who "don't leave home," I migrate just south of the Montana border to track the story of Ennis Del Mar and Jack Twist in Annie Proulx's "Brokeback Mountain." That Wyoming story, of course, belongs in precisely the same rural, ranching culture characteristic of Savage's *Power of the Dog,* which, after all, is set along Montana's southwestern border. Proulx and Savage were friends, Proulx has abetted the current revival of Savage's reputation, and it is tempting to speculate about the ways in which *Power* influenced the writing of "Brokeback Mountain," first published in *The New Yorker* (13

October 1997) and subsequently in book form (1999). It won Proulx both an O. Henry Short Story Award and a National Magazine Award (1998), and she unsurprisingly chose it to close *Close Range*. Ang Lee's film adaptation (2005), with screenplay written by Diane Ossama and Larry McMurtry, has garnered a number of awards and made this story Proulx's most famous by far. Ennis and Jack continue the story only imagined by Phil Burbank with Peter Gordon, and its unhappy bumps, with Jack's violent death and Ennis's lingering sorrow and emptiness, question whether any climate of greater sexual tolerance has emerged in the 1960s or 1980s in comparison with *Power*'s 1924 setting. In his edited oral history, *Farm Boys: Lives of Gay Men from the Rural Midwest*, Will Fellows could be describing tortured Phil Burbank when asserting, "coming of age between the mid-1920s and the mid-1960s meant bearing a burden of unequivocally negative feelings toward their emerging selves" (32). Assessing the experience of gay men coming out from the mid-1960s to the mid-1970s, Fellows dismally predicts the fate of Proulx's two young Wyomingites: "It was apparent that this kind of alternative lifestyle would have to be lived clandestinely, or as part of a fringe community in a large city, and neither of these prospects seemed feasible to many men" (130). Those sexual minorities not leaving rural homes, like Phil Burbank or Ennis Del Mar, enact Phil's credo (i.e., my first epigraph) more than they could ever understand.

Gretel Ehrlich, who lived in Wyoming for several years in the 1980s, probes and revises masculine stereotypes in a way that measures the dilemma facing Proulx's gay men. In *The Solace of Open Spaces*, Ehrlich concludes early on that "the toughness I was learning" consists of "the art of accommodation": "To be tough is to be fragile; to be tender is to be truly fierce" (44). Her instructive inversion of the tough-tender polarity so ingrained in western experience (e.g., Jane Tompkins's anatomy of it in *West of Everything*), and privileging of tenderness, plots Phil Burbank's tragedy and deflates the received stereotypes of machismo. It also forecasts, in some respects, the lonely path Ennis and Jack walk. In "About Men," Ehrlich rebalances the so-called polarity, depicting toughness as merely facade: "If [a rancher or cowboy is] gruff, handsome, and physically fit on the outside, he's androgynous at the core. Ranchers are midwives, hunters, nurturers, providers, and conservationists all at once. What we've interpreted as toughness—weathered skin, calloused hands, a squint in the eye and a growl in the voice—only masks the tenderness inside" (51). Has Ehrlich merely revalidated John Wayne clichés and old cowboy songs? By proclaiming "to be tender is to be truly fierce," she shifts the emphasis and opens new gender space. While one can quibble with Ehrlich's response to

Katherine G. Morrissey's "gendered West" with which I began, the real issue is the masking of tenderness: its social origins and residual pressures. With Phil Burbank and his horny hands, the masking proves potent and fatal; Ennis Del Mar and Jack Twist pursue their own unmasked tenderness at a similarly high price. The world of John Wayne makes no room for the "something wrong" with these boys.

Brokeback Mountain—the setting where the two teenagers discover their sexual passion for one another (Proulx 261–62) and that symbolizes their sexual idyll (277–79)—suggests, by its shape and name, their doomed lives as lovers. It is "'some pretend place where the bluebirds sing and there's a whiskey spring,'" in ironic reference to "The Big Rock Candy Mountain," a famous folk song whose fantasy life is now opened to sexual minorities.[3] Their gay awakening is premised on being spied on (262), their cowboying life (267), and their self-denial (268). They will not admit they're "queers" even though they're found out. Married lives mask their occasional trysts and further marginalize their status. These two hardly have a chance together as Proulx describes Ennis's father's violent homophobia and the tire iron death of old Earl, a gay rancher (270), which foreshadows Jack's same death (279, 282). Later the reader learns that Jack's father, who was uncircumcised, symbolically emasculates Jack as a young boy by urinating all over him (282). So much for masked tenderness. The story even questions their awareness of their gayness. Jack angrily accuses Ennis of precluding a life together: "'What we got now is Brokeback Mountain. Everthing built on that. It's all we got, boy, fuckin all, so I hope you know that if you don't never know the rest'" (277–78).

The site of their adolescent coming out becomes the benchmark against which their subsequent relationship falls forever short, and the story defines its most intense memory as a "sexless hunger": "That dozy embrace solidified in [Jack's] memory as the single moment of artless, charmed happiness in their separate and difficult lives. Nothing marred it, even the knowledge that Ennis would not then embrace him face to face because he did not want to see nor feel that it was Jack he held. And maybe, he thought, they'd never got much farther than that" (279). Though the lovers kiss subsequently (265–66), the suggestion is that there lingers something immature, even infantile, in their love affair. This gay relationship, spied out from the beginning (269) and realized infrequently across decades, stumbles toward Jack's tire iron death. The story's brief mention of the men's fathers—macho parodies bereft of any tender emotion—suggests these two boys discover in one another an affective world missing from father-son relations. "Brokeback Mountain" invites such a conservative psychological reading as if grossly inadequate males, lacking Ehrlich's androgyny, father sons who are gay. The story supports psychoanalysis's etiology of homosexuality, but it also leaves open the possibility of more contemporary, less punitive judgments.

It is hard, though, to dispute the lovers' bleak impasse or the plot's verdicts against them. Ennis and Jack boil over about their lack of options: "'But if you can't fix it you got a stand it,' [Ennis] said. 'Shit. I been looking at people on the street. This happen a other people? What the hell do they do?' 'It don't happen in Wyomin and if it does I don't know what they do, maybe go to Denver,' said Jack" (271). Beth Lofreda reports that in Wyoming, "there isn't a single gay bar, bookstore, or permanent, public gathering place," so that "talking about the closet means something quite different when there are simply very few places to be outside of it." As a result, "friendship, companionship, and community can be much more difficult to discover than sex" (63, 70).[4] The rural-to-urban migration sketched by Jack corroborates the experience of many gay men. For example, in *Farm Boys*, editor Will Fellows, who divides his thirty-seven oral histories into three decades in the twentieth century's second half, states in the preface, "It is not uncommon for gay men who grew up on farms to regard their rural roots as irrelevant or embarrassing." Presumably the latter derives, at least in part, from homophobia that often lingers in, for example, the rural Northern Rockies. Fellows tells a common story of out-migration: "A large majority of these men have left farming and rural communities, choosing to live in or near relatively large midwestern cities" (xi).[5] By keeping her gay pair at Brokeback Mountain, Proulx reinforces Julia Watson's conclusion with which I began. "Adventurous living" results in a tire iron verdict; short of that, the story closes by echoing and endorsing Ennis's bleak stoicism: "There was some open space between what [Ennis] knew and what he tried to believe, but nothing could be done about it, and if you can't fix it you've got to stand it" (285). Neither Ennis nor the reader takes much solace from this "open space," which may prove illusory (e.g., "tried to believe").

The critical and popular reception of Ang Lee's *Brokeback Mountain* raises a range of questions beyond the scope of this essay, some of which I have addressed, with three colleagues, in another essay.[6] Clearly, this film had arrived at its own proper time, and it makes a fascinating case in reception aesthetics in the early twenty-first century. Its popularity suggests some change in tolerance among audiences, yet the film's problematic relation to the Western film genre suggests that the sexually marginal will remain, mostly, marginal.

On my own campus, where the Rodeo Club and Team command a powerful presence, most of the guys, I was told, would not attend a campus screening (spring 2005) and subsequent discussion of the movie, because they would feel "too uncomfortable." Despite this fact, I presume most Montanans and Wyomingites who opted to see the movie, liked it.

Proulx's characters cannot voice their milieu's "queer" verdict, but the story's "open space" leaves open our loud embrace, rather than silent avoidance, of it. We can imagine and enact alternatives to shame and silence. The story prompts our imagining a radically different *I*, as articulated by queer studies, than that granted old Earl or Jack Twist. Again quoting Sedgwick: "'Queer' seems to hinge much more radically and explicitly on a person's undertaking particular, performative acts of experimental self-perception and filiation. . . . There are important senses in which 'queer' can signify only *when attached to the first person*. . . . What it takes—all it takes—to make the description 'queer' a true one is the impulsion *to* use it in the first person" (quoted in *Regarding* 8). The editors of *Regarding Sedgwick* define *queer* as "a crossing of temporality with force" (8) and laud the expressive diversity and aggression of Sedgwick's *I*, itself tantamount to queer representation (19). Of course, the widest space the reader must imagine crossing exists between Sedgwick's confident, performative *I* and the mute queers in Proulx's rural North Rockies, for whom the 1990s Queer Moment remains unavailable.

IV

Literature, I have been suggesting, takes a lead in trying to "fix it" even as it chronicles gay or lesbian characters who struggle, and sometimes fail, to "stand it." A lesbian Montana writer, Patricia Nell Warren, published three "gay-positive novels" (Fellows 221) in the 1970s, thus providing a more optimistic response to Watson's indictment of regional myths. One of them, *The Fancy Dancer* (1976), is set in part in Dillon, Savage's own literary place. It is worth noting, however, that Warren left her native Deer Lodge for urban Southern California decades ago, following the curve plotted by Fellows and Sedgwick, among others. It is also worth noting that if, as Proulx's Jack avers, "'it don't happen in Wyomin,'" the Matthew Shepard murder and subsequent film, *The Laramie Project* (2001), show fiction and fact again dovetailing. That case held up the mirror not just in Wyoming but also in Montana and across the country as it painfully probed the nature of homophobia in rural America. The two young homophobic killers of Shepard, a gay college student from out of state, are residents of Wyoming's only university city and could have stepped from the pages of Proulx's story, tire irons in hand. *The Laramie Project*, which received critical acclaim at the 2001 Sundance Film Festival, exposes this homophobia even as it asks for forgiveness and pleads a greater sexual tolerance, which, I have been suggesting, is an implicit element of Savage's novel and Proulx's short story.

In the afterward to his oral history, Will Fellows does not open up much more space than is suggested by the closing of "Brokeback Mountain." Generalizing about his myriad case histories, Fellows concludes that "something fundamental in their natures makes misfits of them in farm culture" (311):

> If the prospect of staying in their rural communities had not appeared to be so incompatible with leading honest, unconstricted lives, more of these men might have made their homes in farm communities—some of them as farmers, perhaps. If they had been able to live in these places as openly gay men, they might have helped to diminish the silence, ignorance, and prejudice that surrounds homosexuality by demonstrating to their rural communities the possibilities of living fulfilling, meaningful, "wholesome" lives outside the mainstream world. (314)

When will "wholesome" include sexual minorities? There is something both wistful and deeply tragic about these conditional statements that explain "what [Ennis Del Mar] tried to believe." For such gay men, affirming their status requires out-migration and if you go home again, you pay a terrible price. Glancing at the linkage, in the popular mind, between AIDS and gayness in the past fifteen years, Fellows concludes, "Many of the HIV-infected men who have returned to their home communities have found that attitudes toward homosexuality remain grounded in ignorance and prejudice" (315), particularly to the extent that gay men remain scapegoats of the world's heterosexual epidemic. What has changed in the twenty-first century's dawn?

The relationship between literature advocating space for gays and lesbians and genuine social change is complex beyond the bounds of this essay. Savage and Proulx and Warren, for example, bravely point the way, yet my years in Savage's home ground make me wonder when homophobia will lessen. Local and state circumstantial evidence suggests that many either don't understand or don't accept Gretel Ehrlich's tough-tender inversion and paradoxical credo. Some years ago there was a hate crime directed against Pansy Bradshaw, one of our community's few visible gay men, and the subsequent candlelight vigil and demonstration march movingly suggested Dillon's support for gay men. During the march, we watched the two young perpetrators of this crime, propped against an old car, watching us marching and singing, and I remember wondering what, if anything, they learned about sexual tolerance. Were they at all unsettled in their unquestioning, inherited homophobia? I'm not counting on it.

A few years ago a close friend, English professor Henry Gonshak of Montana Tech, taught the first Gay and Lesbian Studies course in Butte, and the resulting firestorm lead to inquiries from *USA Today*, conference appearances, and publications including an essay on the back page of *The Chronicle of Higher Education*. In "Setting the Record Less Straight: My Skirmish with the Religious Right over Gay Studies in Montana," Gonshak reminds readers of Montana's antisodomy statute that "explicitly criminalizes homosexual sex between consenting adults," and points out that Butte's "sizeable gay population" "has always remained almost totally closeted," the local Gay Pride chapter meeting in secret locations. Gonshak faced considerable pressure in offering the course the first time, ending up modifying its title and content: "I regret that by restructuring the class this way, we in a sense 'closeted' homosexuality by concealing it among a cluster of other 'lifestyles.'" Though Gonshak has subsequently taught the course with little opposition, that initial experience raised a series of questions: Is there a connection between homophobia and big business? Are the captains of industry, sworn as they are to preserving the status quo, thus pledged by definition to thwarting the aspirations of historically marginalized groups? Is the dog-eat-dog ethos of laissez-faire capitalism antithetical to a commitment to justice for the oppressed? Is there a tie between the corporate machismo so rife in the business world and the traditional macho revulsion at the perceived effeminacy of gay men?

I find these speculations hard to resist, as I do Gonshak's conclusion: "Disenfranchised economically, watching as their traditional ways of life collapse, such Americans [especially poor, white, rural Christians] are looking for someone to blame. Now that, with the end of the Cold War, communists are no longer available as all-purpose bogeymen, homosexuals are among the only ideal scapegoats left." Gonshak's article suggests that the out-migration Fellows plots focuses on large urban areas, not Montana or Wyoming "cities." In the spring of 2002, arsonists torched the home of two Missoula lesbians, one of them a University of Montana professor, and their young child, who escaped with their lives. According to the state leaders of PRIDE, the investigation had insinuated that the lesbians themselves were suspects in this hate crime. All this in Montana's university town always deemed the most liberal in the state. By mid-2003, the case was officially closed, unsolved—another dismal episode in the endless history of scapegoating. The Montana University system only recently changed course to provide health benefits for same-sex marriage partners. On my own small campus the Lambda Alliance, a student club for lesbians and gays, was formed a few years ago, shepherded in part by my wife, UM-Western's primary counselor. As of this writing, few lesbians and fewer gays regularly attend. We've a "Tolerance Club" on campus, too, but in the town Savage variously calls "Herndon" and "Grayling," it's daunting to come out if you're gay.

When finishing high school, our older son occasionally mentioned the newest antigay jokes heard at school. One May, at the annual Youth Legislature in Helena, he was stigmatized by the rest of the school delegation for supporting a bill endorsing same-sex marriage. In the August 2002 issue of my *Human Rights Network News*, published by the Montana Human Rights Network (MHRN), I read the column by Betty Kijewski, who attended a conference at Indiana University on Sexual Minority Youth. Kijewski describes her "sense of the absolute isolation faced by GLBT [Gay, Lesbian, Bisexual and Transgender] youth," and notes that the conference keynote speaker characterized them as "the most isolated of all minorities, marked by high suicide, addiction and homelessness rates." According to the "GLSEN School Climate Report 2001," printed in a box accompanying the article, "85% of all youth report hearing homophobic remarks frequently; 24% of these youth report hearing homophobic remarks from faculty or school staff; 61% reported verbal harassment; 47% reported sexual harassment; and 28% reported physical harassment (shoving, hitting)." Kijewski, a community organizer for MHRN, made, with her gay son, a half hour documentary, *The End of Silence: Montana Gay Youth Speak*, which she subsequently toured across our state. She showed it at the 2003 MHRN Conference (25 October 2003, Missoula) in a workshop, discussing its genesis and reception. The documentary interviews a dozen gay and lesbian high school students in Montana who discuss, in harrowing terms, their experiences of intimidation, bullying, and harassment. Most poignantly, they plea for changes in attitudes and school policies so that other sexual minority youth won't feel as consistently threatened and marginalized. To the extent high schoolers enact, unmasked and unvarnished, adult opinions, *The End of Silence* verifies abiding homophobia. To the extent that the population tacitly condones such demonizing, it's sometimes a short step to tire iron scapegoating—Matthew Shepard's murder, for instance. But a documentary film, like a novel or short story, ends silence.

That ancient and current tendency to scapegoat derives, according to Michael Warner in his recent provocative book, *The Trouble with Normal: Sex, Politics, and the Ethics of Queer Life*, from "The Ethics of Sexual Shame," the title of his first chapter. Warner's analysis spins out from a pair of statements surrounding a key question in his opening: "Most people cannot quite rid themselves of the sense that controlling the sex of others, far from being unethical, is where morality begins. Shouldn't it be possible to allow everyone sexual autonomy, in a way consistent with everyone else's sexual autonomy? As simple as this ethical principle sounds, we have not come close to putting it into practice" (1). Warner concludes "Homo-Narcissism; or Heterosexuality" (1990) by turning the psychoanalytical explanation of homosexuality on its head: "Modern heterosexuality needs a discourse about homosexuality as a displacement of its own narcissistic sources" (563). A colleague wears a button that proclaims "HOMOPHOBIA Is a Social Disease." Warner's idealistic "ethical principle," no doubt unacceptable to those who embrace that "sense" of "controlling the sex of others," returns us to Phil Burbank, Ed Brewer, Ennis Del Mar, and Jack Twist. No golden rule governs "sexual autonomy," the anthrax or tire iron verdict of majority culture documenting Phil Burbank's "odds" or Ennis and Jack's chances of "standing it." There is nothing new about literature advocating ways to "fix" the cruel oppression of sexual minorities, sometimes initiating discussion of social change well ahead of its time; as the *Great Falls Tribune* suggested in that brief mention of Savage, *Power* seems decades "ahead of the curve."

The dark tale I have told extending from Phil Burbank/Ed Brewer and Bronco Henry (or Peter Gordon) through Ennis Del Mar and Jack Twist, which elaborates Annie Proulx's reading of *The Power of the Dog*, is not, of course, the only Thomas Savage story. *Power* and *Sheep Queen* have many other claims to literary distinction, and then there are the other eleven novels. However, his conception of Phil Burbank—so bright and talented and hateful, as repressed as any of Nathaniel Hawthorne's Puritans—temptingly links itself in my mind with Savage's obscurity and neglect. Burbank holds readers by the throat with his sustained cruelty, and we cannot avoid his breath or voice even as our hatred, like Peter Gordon's, grows. A drought of many years in Montana's southwest corner resulted, by late summer in 2002 and 2003, in large Clark Canyon Reservoir emptying to less than 10 percent capacity. One bizarre result of this 1964–65 reservoir nearly emptying has been the exposure of the town site of tiny Armstead, Montana—Savage's "Beech," which he knew well and wrote about repeatedly as he has Dillon, the county seat. My family and I, along with many county residents, find it uncanny to poke about these archaeological remains, particularly Armstead School, unintentionally "resurfaced" after thirty-seven years underwater. Thanks to Emily Salkin Takoudes when she was at Little, Brown, Savage's literary reputation has been buried less time. I hope the current minirevival restores Savage to an appropriate position on the literary map of Montana and the American West. And I hope that in my big, "empty" county and in comparative counties across the Northern Rockies, gays will out and the local, heteronormative majority will embrace them in their difference.

NOTES

1. This "Queer Moment" in literary criticism was part of a much broader social movement that closed the twentieth century. Beth Lofreda reminds us that "in the late 1990s, homosexuality and vehement opposition to it were everywhere in American public culture and politics" (24).
2. Lofreda unsurprisingly develops the theme of pervasive homophobia in her study: "Discriminatory violence is rarely fully plotted—even in its most grotesque manifestations, it is far more often a bleak and ugly blur of knee-jerk discomfort, semiconscious revulsion, false visions of vulnerability, opportunistic rationalization, and relieved retreats to familiarity and sameness" (144).
3. In this context, Leslie Fiedler again provides the long view when mythologizing Twain's big river and Melville's South Seas: "The immensity of water defines a loneliness that demands love; its strangeness symbolizes the disavowal of the conventional that makes possible all versions of love" ("Huck Honey!" 148). Substitute mountains, specifically Northern Rockies, and mountain valleys for Old Man River or ocean, and the setting for homosexual love becomes the same.
4. In her study, Beth Lofreda analyzes in detail the "guardedness" that characterizes gay and lesbian life in Wyoming: "You'd lose something of the texture of their lives if you failed to acknowledge that background hum of calculation, the daily quick math that accompanies gay life, where each act of openness must be weighed against the potential friends, acquaintances, jobs, happiness lost" (68). As one lesbian remarks, "Wyoming is *run* by people who have a great deal invested in making sure nothing changes. And that includes civil rights" (61).
5. Eve Koslovsky Sedgwick plots much the same curve in her readings of Balzac and Proust:

   > The more than Balzacian founding narrative of a certain modern identity for Euro-American gay men . . . vibrates along a chord that stretches from provincial origins to metropolitan destinies. As each individual story begins in the isolation of queer childhood, we compulsorily and excruciatingly *misrecognize* ourselves in the available mirror of the atomized, procreative, so-called heterosexual pre- or ex-urban nuclear family of origin, whose bruisingly inappropriate interpellations may wound us—those resilient or lucky enough to survive them—into life, life of a different kind. The site of that second family and belated life, those newly constituted and denaturalized "families," those tardy, wondering chances at transformed and transforming self- and other-recognition, is the metropolis. (quoted in *Regarding* 16)

6. See "Conversing *Brokeback Mountain*'s Varied Spaces and Contested Desires," an article in four voices—Scott L. Baugh, Donovan Gwinner, Sara L. Spurgeon, and O. Alan Weltzien—in *Intertexts* 10, 2 (Fall 2006): 155–79. In this article we analyze several aspects of the film and draw a range of connections between the short story, the screenplay, and various visual elements in the film.

WORKS CITED

"Ahead of the Curve." *Great Falls Tribune*, 11 December 2001, B2.

Barber, Stephen M., and David L. Clark, eds. *Regarding Sedgwick: Essays on Queer Culture and Critical Theory*. New York: Routledge, 2002.

Bevis, William W. *Ten Tough Trips*. Seattle: University of Washington Press, 1990.

Egan, Ken, Jr. *Hope and Dread in Montana Literature*. Reno: University of Nevada Press, 2003.

Ehrlich, Gretel. *The Solace of Open Spaces*. New York: Viking Penguin, 1985.

Fellows, Will, ed. *Farm Boys: Lives of Gay Men from the Rural Midwest*. Madison: University of Wisconsin Press, 1996.

Fiedler, Leslie. *An End to Innocence: Essays on Culture and Politics*. Boston: Beacon Press, 1955.

Gonshak, Henry. "Setting the Record Less Straight: My Skirmish with the Religious Right over Gay Studies in Montana." *Open Lives, Safe Schools*. Ed. Donovan R. Walling. Bloomington IN: Phi Delta Kappa Educational Foundation, 1996.

Hart, Sue. *Thomas and Elizabeth Savage*. Western Writers Series No. 119. Boise: Boise State University Press, 1995.

Kijewski, Betty. "Road Trip with Betty: Planes, Shuttles, and Gay Youth." *Human Rights Network News*, Montana Human Rights Network (August 2002), 9.

———. *The End of Silence: Montana Gay Youth Speak*. Montana Human Rights Network, 2002–03.

Lacan, Jacques. "The Mirror Stage as Formative of the Function of the I as Revealed in Psychoanalytic Experience." *Contemporary Literary Criticism*, 3rd ed. Ed. Robert Con Davis and Ronald Schleifer. White Plains NY: Longman, 1994. 382–86.

The Laramie Project, directed by Moisés Kaufman. Cane/Gabay Productions, 2002.

The Last Best Place: A Montana Anthology. Ed. William Kittredge and Annick Smith. Helena: Montana Historical Society Press, 1988.

Lofreda, Beth. *Losing Matt Shepard: Life and Politics in the Aftermath of Anti-Gay Murder*. New York: Columbia University Press, 2000.

Morrissey, Kathleen G. "Engendering the West." *Under an Open Sky: Rethinking America's Western Past*. Ed. William Cronon, George Miles, and Jay Gitlin. New York: Norton, 1992.

Proulx, Annie. "Brokeback Mountain." *Close Range: Wyoming Stories*. New York: Simon & Schuster, 1999; Scribner Paperback Fiction Edition, 2000.

———. "Afterword." *The Power of the Dog*. By Thomas Savage. Back Bay Edition. Boston: Back Bay, 2001.

Savage, Thomas. *The Power of the Dog*. Boston: Little, Brown, 1967; reprint, Boston: Back Bay, 2001.

———. *The Sheep Queen*. (First published as *I Heard My Sister Speak My Name*.) Boston: Little, Brown, 1977; reprint, Boston: Back Bay, 2001.

Tompkins, Jane. *West of Everything: The Inner Life of Westerns*. New York: Oxford University Press, 1992.

Warner, Michael. "Homo-Narcissism; or Heterosexuality." *Contemporary Literary Criticism*, 3rd ed. Ed. Robert Con Davis and Ronald Schleiffer. White Plains NY: Longmans, 1994. 549–65.

———. *The Trouble with Normal: Sex, Politics, and the Ethics of Queer Life*. Cambridge MA: Harvard University Press, 1999.

Watson, Julia. "Engendering Montana Lives: Women's Autobiographical Writing." *Writing Montana: Literature Under the Big Sky*. Ed. Rick Newby and Suzanne Hunger. Helena: Montana Center for the Book, 1996. 121–62.

PART IV Native Revisions/The Problems of History

CHAPTER EIGHT

"He Never Wanted to Forget It": Contesting the Idea of History in D'Arcy McNickle's *The Surrounded*

JIM RAINS

Early in *The Surrounded*, D'Arcy McNickle's first novel, Archilde Leon pauses to reflect on his home on the Flathead Reservation in Montana: "Nowhere in the world, he imagined, was there a sky of such depth and freshness. He wanted never to forget it, wherever he might be in times to come. Yes, wherever he might be!" (5). Like other Montana writers, McNickle emphasizes the importance of the western landscape and its centrality in establishing the identity of his characters. This sense of place, one of the defining characteristics of western literature, acquires added significance in McNickle's fiction, however. McNickle's fiction naturally reflects his dual cultural identity as a member of an American Indian tribe and a westerner; and as a Native American writer and a resident of the American West he writes purposefully to resist the marginalization of his home and his people. Through his fiction he endeavors to shatter the mythic, romantic historical narrative of the West. In its place he offers a more accurate account of its people and events as well as the impact of national expansion and its devastation on indigenous cultures.[1]

In a letter to anthropologist William Gates, McNickle states, "I am writing of the West, not of Indians primarily, and certainly not of the romantic West which best-selling authors have exploited to the understanding of the meaning of the West, the Frontier, in American life."[2] In an effort to explain Native American cultures to non-Indian America and in attempt to achieve understanding among cultures, McNickle chose to focus on the one crucial aspect of the American Indian experience that he believed had been most neglected and had accounted not only for conflicts in the past but also for unresolved issues in the present: Native American history.

"It is asking too much when a man is required to close the book of the past, to forget that it had ever been" (108). The narrator is referring to Max Leon, a white character, Archilde's father, but in a larger sense McNickle is making a statement about the Native American subjects within his novel who, by the beginning of the twentieth century, have been pressured to abandon their traditional cultural beliefs and practices in favor of Euro-American culture. McNickle's Native American characters are trapped between two cultures (Euro-American and Salish), and they are entangled in the agonizing stages of a culture in transition. Life for many Native Americans residing on reservations in the early decades of the twentieth century, like the Flatheads in this novel, reflected the confusion and instability caused by such a transition. Poverty, illiteracy, disease, and despair were typical problems endured by many tribal communities. As Native American people struggled to negotiate the effects of sudden and profound cultural change, their efforts to act were impeded by the marginalized identity that had been conferred on them by Euro-American historical discourse. For example, it was futile for American Indians to resist assimilation because, many in white America assumed, it was the inevitable outcome of American progress. American Indians were regarded as people without a history of their own; each tribe and its history was subsumed by the broader category and narratives of American history.

McNickle was among the first Native American writers to reject this condition, and in his first work he challenged the appropriateness of conventional history for American Indians. *The Surrounded*, published in 1936, was, upon its publication, heralded as a "new Indian literature."[3] Critics seized on the novel's "authenticity," its "Indianness"; but the most noteworthy aspect of this early-twentieth-century novel is the emphasis the author placed on history and its vital, ongoing importance to the future of Native American cultures. McNickle wrestled with the problem of history throughout his life: "If Indians are to write their own histories, and if history is a reflection of the people about whom it is written, I would expect and would hope for some of these qualities to show up in the writing. I don't see how it is possible for an Indian (or any native person) to write about his people if he is required to use the model designed by and for a different set of cultural imperatives."[4] This statement evidences McNickle's lifelong concern with American Indian history. He valued an Indian-authored history and argued for its emergence.[5] He ultimately gained recognition as a professional historian of Native American cultures, but he found in fiction an effective means by which to explore and contest the very idea of history.

In an article titled "Interpreting Native America," McNickle summarizes the need for a specific Indian history: "Most attempts to write about Indians in American history turn out to be accounts of what happened after contact with whites—a history of Indian-white relations in which the Indian is seen only in reaction to an incoming society and usually at a disadvantage. His own society is only dimly perceived, his motives are guessed at, his destiny is under a cloud" (599). This statement suggests guidelines for writing Indian history. It should not limit itself to merely recording Native cultures' reactions to white invasion; it should, rather, convey the nature of the Native cultures and endeavor to articulate their unique perspectives. McNickle also implies that the future of Native American cultures will be determined by their ability to narrate their own experiences and values.

In *The Surrounded* Archilde returns to the Flathead Indian Reservation. He intends to visit only briefly, but his return is extended when he becomes entangled in the affairs of his family. His visit, however, unexpectedly causes him to reflect on unresolved aspects of his own identity. As he reinvolves himself with his family, he begins to confront his own ambivalent feelings toward them and his own identity as a mixed-blood member of the Flathead tribe.[6] *The Surrounded* is a narrative about Archilde's personal journey of identity. It is a Native-authored text that attempts to address what the author perceives to be a fundamental misunderstanding of Native American people. *It* is a book about history: how Native American cultures have been constrained and limited by conventional histories and how they as distinct cultures perceive and practice history differently from Euro-Americans.

McNickle is reopening the "book of the past," challenging the idea of history, complicating conventional national narratives, and posing alternative ways of organizing the past. He believes that historians have not represented Native American cultures accurately and fully: "The so-called Red Race has yet to overcome the disadvantages of its condition at the time of Discovery—of being a people without a written history. . . . The consequence of this critical handicap was to place in the hands of strangers, invariably misinformed, often hostile, the delicate task of transmitting to the world information about one of its major population groups" ("Sociocultural" 2). *The Surrounded* is McNickle's effort to revisit the concept of history in a critical way and initiate, through fiction, a different way of regarding Native Americans and their relation to history.

The Oxford English Dictionary defines *history* as "a relation of incidents; a narrative, tale, story." There is, of course, no single history of Native Americans, no one narrative that takes into account the many histories of the diverse cultures included in the term *American Indian*. Another definition of *history* offered by OED is "that branch of knowledge which deals with past events, as recorded in writings or otherwise ascertained; the formal record of the past, esp. of human affairs or actions; the study of the formation and growth of communities and nations." McNickle challenges conventional history by narrating *The Surrounded*'s characters' particular stories and "relation of incidents." *The Surrounded* does not represent a formal history, of course; rather it complicates conventional histories of the American West, proposes alternative ways of experiencing history, and in the end, challenges the very idea of history. The novel also demonstrates the way in which America's history could—and should—be forced to accommodate the diverse individual histories of the disparate cultures that comprise the nation.

Until recently the histories of Native American cultures have been relegated to a subcategory of a larger national history of the American West. The story of the American Indian was subsumed by the kind of historical narrative put forth by historians such as Fredrick Jackson Turner who interpreted the region as the unfolding of the westward course of empire. Turner's "Frontier thesis" defined the American West as an area of undeveloped free land that marked the lines of settlement for the expanding nation. Furthermore, the settling of that land helped shape the national character. Subsequent scholarship has, naturally, rethought Turner's historical perspective, and many historians agree that his view now appears to have relied too heavily on myth, specifically the national myth of progress. Donald Worster summarizes that myth like this: "We have had many myths about the West but the principal one was a story about a simple, rural people coming into a western country—an ordinary people moving into an extraordinary land, as Robert Athearn has put it—and creating there a peaceful, productive life. In this great good place human nature was supposed to rise out of its old turpitude and depravity to a new dignity: sturdy yeoman farmers would have here the chance to live rationally and quietly, free of all contaminating influences" (6). For Turner, the American landscape underwent a transformation from wilderness to civilization; and, almost instantly, his interpretation became the central, defining historical narrative of the nation. Native American cultures, one of the casualties of the transformation, were reduced to a footnote within the broader history of the region and the nation. They became, in the frontier thesis, simply another obstacle to overcome as America transformed its wilderness into civilization.

The progress myth, and its concomitant erasure of the Native American experience, dominated the written histories of the region. William Cronon concludes, "In countless versions both before and after it acquired its classic Turnerian form, this story of frontier struggle and progress remains among the oldest and most familiar narratives of American history. In its ability to turn ordinary people into heroes and to present a conflict-ridden invasion as an epic march toward enlightened democratic nationhood, it perfectly fulfilled the ideological needs of its late nineteenth-century moment" (1352). The defining power of this myth and its allure as a metanarrative of America as a nation endured until the emergence of the new western history, which appears in Patricia Limerick's *The Legacy of Conquest* (1987). Limerick, Cronon, Worster, and Richard White challenged the assumption on which Turner's interpretation was based. They also noted the exclusion of the voices of women and minorities in the extant histories.

The frontier thesis is a historical discourse of nation building that relegates the role of Native American cultures to victims of progress; they were destined to vanish over time. Such a narrative subsumes the histories of individual tribes and individuals within the tribes. Omitted are the countless stories that contradict the national narrative, alter it in significant ways, or contribute new understandings to it. Colin Calloway notes the subversive potential of such stories:

> The history of the millions of Indian people who have inhabited North America, and of the few million who still do, is important in itself, but it also provides alternative perspectives on the history of the United States. It reminds us that one people's triumph often means another's tragedy; that building a new nation often entails conquest of other, older nations; and that we recognize invasion, racism, and acts of genocide, along with pioneering, liberty, and equality, as part of America's history, and that Native struggles to protect their resources and rights continue today. It is a story of conquest and colonization, but it is also a story of resilience, innovation, and survival. (4)

Calloway's observation identifies compelling reasons for the inclusion of Native American historical perspectives: millions of people who identify themselves as Indians and who still live in this country today possess a distinct history; their histories will yield alternative perspectives on the conventional national narrative of nation building; the building of this nation was coincidental with the destruction of other nations; those other nations suffered in the process of conquest; the themes of pioneering, liberty, and equality—essential aspects of the national narrative—are mitigated by historical acts of invasion, racism, and genocide; and those same millions of people continue to struggle today to protect their resources and rights. Calloway also notes that in spite of these untold aspects of history, Native American cultures can claim, simultaneously, a history that is composed of stories of "resilience, innovation and survival." A national historical narrative that omits the underside of nation building is pernicious in itself, for it conveniently obscures the realities of the past; however, the act of suppressing the accompanying stories of resilience, innovation, and survival of such cultures also threatens to limit their future as well. Calloway concludes, "The past is a complex story, made up of many interwoven lives and experiences. American history without Indians is mythology—it never happened" (8).

For Native American cultures to gain a historical voice, however, they first have to produce historical narratives that convey the uniqueness of their experiences. Consider, for example, the importance of the production of history for those cultures affected by the colonial experience. Bill Ashcroft, Gareth Griffiths, and Helen Tiffin argue that official histories of the colonizers play a predominant role in the conquest of an indigenous people. They write, "For the emergence of history in European thought is coterminous with the rise of modern colonialism, which in its radical othering and violent annexation of the non-European world, found in history a prominent, if not *the prominent*, instrument for the control of subject peoples" (355). They continue, "At base, the myth of a value-free, 'scientific,' view of the past, the myth of the beauty of order, the myth of the story of history as a simple representation of the continuity of events, authorized nothing less than the construction of world reality" (355). Native American cultures have been significantly and permanently altered by the imposition of European and Euro-American cultures and, therefore, exist under similar colonial conditions.[7] For Native American people to reestablish their own identities, they must first reclaim their right to produce their own cultural histories. They must resist "the construction of world reality" that has silenced their narratives of the past. "Clearly, what it means to have history is the same as what it means to have a legitimate existence: history and legitimation go hand in hand; history legitimates 'us' and not others," write Ashcroft, Griffiths, and Tiffin (355).

The Surrounded demands a rethinking of the idea of history as it impacts the telling of the Native American experience. Within *The Surrounded* a new Native American voice does indeed emerge, and that new voice attempts to historicize that experience. In *The Surrounded* McNickle is challenging the dominant national historical narrative and arguing for the acknowledgment and inclusion of historical narratives originating within Native American cultures.[8] McNickle is suggesting that Euro-America relies on formal history to transmit knowledge of its past, while Native American cultures rely on stories. He demonstrates this difference through the stories of Modeste and their transforming effect on Archilde. Throughout this novel Archilde looks to the past to locate himself in the present. *The Surrounded* opens with Archilde returning home. He believes that he has returned home to say a final good-bye. His family's failings at first put him off: "Already he was hearing the old stories—quarreling, stealing, fighting" (4). The reservation appears now just as he had left it, and although it is his home, he intends to leave again.

In spite of his misgivings, however, Archilde maintains a strong memory of place. His identity is bound up with the memories he has of home: "Tomorrow he would go fishing. He would look at the sky some more. He would ride his horse. Then wherever he might go, he would always keep the memory of these things" (14). His mission school education, his participation in tribal life, his recreation in the Montana countryside—these experiences contribute to his identity. Archilde himself is surprised by the hold that his home and family still have on him: "It was a peculiar thing how images of such things entwined themselves into one's life; they were nothing that could be touched and yet they had strength and substance. He had come a thousand miles because they might pull him from across half the world" (16). Archilde is realizing that one does not easily escape his past.[9]

Archilde experiences a radical redefinition of identity over the course of the novel. In the beginning, Modeste and Catharine past are not "real" to him. He resists his mother's efforts to include him in a traditional feast, and her clinging to the past repulses him: "Actually, in the way he was learning the world, neither Modeste nor his mother was important. They were not real people. Buffaloes were not real to him either, yet he could go and look at buffaloes every day if he wished, behind wire enclosure of the Biological Survey reserve. He knew that buffaloes had been real things to his mother, and to the old people who had come to eat with her tonight" (62). Initially, Archilde does not share his mother's interest in the tribal past. There is a significant distance between the traditional world of his mother and his experience of the world. Tribal elders, like the buffalo, are remnants of a former way of life. They belong to the past and therefore lack relevance for him.

The tribal elders maintain the reality of the past through stories, feasts, and dances. As long as they gather and tell stories, the past is not completely lost. Telling stories of the past is the means by which they preserve a tribal identity and teach its values. Archilde dislikes the gatherings: "That was something he had forgotten to include in his visit—the old lady and her feasts! You gorged yourself on meat until you felt sick, and a lot of old people told tiresome stories. He frowned. He ought to refuse" (4). As the feast begins, Archilde feels uneasy: "The deeper feeling was impatience, irritation, an uneasy feeling in the stomach. Why could he not endure them for just these few hours? Why did they make him feel sick?" (62). Archilde admonishes the elders for clinging to the memories of the old days: "You people talk about the old days as if they were here. But they're dead and gone" (63). He cannot see the value in holding on to the past. During the feast that his mother holds for him, Archilde's responsiveness to the old stories begins to change. He is moved by the earnestness with which the tribal elders tell their stories: "The first story was told by an old woman. Her scarcity of teeth gave an odd sound to some of her words but the story was an old one and nothing was lost" (64). As he begins to listen to the old stories told by the elders, such as "The Thing That Was to Make Life Easy" and "The Story of Flint," and Modeste's story of the Blackfeet and the black-robes, they begin to "speak" to him.

Archilde surprises himself when the old stories begin to move him: "Archilde had not intended to listen, yet he had heard every word. The story had amused him in spite of himself. It left a spark of gay remembrance in his mind" (66). The stories are amusing and memorable; they are provocative. "Archilde heard that story also. He wondered at it. And the more he reflected on it the more wonderful it grew. A story like that, he realized, was full of meaning" (69). Within the oral tradition, stories compel active listening and they grow in meaning as one reflects on them. As Archilde listens, something powerful begins to draw him back into an affinity with his tribe. The Salish stories, sincere and compelling, move him toward a newfound identification with the tribe: "For the first time he had really seen it happen. First the great numbers and the power, then the falling away, the battles and starvation in the snow, the new hopes and the slow facing of disappointment, and then no hope at all, just this living in the past. He had heard the story many times, but he had not listened. It had tired him. Now he saw that it had happened and it left him feeling weak. It destroyed his stiffness toward the old people" (74). The tribal past is at last made "real" to him. He shares the sense of loss and bewilderment of the Salish elders. McNickle describes the effect on Archilde: "Modeste's story about the old days was the first one, and he had heard many, that Archilde had listened to with his mind. It was the first story about his people that he understood. He could not explain why he had listened and understood, but since it had happened he was continually thinking about the old chief" (194).

Modeste's story is not history in the conventional use of the term. It is, however, a narrative that transmits important cultural information; and it contains a power that changes Archilde's view of the Salish people—and himself. Modeste's story embodies the suffering and weakening of the Salish people, but it also acknowledges their ability to adapt; it demonstrates their collective resolve to adjust. Modeste's stories provide the reader with a distinct perspective on the events that altered the lives of the Salish people. The stories are narrated in terms of his experience and memory.

Modeste interrupts his story to tell Archilde, "Perhaps this talk of fighting and men dying means little to you. It is a little thing now, but when it was happening it seemed big" (72). By retelling the stories Modeste succeeds in elevating the importance of their tribal history for themselves and for Archilde. For the values and traditions of the Salish culture to be transmitted to the next generation, the young, like Archilde, must learn to listen to them, identify with them, and someday retell them. If this does not occur, in time the Salish people will lose the ability to narrate their own past, and the cultural identity that is conferred by a historical discourse will diminish. Modeste says, "Our voices, they said, no longer reach Amotkan. Maybe he has gone too far away or maybe our voices have become weak, but when we speak in the old ways we are not heard" (73). In the admission that their voices have grown weak Modeste identifies the central problem for the Salish people. The concept of a diminished voice offers a powerful metaphor for cultural loss. Their tribal past recedes in the face of the constant pressure to assimilate Euro-American culture as their own voices grow weaker. McNickle states: "The American Indian history is a most welcome prospect. The American Indians have had to contend with many disabilities, in my judgment, as their lack of a written history setting forth their achievements, their insights and their value orientations. No people should have to depend on another and possible hostile party to give its account to the world."[10] The old stories are one of the sources for a kind of history. An Indian-centered history would inevitably reflect their accomplishments, their wisdom, and their spiritual values; and as they, in time, selectively assimilate the writing tools of the dominant culture, they can set the record straight by authoring their own histories. Donald Fixico argues for the importance of such histories:

> Historians now have an opportunity to study and learn about the internal nature of Indian communities at the tribal or urban levels. This means using ethnohistory or anthropology to comprehend the cultural development of the community. In considering Indian history in this manner, it is necessary to use introspective analysis of how Indians perceive history with

> regard to tribal language, values, kinship relations, infrastructure, societal norms, tribal beliefs, and worldview. To further this consideration, historians must be willing to acknowledge other means of analyzing history and other sources of facts. (92)

Tribal stories are an essential source for writing accurate tribal histories; such stories contain vital information about beliefs and values that define tribal communities. John Mack Faragher echoes this critical need for the inclusion of diverse voices in the construction of historical narratives of the West: "The story of America's frontiers is no longer told as a simple tale of civilization and savagery, of conquest and colonization, but as the complicated history of the encounters between diverse peoples and cultures" (454).

Archilde's transformation could be regarded as the development of a historical consciousness. A similar development occurs with James Welch's unnamed narrator in *Winter in the Blood.* Paul Eisenstein argues that the narrator's conflict centers on his lack of a cultural history. For Eisenstein a cultural history not only provides identity but also offers a "survival lesson" (3). Upon hearing Yellow Calf's revelation about his own ancestry, the narrator acquires a "sense of the permanence" (3). Eisenstein compares Welch to Hemingway and other modernists whose characters learn "to live in relation to time in a new way" (3). Eisenstein writes, "Welch wants to imply the historical/ancestral cause of the narrator's malaise, that is to say, how this thirty-two-year-old man's inability to connect is, at least in part, determined by the void which characterizes his and other Native American's (and the dominant culture's) historical consciousness" (4). Archilde's resemblance to Welch's narrator is striking. Archilde's "unconnectedness" is a result of the lack of a cultural consciousness. Archilde is seeking a history of his own:

> The dominant culture's writing of history may record events (i.e., land surrendered, treaties signed), it may even extol a handful of minority individuals for their achievements, but its discourse cannot include the recounting of events that threaten the image of itself it must maintain. That image, the product of power relations that construct it, at every step determines what does and does not get told; stories of cruelty committed in its name are either concealed or rewritten for absorption into America's monocultural narrative. Beholden to the self-image that narrative is bent on reproducing, such telling only continues the cruelty. The history produced may protect the interests of its writers, but to do so, those writers must distort or leave out altogether certain occurrences, thus burying (and doing violence to)

> the larger body of communication that conveys the way of life and way of seeing of those they have subjugated. For minority cultures like those of Native Americans to resist absorption, for them to maintain identity, this body of communication—heretofore lacking, heretofore omitted—must be articulated. (Eisenstein 4)

Since the dominant culture's "discourse cannot include the recounting of events that threaten the image of itself it must maintain," Native American cultures, to preserve identity, must create a space in which to articulate their own histories. Eisenstein argues that Welch's narrator, with the assistance of a tribal elder, learns to articulate the "omitted history." Archilde accomplishes something similar. By listening to Modeste's stories, and by examining and rethinking his own memories, Archilde accepts the Salish version of history, not the Euro-American version. Eisenstein claims that once history is communicated, the Blackfeet worldview is restored for Welch's narrator. Similarly, once Archilde feels the "reality" of the past in Modeste's stories, he begins to share the communal past with his people.

Archilde's appreciation for the old stories leads to a renewed relationship with his mother, which in turn allows him to begin to see the Salish people differently. Catharine's retention of her sense of traditional practices impresses Archilde. Her example "started him on a new train of thought regarding not only his mother but all the old people. He had really understood their struggle as it was told that night; he was moved by it" (113). Catharine embodies the spirit of the old stories: "There in his mother's tepee [Archilde] had found unaccountable security" (222). Catharine's identity derives from the past and her connection to it. By simply watching her, Archilde can glimpse the past in her "minute observances" (215). Catharine's physical movements reveal her link with her tribal past: "Archilde could see that for his mother this was a real thing. . . . For these old people it was real, almost real enough to make it seem like a spirit come from the grave. Watching his mother's experienced hands, he could guess how she lived, what she had thought about in her childhood. A great deal had happened since those hands were young, but in making them work in this way, in the way she had been taught, it was a little bit as if the intervening happenings had never been" (215). Traditional practices keep the past alive for the Salish. Catharine's actions eclipse the time that has passed and connect her to traditional Salish culture. "She was pleased with her duties in the way that only an old art or an old way of life, long disused, can please the hand and the heart returning to it" (215). Archilde notes that "her hands had taken her far back into the past that day and he would not drag her forth again" (221). McNickle once lectured about "symbiois," a concept that identifies that relationship of the past to the present. He defines it this way: "Symbiosis—the past functioning in the present. Sometimes that past is hard to discover; it may be fragmentary and distorted, yet inevitably it crops out."[11] For McNickle, the past perpetually resides in the present. Catharine keeps the past alive through her observance of tradition in her practiced, ritualistic physical movements.

McNickle offers no simple resolution for the problem of history in *The Surrounded.* While McNickle contests conventional American histories and posits the possibilities for a Native American alternative to national history, Archilde's journey toward a full traditional Salish identity is never completed. Before her death Catharine makes Archilde take her on a hunting trip. The hunting trip convinces Archilde how much things have changed. "Archilde and his mother had to ride on and on, trying to go backward in time rather than onward in mountain fastness" (116). While his mother values the mountains, for Archilde the trip forces a sharp contrast between the past and the present: "This was how it would have seemed years ago. . . . But it was different. The mountains were empty of life, that was the difference" (116). Although Archilde is beginning to recognize the power of traditional stories, the mountains represent the past to which he and his family cannot ever return. The mountains "were empty of life." In spite of his growing acceptance of his family, Archilde comes to the realization that the mountains (the past) are no longer *his* home.

Archilde also realizes that he cannot help his family in a meaningful way. He is sympathetic with his young nephews, Mike and Narcisse, because of their forced enrollment at the boarding school. Archilde recalls his own experience at the Indian boarding school, and he wants to tell Mike that he need not be afraid. "Tell him it's all lies, what the priests say. It's all lies about the devil. Tell him to look at the birds. They fly around, and they don't know nothing about the devil. Look at them fly!" writes McNickle (192). Archilde desperately wants to communicate his own experience and articulate his own liberation from oppressive Christian beliefs and relieve his nephew's fear, but he is frustrated by what he perceives to be the limitation of words.

Unable to act, unable to communicate, unable to affect the lives of those around him, Archilde appears to offer little hope in resolving the problems facing his family and his people. Rather than resolving Archilde's identity conflict in an idealistic ending, McNickle ends Archilde's journey with a newfound awareness of his Salish culture. Archilde learns two things. First, he achieves an understanding that reconciles him with his Salish elders who stubbornly strive to cling to their traditional values and practices in the face of the pressures to assimilate Euro-American ways. Archilde acquires sympathy for and pride in them. He learns also that he cannot directly influence their lives as he might wish: "He was always forgetting that his way of seeing things was his own. His people could not understand it, but thought he was chasing after damn fool notions. All ideas were damn fool until they were understood and believed; and it was useless to wish them on to anybody else until the other person had come to them in the same way—by understanding and believing. In his present evolution he could admit this lack of insight in his people without getting angry" (247). For the first time in his life, Archilde accepts the Salish people on their own terms. He realizes that he cannot impose his understanding of the world on them. The Salish will accept his views only if and when they recognize value in them. Rather, what the Salish want—and require—is this: "All they asked was to be let alone, and perhaps this time he would not forget it" (247). McNickle adds, "Mike and Narcisse taught him something—it did no good to make a fuss about things; just go ahead and do what you liked, and ask only to be let alone" (248). Archilde's conclusion reflects McNickle's own political position, one that would guide his career under John Collier at the Bureau of Indian Affairs: leave Native American people alone and let them find their own way. In the end, Archilde decides to leave, but he feels the pain that comes with having gotten closer to the Salish people: "Instead of learning to live at peace with their limitations he ought to have kept his distance, then he could have enjoyed going away" (248).

Archilde also learns how a people become a community through shared stories. He realizes that people's lives grow together; they become "entangled." The passing of time is an important aspect of the human condition; time bonds people. People create stories about the past that, when told, connect the teller and his or her listeners with the communal past. The stories contain shared experiences and values and contain the power to unite a people:

> People grew into each other, became intertwined, and life was no mere matter of existence, no mere flash of time. It was time that made the difference. The time that was consumed in moving one's feet along the earth, in learning the smell of coming snow, in enduring hunger and fear and the loss of pride; all that made a difference. And a still greater difference was this entangling of lives. People grew together like creeping vines. The root of beginning was hard to find in the many that had come together and spread their foliage in one mass. (258)

The foliage metaphor in the context of history is effective. The image of "growing together" suggests the organic nature of communal experiences.

Euro-American culture organizes the passing of time differently from the Salish. Through narrative it organizes time in a thematically structured linear progression. The past explains and justifies the present, affirming present values. The Salish, however, tell stories about the past to preserve a sense of communal identity and to express common values. The storytellers order the past through stories in such a way that it makes one, like Archilde, reflect on their meaning.

In the end the stories cannot save Archilde. When he is arrested for a killing that his mother commits, his life appears to end. Imprisonment, or worse, awaits him. He is "surrounded"; he cannot escape. He seems to accept his fate when McNickle writes, "but as for himself—he too belonged to the story of Sniel-emen" (275). The ending is curiously ambiguous. Archilde's passivity is remarkable. He appears to let the women in this novel—Catharine and Elise—determine his future. At novel's end, in spite of his potential, he succumbs to the same fate as his brothers. He is now utterly at the mercy of the U.S. government. "You can't run away nowadays," he tells Elise (287). What might this statement mean? Perhaps Archilde means he (like all Native Americans) cannot escape to the past. That way of being Salish is gone forever. When Agent Parker declares, "You had everything, every chance, and this is the best you could do with it! A man gets pretty tired of you and your kind," he invokes a controlling stereotype (296). Ironically, he does not comprehend the complexity of Archilde's life that ultimately differentiates him from such stereotypes. From a white perspective this seems to be the "same old story," but Archilde's life has been unique. The fact that he, too, fails to escape the grasp of this colonized life, suggests the extent of the control that Euro-America has over the American Indian people. Education, success in the white world, inheritance from a white father, admiration of the white reservation officials and priests—none of this protects him from being falsely accused and arrested for murder.

One cannot ignore the apparent pessimism of the ending. Perhaps McNickle is expressing the hopelessness of the predicament for Native Americans in the twentieth century. Archilde's arrest may symbolize the end of one way of "being Indian." The only Native Americans who are likely to survive and prosper in twentieth-century America, he may be saying, are those who successfully balance the values of a traditional past and the demands of the changing present. Another possibility is that McNickle is more interested in demonstrating the scope of the problem—the disenfranchisement of indigenous cultures—than he is in proposing a solution. However one reads *The Surrounded*, this much can be stated with certainty: the novel does raise the reader's hopes and expectations for Archilde's future before finally dashing them with a conventional tragic conclusion. The reader's ultimate disappointment, however, does not minimize the revelatory insights he or she gains by glimpsing into the complicated and poignant story of Archilde Leon's life.

McNickle once stated, "It may yet be possible, given this emerging awareness, to see Indians in the perspective of their own time-space experience and to write about them within the moral order created by those experiences."[12] This is what *The Surrounded* appears to be doing: compelling the Euro-American reader to see Native American cultures from the perspective of the moral order out of which those cultures operate. If Americans in 1936 regarded Indians and their histories as a subcategory of national history and drew from that certain stereotypes and conclusions about why Native Americans live and behave as they do, then McNickle's characters force them to consider the many factors that converge in this historical moment. McNickle embedded in his novel an articulation of some of those factors as Native Americans experienced and interpreted them: "Theirs is the story to be told and they are the ones to tell it."[13]

The Surrounded reveals critical insights about the problematic nature of the idea of history. For McNickle, like recent historians, writing history involves critically questioning epistemological assumptions. In a discussion about the problems of history, Cronon argues that all histories bear "serious epistemological problems": "Because stories concern the consequences of actions that are potentially valued in quite different ways, whether by agent, narrator, or audience, we can achieve no neutral objectivity in writing them. Historians may strive to be as fair as they can, but as these Plains examples demonstrate, it remains possible to narrate the same evidence in radically different ways" (1370).

In *The Surrounded*, McNickle juxtaposes stories about westward progress, Christian conversion of the Salish, and Archilde's own search for identity. The reader takes away from the novel an appreciation for the many particular narratives that a broad history naturally obscures. He or she is exposed to multiple orderings of the past, and—McNickle would hope—a new appreciation for the complexities of history and, most importantly, the realization that he or she is reading an appeal for the inclusion of Native-centered accounts of the past.

"Then he told a story—nothing was ever done without telling a story" (211). For the Salish, all actions require a story. Each story contextualizes conduct and connects it to the past. Archilde is a casualty of the many conflicting forces present on the reservation; he will not survive, but his story will. Storyteller is the one role all generations must embrace. The Native American means of preserving history requires new generations of storytellers. Throughout his life, McNickle never stopped attempting to articulate and appeal for an understanding of Native American cultures: "They came out of an Indian past, not a white man's past, and the future is something they will make out of what they had to begin with" ("American Indians That Never Were" 24–29). Long after the publication of *The Surrounded*, he was still linking the future of Native American cultures to a valuation of the past, and demanding that Euro-America acknowledge and include their stories of the past, even as such stories complicate and contradict their own cherished histories.

NOTES

1. I have often wondered whether McNickle was inspired to write about his experience as an American Indian in Montana by the success of Oliver LaFarge's *Laughing Boy*, which won the Pulitzer Prize for fiction in 1930, much as the regional African American writer Charles Chesnutt was inspired to write about his experiences in the South when he observed the success of white writers capitalizing on southern black characters in their regional fiction. Richard Brodhead identifies Chesnutt's writing strategy: "Chesnutt here seizes the idea that if the forms of literary expression must be found in a dominant culture, they can still be used in the interest of subordinated peoples. He grasps that if writing must be directed to Northern white audiences, it can nevertheless aim to further black causes with those audiences—can make itself a means to enter the minds and remodel the mental habits of white readers as they read" (*Cultures of Letters* 195).
2. McNickle to William Gates, 14 May 1934, General Correspondence, McNickle Papers, Newberry Library, Chicago.
3. Even though Harcourt Brace and Co. rejected an early manuscript of what would eventually become *The Surrounded*, an editor at Harcourt recognized the potential of McNickle to become a new voice for Native American writing. See Harcourt, Brace & Co. to McNickle, 6 April 1929, General Correspondence, McNickle Papers, Newberry Library, Chicago.
4. McNickle to Richard Pope, 15 March 1975, General Correspondence, McNickle Papers, Newberry Library, Chicago.
5. Susan K. Bernardin raises important questions concerning assumptions about the authority of American Indian authorship. She asks, "What kinds of discourse 'count' as culturally authoritative and persuasive and according to whose cultural authority?" ("Mixed Messages" 487). Bernardin cites *Cogewea* as "a radical departure from the conventional reliance on autobiographical and ethnographic narrative forms to present 'Indian' experience to mainstream audiences" (488). Bernardin

also identifies the "liminality of mixed blood identity" as the central theme of twentieth-century Native American literature. McNickle's father was Irish while his mother was Metis. He possessed probably one-quarter or less degree of Native American blood; yet because of his childhood he identified with his Native American heritage. Bernardin considers Mourning Dove a "literary intermediary" because of her bicultural childhood. Similarly, McNickle is regarded by many as a cultural broker, a writer who has experienced both Indian and white worlds throughout his life. His ability to write well made him uniquely qualified to mediate between these two cultural identities. Bernardin questions "the ultimate inability of Euro-American literary forms to 'bear the burden' of the experiences of marginalized peoples" (Mixed Messages" 504). McNickle believed quite earnestly that they could.

6. McNickle's grandfather, Isidore Parenteau (1849–1925), descended from the Metis settlers from the Red River Settlements in what is now Winnipeg, Manitoba, Canada. McNickle was adopted into the Flathead tribe on May 5, 1905, at the age of one. For a biography of McNickle see Dorothy Parker's *Singing an Indian Song: A Biography of D'Arcy McNickle* (Lincoln: University of Nebraska Press, 1992).
7. Critics question the appropriateness of the application of postcolonial theory to the reading of American Indian–authored texts. For example, Arnold Krupat agrees with Ashcroft et al. that Native American literatures "emerged in their present form out of the experience of colonization and asserted themselves by foregrounding the tension with the imperial power, and by emphasizing their differences from the assumptions of the imperial centre" (Ashcroft et al. *The Empire Writes Back* 2); however, Krupat argues that "contemporary Native American literatures cannot quite be classed among the postcolonial literatures of the world for the simple reason that there is not yet a 'post-' to the colonial status of Native Americans. Call it domestic imperialism or internal colonialism; in either case, a considerable number of Native people exist in conditions of politically sustained subalternity" (30). In contrast Louis Owens argues that "for American Indians, the problem of identity comprehends centuries of colonial and postcolonial displacement, often brutally enforced peripherality, cultural denigration—including especially a harsh privileging of English over tribal languages—and systematic oppression by the monocentric 'westering' impulse in America" (4). This essay does not seek to resolve the postcolonial theory debate; however, inasmuch as such critics agree on the experience of colonization—even if full independence has not been achieved by all Native Americans—it is an especially useful critical framework in which to understand the dynamics of literary production out of which American Indian writers like McNickle rose to authorship.
8. Birgit Hans contextualizes McNickle's concern for history in "Rethinking History: A Context for the Surrounded" in *The Legacy of D'Arcy McNickle: Writer, Historian, Activist*, edited by John Lloyd Purdy (Tulsa: University of Oklahoma Press, 1996). Hans notes McNickle's initial faith in conventional Euro-American history, as evi-

denced by early drafts of *The Surrounded*, and then identifies specific texts to which the author begins responding with a new Indian history. Among those texts are Theodore Roosevelt's *The Winning of the West* (1886), John Truslow Adams's *The Epic of America* (1931), Leo Huberman's *We, The People* (1932), and Ellsworth Huntington's *The Character of Races* (1925).

9. Contrasting plots of novels produced by mixed-blood writers (including McNickle) and canonical American white writers, William Bevis observes that "American whites keep leaving home: *Moby Dick, Portrait of a Lady, Huckleberry Finn, Sister Carrie, The Great Gatsby*—a considerable number of American 'classics' tell of leaving home to find one's fate farther and farther away" (93). Native American writers, on the other hand, "are not about going out, diverging, expanding, but about zooming in, converging, contracting" (94).
10. McNickle to Matt P. Lowman, II, February 2, 1971, General Correspondence, McNickle Papers, Newberry Library, Chicago.
11. "Memorandum for the Press." Speech to the Missouri Archeological Society, Kansas City, 1940, McNickle Papers, Newberry Library, Chicago.
12. Speech at the Convocation of American Indian Scholars. Princeton University, March 1970.
13. Speech to the American Indian Institute, Bozeman, Montana, ca. 1972.

WORKS CITED

Ashcroft, Bill, Gareth Griffiths, and Helen Tiffin, eds. *The Post-Colonial Studies Reader*. London: Routledge, 1995.

———. *The Empire Writes Back: Theory and Practice in Post-Colonial Literatures.* New York: Routledge, 1989.

Bernardin, Susan K. "Mixed Messages: Authority and Authorship in Mourning Dove's *Cogewea, The Half-Blood: A Depiction of the Great Montana Cattle Range*." *American Literature* 67, 3 (September 1995): 487–509.

Bevis, William W. *Ten Tough Trips: Montana Writers and the West.* Seattle: University of Washington Press, 1990.

Brodhead, Richard. *Cultures of Letters: Scenes of Reading and Writing in Nineteenth-Century America*. Chicago: University of Chicago Press, 1993.

Calloway, Colin G. *First Peoples: A Documentary Survey of American Indian History*. Boston and New York: Bedford/St. Martin's, 1999.

Cronon, William. "A Place for Stories: Nature, History, and Narrative." *The Journal of American History* (March 1992): 1347–76.

Eisenstein, Paul. "Finding Lost Generations: Recovering Omitted History in *Winter in the Blood*." *Melus* 19 (Fall 1994): 3–18.

Faragher, John Mack. "The Social Fabric of the American West." *The Historian* 66, 3 (Fall 2004): 442.

Fixico, Donald. "Ethics and Responsibilities in Writing American Indian History." *Na-*

tives and Academics: Researching and Writing About American Indians. Ed. Devon A. Mihesuah. Lincoln: University of Nebraska Press, 1998.

Krupat, Arnold. *The Turn to the Native: Studies in Criticism and Culture.* Lincoln: University of Nebraska Press, 1996.

McNickle, D'Arcy. "American Indians Who Never Were." *Indian Historian* 3 (1970): 4–7.

———. "American Indians That Never Were." *New University Thought* (Spring 1971): 24–29.

———. "Interpreting Native America." *The Nation* 219 (December 7, 1974): 599–600.

———. "The Sociocultural Setting of Indian Life." *American Journal of Psychiatry* (August 1968): 115–19.

———. *The Surrounded.* 1936. Reprint, Albuquerque: University of New Mexico Press, 1990.

Owens, Louis. *Other Destinies: Understanding the American Indian Novel.* Tulsa: University of Oklahoma Press, 1993.

Worster, Donald. *Under Western Skies: Nature and History in the American West.* New York: Oxford University Press, 1992.

CHAPTER NINE

A Haunted Nation: Cultural Narratives and the Persistence of the Indigenous Subject in James Welch's *The Heartsong of Charging Elk*

ANDREA OPITZ

The primitive has somehow escaped from control.
—Stuart Hall, "The Local and the Global"

Nothing that has ever happened should be regarded as lost for history.
—Walter Benjamin, "Theses on the Philosophy of History"

THE "EMPTY" SITE OF PERFORMANCE

In 1889 Marseille, France, one of the Oglala Lakota performing in Buffalo Bill's Wild West awakens in the hospital after falling from his horse, left behind by the show that has traveled on to Italy. Abandoned in a foreign country where no one speaks his language, James Welch's protagonist in *The Heartsong of Charging Elk* (2001) has exited the "safe" containment of Buffalo Bill's history lesson—in which he was cast as "first citizen"—and so has quite literally exited the narrative space of American national history and culture; the "primitive," as Stuart Hall so poignantly puts it, "has escaped control" ("The Local" 187). Charging Elk escapes from the hospital and wanders around Marseille for several days. He finally comes to a site that he recognizes as the place where the Wild West show had performed. He crosses the roundabout and walks up a wide street, eager to reach the field where the show had been erected. However, he finds that "there was nothing there. Not one tent, not one hawker's stand, not even a fire pit where the Indian village had stood. He walked over to the large trampled circle of earth where the portable arena had been set up. The ground had been raked smooth. There was not a hoofprint on it, not one sign that the Indians, the cowboys, the soldiers, the vaqueros, the Deadwood stage, the buffaloes and horses had acted out their various dramas on this circle of earth" (48). Charging Elk's "reading" of the former performance site reveals no trace, seemingly, of the show ever having been in Marseille. In vain, he looks for any evidence of the fire pits or the enactment of the drama of western conquest. However, he discovers that the enactment of dreams and fantasies does not leave any retrievable trace, and while the show was a real experience for him and the other performers who had cooked on those fire pits, the performance is only representative of something fabricated. Even though at first glance "there was nothing there" Charging Elk remembers what had been there and so reveals the presence of an absence. Competing against the powerful forces of a cultural narrative that enacts what will soon become the dominant story of the West (and by extension the nation), he cannot recover the material and social histories and experiences that have been erased. Yet, he is able to witness and expose how every attempt has been made to "rake[] smooth" any trace left by these histories—traces that might disrupt the official narrative of the American nation and its conquest of the West. In this novel, what is produced by the Wild West show as the "vanishing Indian" emerges as a "ghost" in an alternative space—outside the "historical" narrative and thus outside the nation space—and reveals that "other" material and social histories indeed leave traces that are in excess of U.S. cultural and national narratives.

Extending the revisionist and decolonizing work he began with *Fools Crow* (1986) and continued with *Killing Custer* (1994), Welch examines in his last novel the relation between U.S. government policies of removal, extinction, and assimilation, and the ways in which cultural and national narratives—as produced, for example, by Buffalo Bill's traveling Wild West—work to "naturalize" how indigenous peoples imagine themselves in relation to these narratives. Welch's work critically intervenes in the kinds of inquiry American Indian literature, as well as Montana literature, can pose. *Heartsong*, which is based on a true story and set primarily in late-nineteenth-century France in the context of Buffalo Bill's Wild West touring Europe, not only imagines a site of competing histories but also *re*imagines the relation of the indigenous subject to the American nation and its national narratives. In other words, Welch's project is as much concerned with offering an alternative narrative as it is with theorizing what it means to be an American Indian and what it means to be an American in a national context that is highly racialized. Framing Charging Elk's development and his subsequent—and highly complicated—merging into the French social order with his remembering of pre-reservation life as well as his exit from Buffalo Bill's "history lesson," the novel traces and exposes the competing and often paradoxical narratives within which Charging Elk is caught. Further, by examining the (im)possibilities of Native American subjectivity within a national context, the novel opens up questions of citizenship, the erased traces of material histories, and the relation of racial violence to systems of representation. In order to flesh out this argument, I consider how, in this novel, bildungsroman conventions produce a contradictory subject, before I conclude with a discussion of the continued emergence of the indigenous ghost despite bureaucratic, political, and legal attempts to erase it.

The literal shift from the western United States to Marseille, France, as the primary setting enables Welch to move his examination of Native American subjectivity beyond an exclusively Native or western American literary and cultural context. Shifting this story from the United States to Europe by way of the traveling narrative of national conquest (Buffalo Bill's Wild West)—meant to test and legitimize the coherence of America's national narrative in the eyes of the world, and its beginning hegemony internationally—the novel implicates Europe as a necessary part of this performance. However, it also casts Europe as the site that reveals the crisis and anxiety with which the nation approaches the integration of its Others into the national narrative in order for the ideology—performed and presented by Buffalo Bill's Wild West—to work. Emerging at this site, cast as "permanently external to the nation yet absolutely immanent to the national integrity" (Pease 13), the Native materializes as that which colonial narratives of western expansion have tried to foreclose. What emerges in this site of radical displacement is a space in excess of the nation and yet painfully tied to it, a space in which the American Indian articulates the uncanny relocation of self that is in conflict with the American nation.

A "CROSS-RACE AND CROSS-NATIONAL" PROJECT

Welch's analysis of the ways in which American Indians are constructed as a necessary, and yet excluded, part of the U.S. nation and its historical and cultural narratives offers insightful parallels between *Heartsong* and the model of cultural critique that Lisa Lowe develops in her study of Asian American cultural politics, *Immigrant Acts*. For my reading of *Heartsong*, three of Lowe's ideas are particularly compelling: examining the citizen-subject as formed by cultural narratives, reconceptualizing "minority" discourse as a site of cultural critique, and reading "minority" communities in alternative relations to national systems of representation. The critical model Lowe develops by analyzing Asian American texts in relation to U.S. dominant cultural productions is suggestive because of her reading of Asian American culture as a site in which alternative identities and practices emerge, a reading, as she herself suggests, that could also be applied to African American, Native American, or Mexican immigrant cultures. Lowe's project proposes a way of reading cultural productions and historical narratives as spaces that have to be interrogated and theorized continuously, because "it is through culture, rather than government, that alternative forms of subjectivity, collectivity, and public life are imagined" (22). A cultural critique such as this considers different, particular histories of indigenous, immigrant, migrant, and diasporic experiences in the United States as a way to reimagine the relations among various groups and to the "dominant" culture so that the national cultural terrain can be questioned and reshaped.

Lowe argues that Asian American and Asian immigrant cultures challenge the idea that the "minority" position is the "only form of inclusion within the universal postulates of the nation" (29). Lowe is primarily concerned with the ways in which U.S. culture is employed to assimilate immigrants into the nation through narratives of inclusion and equal access to representation within the political sphere. She illustrates how the immigrant en route to American citizenship passes through a terrain of culture: "a terrain introduced by the Statue of Liberty, discovered by the immigrant, dreamed in a common language, and defended in battle by the self-made man" (2). This immigrant subject is thus "immersed in the repertoire of American memories, events, and narratives and comes to articulate itself in the domain of language, social hierarchy, law, and ultimately, political representation" (2). The state offers the promise of freedom and an end to material inequality to transform the immigrant from alien into citizen, all the while working to disavow histories of racialized exclusion and labor exploitation (10). Here the state engages cultural narratives to create a national culture with which the immigrant can identify by believing in the nation and its promise. At the same time, this abstracting identification results in the immigrant, now subject-citizen, being split off from the material and social particularities of diverse immigrant experience and life in the United States. Lowe argues that the "promise" is never kept, and Asian Americans, like other racialized groups, do not find equal representation, but instead constitute a body of continuing conflict in relation to the "dominant" U.S. culture.

In these contradictions Lowe sees the potential for radical cultural—and consequently, national—critique. For, within contemporary Asian American cultures, the memories of different immigrant experiences—such as the very different memories of war and displacement by Japanese Americans, Korean Americans, and Vietnamese Americans—constantly contest the question of what America is and how Asian immigrants imagine themselves as part of America. Lowe makes clear, however, that she is not content to consider continuing material inequality of racially subordinated groups as a failure in assimilation. Neither is she content with the marginal spaces to which U.S. laws and institutions continue to relegate Asian immigrants (the "model minority" box is no exception). In other words, Asian American culture is neither merely a "minority" nor a multicultural topic for occasional study, but instead a site that imagines alternative narratives and histories and allows for the emergence of new forms of subjectivity. Recovering sites of contestation for a cultural critique that intends to destabilize existing structures of power and national narratives must work against homogenizing classifications of Asian Americans, just as it needs to be imagined as a "cross-race and cross-national" project.

TERRAIN OF NATIONAL CULTURE AND "FIRST CITIZEN"

Whereas Lowe focuses her argument on Asian American and Asian immigrant formations, I consider how the "national terrain of culture" applies to American Indians as well. I argue that, unlike immigrants, American Indians do not "move through" the national terrain of culture as much as they are constitutive of it: cast as "first citizen" in its originary narrative but constructed as both "savage" and "past" according to a logic of progress. Helen Carr observes that creating indigenous peoples as "primitive" absolved the nation of some of its guilt for destroying them not only because they were "past" but also because they were clearly not going to progress (unless, of course, they assimilated) (20). Such a temporal construction of American Indians, being "already in the past," is thus a necessary requirement for the nation to imagine a future free from the burden of genocide. This construction of the nation, Paul Gilroy argues, "naturalizes" the mechanism by which "racially different groups no longer share[] the same present" (57). So, the construction of linear temporality that accompanies the national narrative enables the naturalization of this temporality and of the "Indian's" relationship to it. As Shari Huhndorf points out in her careful analysis of the 1876 Philadelphia Centennial Exposition and the 1893 World's Columbian Exposition, the Native population had to be narrated as inferior Other to enable the superiority of white civilization over "(Native) savagery," a narrative meant to "deflect difficult ethical questions about centuries of slaughter of Native peoples and usurpation of their resources" (30). Turning "naturalness" and inevitability into a national narrative, the modernist nation thereby progresses with a sense of stability and cohesion meant to hide the internal contradictions between this rapidly developing national ideology and the material reality—between cultural narratives and state policies working to secure Indian removal to and containment within reservations.

Huhndorf has further argued that the figure of the "Indian as first citizen" aligns American Indians into the "dominant" Euro-American narrative of American history so as to provide white Americans with a sense of "authentic" national culture (22). Even though American Indians are considered a figure of difference they are at the same time moved into and absorbed by the national mythology that can then unfold without having to account for that difference. Equipped with a narrative that obliterates not only the violence of genocide and systemic oppression, but also Native Americans' *difference* from Euro-Americans, the American nation thus imagines itself against an interior Other, "fixed" in the past as the first citizen, and repeatedly has to perform this construction as part of its imaginative project. Clearly, what has to be concealed, however—when American Indians are imagined as constituting part of the (white) American national narrative—is that Natives first had to be wiped out, or at least brought to the brink of "vanishing," for this narrative to work. Buffalo Bill's Wild West, for example, was one popular cultural production that helped to create "the Indian" and thus literally removed American Indians into the American and European imagination as "first citizens" of the nation, securely conquered within and tied to this nation's creation myth. By thus displacing the racialized Other as part of the nation's past, the Wild West show plays its part in the drama in which the modernist narrative of the nation relies on cultural practices and productions to imagine the "Indian" as the country's "first citizen," whose perceived primitivism allows the Nation's "civilization" to emerge as a chronological development.

Touring both the United States and Europe, Buffalo Bill Cody's version of the history of the American West was promoted as a "clean, dramatic, and compelling narrative [that] made the conquest of savages central" (White 11). In doing so, Richard White argues, Cody inverted the history of the West by casting the Indians as aggressors, constantly attacking white settlers. Thus Buffalo Bill's Wild West offered a companion version of western history to the one Frederick Jackson Turner laid out in his "frontier thesis" in 1893, in which the Indians "were not so much absent as peripheral; they were not essential to the meaning of his narrative" (White 27). Both narratives proposed to be histories and both stand as founding examples of narratives that link the history of the West with American national identity.[1]

Welch places his critical intervention within the context of the work the Buffalo Bill show did historically—as a cultural production that enabled American national narratives continuously to cast the Indian as an essential (but only original) part—to highlight the anything but natural relationship between cultural narratives and government policies and politics. By examining the paradoxical relationship of American Indians to the cultural terrain, Welch's historical novel reveals how this national narrative and its racializing mechanism work to produce the nation's first narrative of difference. Even though this narrative of difference has served as a model for racialization in the United States, it is often ignored in race discourses. In an argument similar to Lowe's, Welch's novel suggests that government policies of removal and assimilation relied on cultural narratives and practices, such as Buffalo Bill's Wild West, to repeatedly perform the Native's "vanishing act" by presenting the Indian as a howling, aggressive primitive chasing buffalo through the arena within the context of a nostalgic retelling of American history. One of the characters in the novel recalls that in Buffalo Bill's narrative the Natives are "disappearing—like the bison" (137). In fact, Buffalo Bill tells the audience that "their culture is dying and soon they will be gone too," as if there is no reasonable explanation for this disappearing act. Also according to this version, American Indians move "safely" into the narrative of the nation's past so that they emerge as conquered artifacts thoroughly disconnected from their own particular histories.

Welch presents the French audiences as so enraptured by the spectacle that presents itself on posters and programs as a "full and complete history" enacting "vivid and realistic scenes from the Pioneer History of America" that they are unable to distinguish performance from real life. After the shows were over, Charging Elk remembers, audience members would enter "family lodges, as though the mother fixing dinner or the sleeping child in its cradleboard were part of the entertainment" (51). Buffalo Bill meant to show the West as it was, not merely as entertainment, and yet the way history is presented and perceived by the audiences merges entertainment with the after-show activities of the performers so that even their everyday activities become nothing more than products of a culture "long gone," displaced into the past. American Indian histories and their role in national narratives and cultural productions are perceived and constructed, then, as a natural part of the past, not as something continuously repeated. However, Charging Elk's radical displacement from this cultural production reveals that this narrative has to be repeated in order to suggest stability and narrative inevitability. Even though he was initially part of the enactment, by being left behind Charging Elk ends up *not* moving into the Euro-American imagination. Moreover, he is able to witness, remember, and articulate the wiped-out presence—the forgotten socialities—of his people, exemplified in that moment when he reads the "empty" performance site.

"THE PRIMITIVE HAS ESCAPED CONTROL"

Charging Elk's exit from the show throws into relief questions of cultural and national subjectivity and exposes the different discourses complicit in the displacement and racialization of the "Indian." At the beginning of the novel, Charging Elk is already no longer part of the show, which has moved onto Italy and left him stranded in the hospital in Marseille. What we know of the show will be revealed through flashbacks as part of Charging Elk's remembering. During the early parts of the novel in particular, his remembering of the show and his memories of his home in the Dakotas provide an interrelated mosaic against which he is trying desperately to make sense of his environment and himself in it. The novel's prologue—set in 1877, a year after the Battle of the Little Bighorn—stages the removal of the Lakota people onto the Pine Ridge Reservation and places the subsequent story in critical and continuous relation to colonial violence and radical displacement. In addition, Charging Elk is haunted by memories of "back home"—stories of living at the Stronghold with friends who refused to join their families, who by then had already been relocated onto the Pine Ridge Reservation. These young men insist on living the life they knew even if they know this life has become unlivable. They have to search for food and shelter, increasingly scarce, especially during the winter months, and yet they still nurture their contempt for those who had gone to live on the reservation "adapt[ing] to this new life of strangers" (130). These descriptions of Plains life are not meant to cater to romanticized ideas of the Old West. Rather, evoking Indian removal as the novel's frame, as well as disrupting Charging Elk's evolving story in Marseille with these recurring memories, allows Welch to locate his protagonist's conceptual understanding—his ways of knowing—at the moment at which the tribal world of pre-reservation life begins to be radically transformed by removal and assimilation policies.

Further, similar to *Fools Crow*, Welch establishes a distinctly non-Euro-American perspective through language. Describing a historical event otherwise known as the Battle of the Little Bighorn, the prologue's opening sentence reads, "It was early in the Moon of the Shedding Ponies, less than a year after the fight with the longknives on the Greasy Grass, and the people looked down in the valley and they saw the white man's fort and several of the women wept" (1). From the perspective of the Lakota people, who fought in that battle against

Custer's army, the event stands in direct relation to their impending relocation on the Pine Ridge. The scene—shifting from a type of military meeting between the soldiers and the tribal leaders to the perspective of an eleven-year-old boy who witnesses the gathering and the continued movement of this family toward the fort—operates like a threshold, a moving from one way of life to another state of being, a literal transformation and transplantation. This framing clearly invites an allegorical reading of Charging Elk's experiences in Marseille paralleling those he would have lived through had he moved with his family onto the reservation. However, I suggest that the prologue, in particular, functions more as a haunting reminder of the silenced and "naturalized" violence that informs the history of the West and of the nation. And so I argue that rather than offering merely an allegory, the novel theorizes Charging Elk's remembering as the racialized Other's remembering of the past, as an articulation of the present that threatens to reintroduce into the narrative of the nation, the history of racial violence, as well as the forgotten socialities of his people: what was perceived as "dead past" emerges as part of the present and subsequently as contributing to "history."

Progressing from the moment Charging Elk awakens in the hospital to his escape, his capture, and his eventual "adoption" by a French family, the novel sets up the particular perspective of an Indian left behind in a foreign place. The particularity of this setting allows for two very different and contradictory story lines to clash: cultural narratives that work to naturalize a history that contains American Indian experience as a means to exclude it come face to face with the contradictory subject that emerges at the moment it is meant to disappear. In fact, Charging Elk emerges as a contradictory subject at the site where the indigenous subject, in excess of the national narrative, encounters the "Indian" who can only "live" in the U.S. national narrative as the artifact that marks the nation's emergence in the past.

After escaping from the hospital (he fears he has been left to die there so that neither he nor his spirit will find the way back home), Charging Elk spends five days walking through the city. The days before he gets captured map his radical displacement onto the streets of Marseille, which he tries to navigate in the search for food and shelter from discriminating glances. No longer part of the Wild West show spectacle, something to be marveled at, he feels that while he "had entered the city in triumph and the people had welcomed him, [now] they looked at him with suspicion, even with hostility, just as the Americans did" (52). Aware of his racial difference and "visibility" to such a degree that he almost loses any sense of himself, he is overwhelmed by the knowledge that this "visibility" differs from the one he performed as a "wild Indian" in Buffalo Bill's show. Looking at his dark hands, he realizes that he is "not of these people" (9). Desperately trying to "remember[] something about himself," he recognizes the shift in his status: from performing "Indian"—exotic and awe aspiring, someone who causes excitement—to dark Other, exposed (9).

While he was still part of the show, he was part of the narrative and did not recognize or experience his difference in the same way. In fact, he later mentions having been proud of being in the show; further, being "eager to put on a show" for the French creates in Charging Elk a sense of pride in being Lakota (147). He also remembers the pride he felt at being called a "wild" Indian—the reason he was chosen to join the show (130). Yet, although the show provided a place where he could show off what he was good at, make some money, and travel and be with friends, he knew all the while that "it was all fake" (52). He describes the enactment of Custer's Last Fight as "a big show" and remembers how the "young Indians enjoyed the spectacle of themselves reflected in the astonished eyes of the French people" (22). He himself admits that he "knew he was quite a sight" and "couldn't help feeling a great pride that he was part of such a spectacle" (49). He had a place that he recognized, even identified with, even if he was merely performing Buffalo Bill's version of "Indianness." Yet, it is important to recognize that Charging Elk's performance is meant to signify more than what is produced on the stage as entertainment; it illustrates the performativity of "Indianness" that reproduces the racialized subject's relation to the nation. This identification only works within the realm of the cultural production as long as he performs his role in a narrative that *repeatedly* creates him primarily in relation to the dominant imaginary. Once he is thrown out of this narrative, he wakes up in the hospital completely disoriented, not sure whether he is dead or alive. There is then a clear disjunction, of which he becomes painfully aware, between his experience as a performer and that as a "vagabond." Walking the city highlights the way in which the cultural narrative he performed and which performed him, was a safe place not just for the people watching but also for himself.

(THE IMPOSSIBILITY OF) MERGING WITH THE SOCIAL ORDER

Not only because the novel examines the paradoxical construction of the American Indian subject's relationship to the American national and cultural imaginary, but also because it proposes an alternative site for its emergence, it is of great significance that Charging Elk's strange story reads like a classic

European bildungsroman. The first chapter's opening sentence ("Charging Elk opened his eyes and saw nothing but darkness") suggests an awakening into his disorientation that sets the stage on which he has to begin making sense of his immediate and social environments, as well as his racialized difference. The ensuing plot more or less traces the maturing process—development—of this young protagonist, who by the end of the novel marries and emerges in the French social order as subject and citizen.

The ideological function of the story of development echoes the idealized relationship of the subject to the national collective by narrating, as Lowe suggests, the "development of the individual from youthful innocence to civilized maturity, the telos of which is the reconciliation of the individual with the social order" (98). Further, Lowe suggests in a move that critically links the narrative of formation with the national project of abstracting (or universalizing) the individual into an ideal form of citizen, the maturing individual learns to relinquish his or her particularity and difference. Read in this context, Welch's novel illuminates the strangeness of the racialized individual's "merging" into the social order.

Bildungsroman conventions allow Welch to map his protagonist's maturing process and his complicated "merging" into the French (!) social order as subject and citizen. On the one hand, what is supposed to happen to him as a young man, even a young American Indian, developing into a mature, "civilized" subject, indeed happens. After killing Breteuil, whom he classifies as "evil," he spends ten years in prison but is eventually pardoned by the French government that recognizes the legal error it committed trying him as an American, instead of a Lakota, citizen. Because his "tribe is his own separate nation," the treaties between France and the United States do not apply to him (361). Declassified as a political prisoner, he is released. Upon his release he becomes a French citizen at the same time as his citizenship of the Lakota nation is recognized by the French government. On the other hand, through this development, as the subject moves from racial "innocence" into "civilized maturity" or from being a displaced "Indian" to being a French subject, the American Indian emerges as a subject in excess of the U.S. nation, despite his role as "first citizen" within that nation's narrative. Even though he is part of it, he is a figure continuously displaced from the U.S. national terrain. His temporary identification with the "idealized subjectivity" of "first citizen" as well as his initial alienating experiences as he walks through Marseille, sits in prison, and finds a home with the Soulas family, all express a rather uncanny "resolution."

Challenging the demand on Charging Elk to merge with a dominant social order, the novel explores a space in which alienation and the other effects of displacement inform the rearticulation of identity. At the beginning of the novel he only has access to this social order in two "forms": as the object and as the inferior Other constructed and racialized by cultural productions and national narratives. The formation process mapped out in *Heartsong* critiques the abstracting mechanisms by which narratives that demand resolution—the "first citizen" resolved into the national narrative, for example, or the indigenous subject "assimilated" into white America—erase an individual's particularity. Instead, the novel argues for an alternative conceptualization of the subject's relation to the nation's cultural narrative and skews, to borrow from Lowe, "the relationship of the citizen-subject to the nation by challenging the constructions of both ['Indian'] and 'American'" (100–101).

Quite contrary to the narrative of the "vanishing Indian," *Heartsong* conceptualizes cultural identity as *becoming*—an identity that is performed and conceived in relation to the fragmented memories and histories of his own culture, the representations of him as "exotic" and little more than a feathered creature, and legal and political regulations. In short, Charging Elk forms a cultural identity within social, legal, political, and representational relations—an identity that contradicts the universalizing narrative of the "idealized" and unified subject. When Charging Elk encounters the new generations of performers of the Wild West show fourteen years after he was part of that group himself, one of the Lakota he talks to observes, "I can see you are still one of us, yet you are different" (431). While the noted difference might point toward Charging Elk's European dress and possibly his different manners, it also suggests that these new performers, who are all from the reservation, are also different from him, the former "wild" Indian.[2] Despite their differences they share collective cultural knowledge that should, however, not be described as homogeneous. Since they remember and practice their culture in relation to displacement and government policies, and since the present performers experience this cultural terrain and the displacement quite differently from Charging Elk, their common knowledge and memories express a more diverse space than constructed artifacts might suggest.

CONCEPTUAL DISPLACEMENTS

The story of development is clearly the genre best suited to align the reader with the point of view of the protagonist, which is crucial for a story in which that point of view is not necessarily "different" in terms of the position that is occupied, but "different" in what the perspective looks at. In other words, what is alienated at the beginning of the novel is not Charging Elk's point of view itself but the world he sees. In her discussion of the canonical function of the bildungsroman, Lowe says that the "novel of formation has a special status among the works selected for a canon, for it elicits the reader's identification with the bildung narrative" (98). Drawing on this practice, Welch aligns the reader with the point of view of the protagonist so as to achieve an almost exaggerated sense of alienation and displacement when the perspective shifts away from Charging Elk and is instead directed *at* him. So, for example, during the time he is in the prison cell, the narrative distances itself from his consciousness so that for the first time, the reader is not privy to his thoughts and impressions, but to the images, fears, preconceptions, and narratives within which the people around him are caught. The identification that was established with his perspective is radically displaced and the reader experiences a sense of alienation from those rather odd comments people make about Charging Elk, and the way he appears to them. In the eyes of the newspaper reporter St-Cyr, who greedily picks up the story of this *Peau-Rouge*, he is "a figure on a bed," an object, about which a story can be written, and pity evoked. Even though St-Cyr successfully recognizes Charging Elk as a human being, by looking into the man's face and thinking his name, Charging Elk nonetheless figures as little more than as one of "God's simplest creatures" in desperate need of the reporter's help, without which he surely would die (94–96). Trained in reading situations for their entertainment value, St-Cyr can perhaps not be expected to relate to Charging Elk in any other way but to categorize him according to the needs of a future news story. Yet, the process by which this assignment is made complicates the reader's relationship to this scene. In a way, we still share Charging Elk's perspective, so what is "alienated" here is not the "simple creature" on the bed but St-Cyr's reading of it. Here, Welch challenges readers to examine stereotypes of American Indians and to explore their relation to an American Indian's experience of alienation, demanding the reader's involvement in the process of reimagining cultural narratives.

Narratives are exposed here as mechanisms of containment and regulation—after all, once the "Indian" is let loose and out of control, how else to realign him in "proper" relation to the dominant story about him? Whereas René Soulas is only too happy to take in Charging Elk while the authorities figure out what to do with him, his wife's reaction and her perception of the young Lakota show the difficulty of explaining his difference. Reflecting on the Wild West show and how its spectacle made her think that the Indians seemed part beast, Madeleine is afraid to bring home a savage. Consequently, when finally looking at the man's dark skin, she cannot help but think that "he was far from being a normal man" (116). The construction of the racial Other dominates her perception and obliterates whatever humanity lies underneath. While the performing Indian can be admired as the "first citizen" (so pronounced by Buffalo Bill at the beginning of the show), his presence outside the context of such "safe" constructions highlights the ambivalence of his situation, as well as everyone's need to resort to a narrative model that explains his difference to them.

Welch also critically links this preoccupation with containing narratives to larger issues of government policies concerning Indian education and assimilation policies. While he is still "on the loose" in the city, Charging Elk recalls an early childhood experience at the boarding school where he went for a year. The white teacher models a curious reading lesson that bears an uncanny resemblance to the kind of traditional identificatory practice modeled by a bildungsroman narrative. During this lesson, the teacher pointed to him as she explained the word *Indian*:

> He had sat in one of the rows of long tables watching the freckle-faced white woman write her words in white chalk on the black board: Boy. Girl. Cat. Dog. Fish. She showed them colored pictures of these creatures. The humans were pink, the cat yellow, and the dog black-and-white. The fish were orange and fat, unlike any he had ever seen. . . .
>
> He remembered the word "Indian." She had pointed directly at him, then at the board, and said "Indian." She made all the children say "Indian." Then she showed them a picture of a man they could not recognize. He had sharp toes, big thighs, and narrow shoulders; he wore a crown of blue and green and yellow feathers and an animal skin with dark spots. His eyes were large and round; his lips tiny and pursed. The white woman said "Indian." (56)

The shocking conceptual gap that Charging Elk experiences between the feathered "creature" and himself also becomes an alienating experience for the reader. The reader is confronted not only with the paralyzing mechanism of stereotyping that is exposed here, but also with the continued construction of the "fixed" artifact as Other.[3] The reader empathizes with Charging Elk and at the same time has to recognize the (il)logic on which the construction of him as a fixed sign of "exotic" otherness relies. The teacher's move to identify him with the sign of a feathered creature also works to override any other sense he may still have of himself.

The production of the "Indian" and "savage" as artifact is made visible and located within the colonizing system, rather than experienced as "natural" or "inherent" to the object himself. What is constructed here is the figure of prehistoric and fantastic "Indianness," the racist fantasy that needs to project the "Indian" as artifact, as fetish, and as Other. The fantasy operates on three assumptions: that this "Indian" is a stable object of representation, that he is in some strange way identical with the sign, *and* that he identifies himself with it. This scene exposes how the government system—here supported by education—worked to make American Indians internalize cultural, social, and racial hierarchies. The lesson of the Indian is not merely meant to teach the other children what a creature the Indian is, but by identifying Charging Elk with this picture, the teacher means to suggest that he is this—and nothing else—unless he assimilates and relinquishes the particularity of his experience and cultural identity. That way he would have to disidentify himself from this sign, then recognize the creature as that which is him but from which he needs to "Other" himself. To the class the figure is already that which they are not—a sign of seemingly stable representations of difference, contained.

This scene speaks as much to the ways in which racialization relies on "visible" evidence as to the discrepancy between abstracting narratives and material "reality" and to the repeated deferment of subject formation. Quite ironic in other ways as well, the scene explores the idea that boarding schools provide Indian students with the tools for converting their "savage" minds into civilized beings by means of the colonizer's language. Here the idea is parodied as a lesson in the most simple form of reading. In these simple terms the teacher practices most basic boarding school philosophy in which Indian students learn to identify and "embrace a sense of tribal culture as inferior and 'savage'" (Katanski 7). However, she clearly neglects to allow Charging Elk to distance himself from this image, which seems to counter the pedagogy that means to help students "affirm their assimilationist project" (Katanski 7). Also, for Charging Elk's relinquishing of his particularity in order to (try to) assimilate into a more civilized "image" operates within the same type of socializing narrative that bildungsroman conventions prescribe. The classroom is identified as an alien, and alienating, social order, and thus offers an interesting counterpoint to the estrangement Charging Elk experiences trying to establish a life in Marseille.

"A VERY REAL *INDIEN*"

The paradoxical cultural and national imaginings within which Charging Elk is caught and his complicated relationship to the legal discourses around him are most clearly exemplified in the frustration and helplessness with which Vice-

Consul Bell reacts to Charging Elk's situation. I read Bell's role as vice-consul and diplomatic representative for the Indian performers as representative of official cultural and political national discourse. When Bell is first confronted with Charging Elk's disappearance from the hospital and his arrest five days later, he visits Charging Elk in his cell and cannot help but reflect on the Indian as being of a "strange race of people [who were] still attempting to live in the past with their feathers and beads" (82). Bell claims to understand this, "seeing that they had no future to speak of," and concludes along the same lines as the popular narrative: "They were a pitiful people in their present state and the sooner they vanish or joined America the better off they would be" (82). However, Bell's relationship to Charging Elk becomes far more complicated and ambivalent than this. On the one hand he is "burdened" with Charging Elk's case, first visiting him in the hospital and then taking care of the bureaucratic complications that ensue due to his complicated status in relation to the United States and the mispronouncement of his death. Discussing with the prison chief the charges brought against Charging Elk for leaving the hospital and for loitering, Bell finds himself in an awkward situation, not quite knowing how to define Charging Elk's status in terms of citizenship. Even though it occurs to him that Charging Elk is not an American citizen, he still pronounces him a citizen because of a special agreement with the Wild West show under which the performers are entitled to diplomatic representation. Framing his "ward" within a national context gives Bell more leverage, while he himself—off duty, on the way home—finds himself resorting to the generalizing "assimilate or die" narrative.

Yet, Bell is torn among official discourse, cultural narratives, and the actual presence of the Indian, which he cannot himself erase. The first complication of Charging Elk's status erupts when the French officials suggest that he entered the country illegally; "he is not a citizen of the United States, he does not hold a valid passport" (114). This legal fact collides with the cultural narrative that has been traveling across Europe as America's representative. René Soulas tries to correct the officials: "But the law is misguided in this case, *capitaine*. The Peau-Rouge is clearly a citizen of America. He is the original citizen. Buffalo Bill said so" (114). Even the captain has to confess that he finds this fact confusing; he assumed that Buffalo Bill's assertions during the show were true, and only now finds out that the U.S. government claims that the "*indiens* were not real citizens of their own country" (115). The already paradoxical situation turns into a farce when Charging Elk is declared dead (in error) by the hospital officials, and Bell finds himself fighting to correct this mistake, while he himself at times thinks of Charging Elk (and his people) as barely alive. In defense of Charging Elk's life, Bell finds himself not only proclaiming out loud to his boss that Charging Elk is very much alive, but also outraged at the French officials, who apparently didn't "care which Indian lived and which died [since] one Indian is as good as another to them" (160). To this his boss merely retorts, "And what about us, Frank? [. . .] Do we care?" Bell's initial attempt to write off Charging Elk in order not to assume responsibility remains futile, and thus he has to acknowledge not only his responsibility for Charging Elk but also the young Lakota's persisting presence despite his bureaucratic erasure. Bell becomes increasingly frustrated with the French government's handling of Charging Elk's case, and when the official statements claim that there was "no *indien* in the Préfecture on Christmas Eve," he is confronted with the fact that in his stewardship Charging Elk has vanished (179). The Indian has become "nonexistent, a ghost you might say" (178)—a narrative twist that makes the French official story sound very much like the U.S. narrative.

This erasure of the Native exemplifies the bureaucratic practice so similar to the various narrative attempts to render Charging Elk ghostly: from St-Cyr and Madeleine Soulas's initial impressions of him, to Buffalo Bill's "Indian," the white teacher's "feathered creature," to Breteuil, who casts Charging Elk as the exotic, yet conquerable, Native in order to violate him sexually. However, telling René Soulas of Charging Elk's supposed death, Bell comes to realize that, instead of a ghost or an anachrony in the present, "we still have a very real *indien* on our hands" (179). Initially his presence is only recognized as part of the performance of an American historical past. In an insightful study of the presence of ghostly Indians in American literature, Renée Bergland writes that whenever American Indians are figured as ghosts it is done so as a "technique of removal" (4). In spectral form, in other words, Indians are transported into the American imagination and "safely" removed from physical land that needed to be settled. Obviously this Indian ghost has been removed from the (American) land, but Welch writes him as emerging as a ghost elsewhere. This ghost, otherwise erased, not only haunts the present nation but also suggests the ongoing existence and persistence of indigenous peoples.

THE PERSISTENCE OF THE INDIGENOUS SUBJECT

In his last novel, Welch does more than merely offer an alternative memory, or an excavation of that which has been forgotten so that it may be present again. An "untroubled recovery" of the past, to paraphrase Lowe, is not possible, as a return to pre-reservation life is also not possible (140). Being stranded in France highlights Charging Elk's feelings of alienation, displacement, and racialized otherness—feelings his people and other indigenous tribes all over the United States experience in relation to the encroaching American nation. What emerges in this site of radical displacement is a space in excess of the nation and yet painfully tied to it, a space in which the American Indian articulates the uncanny relocation of self that is in conflict with the American nation (of which American Indians are such an integral part), offering a critique of that nation's modernist narrative. So, while the novel is in part about recovery and the subject's longing to return home, the subject's return—spun out of the secure place within the national narrative—becomes an impossibility, and instead the novel constructs something of an alternative relationship of the displaced indigenous subject to his home, and the United States.

By exiting from the show's performance of the vanishing Indian, a performance that repeats the fetishization and othering of the Native, Charging Elk disrupts the perceived stability of national ideology, because the "primitive has somehow escaped from control" (Hall "The Local" 187). While the idea of the "Indian" cannot progress, Charging Elk *does*, and moves into the present. Now, creating his own life, he points to and recovers traces of the materiality and social histories of the social groups that were assumed to be excluded from the history of the modern nation. The effect of the novel can be grasped in Lowe's words, as a "constant interrogation of the discrepancies between canonical historical narratives and what Walter Benjamin would term the material 'catastrophes' that those histories obscure" (100). The legal and representational difficulties that prevent Charging Elk from returning to his homeland also bring Bell, as the representation of the official American national narrative, into active dialogue with what it means to be "American," with who gets to pronounce national belonging, and with the continued violence of pronouncing someone dead who is very much alive. In this novel Welch redirects conventional notions of home, culture, and belonging into a critique of radical displacement policies, which even today leave Native Americans disenfranchised in a segregated place, because remembering and enacting the "first citizen" and forgetting the violence done against Native peoples are still an intricate part of American national narratives.

As part of the national cultural terrain American Indian literatures and cultures occupy a crucial space that should be read and studied as continuously *challenging* the ways U.S. national culture fixes "otherness" in contained, "marginal" places, as *interrogating* the way U.S. cultural productions narrate the nation's histories (the "vanquished Indian" is only one such narrative that needs to be repeated), and as *remembering* the particularities of diverse American Indian histories and cultural practices through histories of violence and displacement, not in an attempt to propose some essential authenticity, but instead to create a space for counterdiscourse. In short, they produce alternative ways of knowing with which to contradict, disrupt, and expose the workings of U.S. national and cultural narratives. Out of the oppositional space of American Indian cultures emerge new forms of subjectivity that contest the models of subject formation on which the nation relies.

NOTES

I would like to thank Chandan Reddy and Alys Weinbaum for their critical and challenging responses to earlier drafts of this paper, and to Lois Welch and Stacy Grooters for their invaluable insight and support.

An earlier version of this essay has been published in *Studies in American Indian Literatures* 18, 3 (Fall 2006): 98–106.

1. Robert Rydell and Rob Kroes suggest, too, that the Wild West functions beyond an American national context, acting also as a vehicle for selling the product of "America"—with its dreams of freedom and a classless society—across the Atlantic. In their reading of European reactions to the show, Rydell and Kroes assert that not only did the Wild West transport this so American of narratives into the European imagination, but it also allowed Europeans to see themselves—at a moment of expanding European colonialism—as protagonists whose "views of Western superiority and the White Man's civilizing mission" seemed to be confirmed—narratively—in front of their very eyes (105–17). Considering Welch's popular reception in France, it would be interesting to read *Heartsong* as commenting, too, on the role of the West in constructing European subjectivity. My focus in this essay, however, is the novel's argument about U.S. nation formation and the paradoxical construction of American Indians' relationship to it.
2. Suzanne Methot, in her review of *Heartsong*, reads the novel as an "indictment of reservation life" and suggests further that Charging Elk's exile "has ensured his perpetual Lakota-ness" and that, in fact, he is the "only true Lakota left in the world" because he has escaped the influence of "reservation life and residential schools." While this is a tempting description, especially if we consider that many of his tribe were killed at Wounded Knee—a fate that could have befallen him had he been there—I find this reading too close to an essentializing understanding of cultural identity, one that does not take into account the effects of alienation, exile, and racialization on the shaping of his identity.
3. Homi Bhabha explores the fixity of otherness within colonial discourses as a paradox: the rigidity of the sign has to be "anxiously repeated" (*Location* 66).

WORKS CITED

Benjamin, Walter. "Theses on the Philosophy of History." 1950. *Illuminations: Essays and Reflections*. Ed. Hannah Arendt. Reprint, New York: Schocken, 1985. 253–64.

Bergland, Renée L. *The National Uncanny: Indian Ghosts and American Subjects*. Hanover NH: University Press of New England, 2000.

Bhabha, Homi K. *The Location of Culture*. New York: Routledge, 1996.

Carr, Helen. *Inventing the American Primitive: Politics, Gender and the Representation of Native American Literary Traditions, 1789–1936*. Dublin: Cork University Press, 1996.

Gilroy, Paul. *Against Race: Imagining Political Culture Beyond the Color Line*. Cambridge MA: Belknap Press of Harvard University Press, 2000.

Hall, Stuart. "The Local and the Global: Globalization and Ethnicity." *Dangerous Liaisons*. Ed. Anne McClintock, Anmir Mufti, and Ella Shohat. Minneapolis: University of Minnesota Press, 1997. 173–87.

Huhndorf, Shari M. *Going Native: Indians in the American Cultural Imagination*. Ithaca NY: Cornell University Press, 2001.

Katanski, Amelia V. *Learning to Write "Indian:" The Boarding-School Experience and American Indian Literature*. Norman: University of Oklahoma Press, 2005.

Lowe, Lisa. *Immigrant Acts: On Asian American Cultural Politics*. Durham NC: Duke University Press, 1996.

Methot, Suzanne. "Review of *The Heartsong of Charging Elk*." Aboriginal Multi-Media Society, http://www.ammsa.com/bookreviews/Heartsong-review.html (accessed May 24, 2007).

Pease, Donald E. "National Narrative, Postnational Narration." *Modern Fiction Studies* 43 (1997): 1–23.

Rydell, Robert W., and Rob Kroes. *Buffalo Bill in Bologna: the Americanization of the World, 1869–1922*. Chicago: University of Chicago Press, 2005.

Scheckel, Susan. *The Insistence of the Indian: Race and Nationalism in Nineteenth-Century American Culture*. Princeton: Princeton University Press, 1998.

Welch, James. *Fools Crow*. New York: Penguin, 1987.

———. *The Heartsong of Charging Elk*. New York: Anchor, 2001.

Welch, James, and Paul Jeffrey Stekler. *Killing Custer: The Battle of the Little Bighorn and the Fate of the Plains Indians*. New York: Norton, 1994.

White, Richard. "Frederick Jackson Turner and Buffalo Bill." *The Frontier in American Culture*. Ed. James R. Grossman. Berkeley: University of California Press, 1994. 6–65.

CHAPTER TEN

"I Have Had Some Satisfactory Times": The Yellowstone Kelly Novels of Peter Bowen

GREGORY L. MORRIS

Over the past several decades, history in general—and western American history in particular—has grown ever more difficult to write. What might be called a crisis in historiography has problematized the ways in which historians conceive of and describe the past. Questions of apprehension, questions about the nature of the historical consciousness, and questions of our intellectual relation to the past have complicated the historian's task. Questions about the nature of the *historical*, about the varied and slippery forms that it might assume have also made the job of writing history an uncertain one. Indeed, when history itself is reconceived as narrative, as a specific form of discourse, subject (one might say) to subjectivity, then how does one go about transforming event into language? When history itself is imagined as text, how does the historian translate that text into yet another?

But such is the state of contemporary historiography. The act of writing history has become, for some, an act of recomposition, of formulating new texts and "new myths" out of the broad lexicon of historical event. Making the enterprise more difficult is the revised relation among many historians to historical "fact." Postmodern historiography is, at best, ambivalent toward the factual. Historical fact has grown indeterminate, subjective; the apprehension of fact has, indeed, become a matter of perception, of the historical angle of vision assumed by the historian writing the history from those facts. As historian Hayden White argues, in constructing and delineating the historical record as text, the historian—like the poet and the fiction writer—selects and deploys various "tropes," an act that basically liberates the historian from the limitations of the factual: "Historians and philosophers of history . . . [are] then freed to conceptualize history, to perceive its contents, and to construct narrative accounts of its processes in whatever modality of consciousness is most consistent with their own moral and aesthetic aspirations" (434). Moreover, if historical event is imagined as text, then the historian engages in the interpretive, hermeneutic act every time she or he approaches those events.

All of this is meaningful for the writer of historical fiction—and, for our purposes, the writer of western American historical fiction—who writes under the influences of this altered historical and historiographical consciousness. The tradition of historical fiction for so many years has been one rooted in the notion of verisimilitude, in the idea of paying faithful and realistic duty to events-as-they-were even while the writer participates in a fictive discourse. This "paradigm of verisimilitude," as David K. Herzberger calls it (7), assumes a relatively confident belief in a knowable reality-of-the-past; it also assumes the writer's objective ability to apprehend and replicate that reality in the language of fiction.

But postmodern historiography has thrown the art of historical fiction into crisis. The paradigm of verisimilitude has broken down; the nature of historical perception has been revealed in all its ambiguity and subjectivity. As Lionel Grossman has noted: "For many . . . the fact that the knower is himself involved in the historical process as a maker of history and is thus unable to achieve the 'objective' view . . . [has become] the very condition of historical knowledge" (215). Consequently, the historical fictionist has had to redefine his or her relation to the past and to the "problem of pastness," as Russel Nye describes it (146). For many writers of recent historical fiction, the aim has been to "transcend the narrowly historistic" (Henderson 12), to dissolve the paradigm of verisimilitude, and to create what various critics—including Barbara Foley—have described as "metahistorical fiction." For Foley, "the metahistorical novel takes as its referent a historical process that evades rational formulation; its documentary effect derives from the assertion of the very indeterminacy of factual verification" (25). Both the novelist and her or his protagonists—especially those who narrate their own stories—become "creative historians" (Foley 195) who self-consciously represent a nonrepresentative object: the amorphous, indefinite flow of historical process.

Complicating the task of the *western* metahistorical novelist's task in particular is the recent critical literary concern with authenticity—or more accurately, with the argument *against* authenticity as a criterion upon which to judge western writing. This argument has been led by Nathaniel Lewis, who in the introduction to his book, *Unsettling the West: Authenticity and Authorship*, declares: "For two centuries readers have had little choice: western literature has been constructed and legitimized primarily in relation to 'authentic history.' Western writing has been evaluated as either 'mythic' or 'real'" (2). Lewis goes on to contend that once "we stop evaluating western writing with the test of authenticity, we can begin to dismantle the burden of realism and can treat western literature as simulation rather than representation" (15). Such "simulation" seems to be at the heart of this metahistorical fiction and its project of disarming certain crippling central myths.

For those writers who pursue a *radical* version of metahistorical truth, history itself becomes a body upon which imaginatively to feed. This particular brand of metahistorical novelist comes to the past along a certain ideological vector, recognizing that the past is in the present and that both are deserving of critique. In David Lowenthal's words, "Fiction criticizes history while cannibalizing it" (228). This seems to be the stance taken by Montana novelist Peter Bowen, who as a writer of historical fiction might well be described as an artful and comic cannibal. In particular, Bowen's novels about the historical figure Luther "Yellowstone" Kelly create what I would call a *ludic history* of Kelly and of his life in the mid-nineteenth-century American West. Bowen takes as his subject the verifiably "real" life and times of this character and shapes and reshapes that life and those times into a modern myth—or, more accurately, an *anti*-myth. Enfolding simulacrum within simulacrum and engaging the historical moment in often carnivalesque ways, Bowen has a great deal of fun with what history gives him and with what he gives back as imaginative and *inauthentic* history. Bowen's historical mode is powerfully comic, but beneath that ludic, playful history lies a more subversive ideological critique of the American mythos and of the American identity. Bowen accomplishes this by making free and imaginative use of his protagonist, Yellowstone Kelly, who himself took part in so much of the historical process that contributed to the making of this mythos and this identity.

The historical Luther Sage Kelly was born in Geneva, New York, in the Finger Lakes region, on July 27, 1849. His education was modest, local, and incomplete: after attending the Geneva Union School, he entered the Genesee Wesleyan Seminary at Lima, New York. The Civil War, however, put an end to Kelly's formal schooling. At the age of fifteen—but claiming to be over eighteen—Kelly enlisted in the Tenth Infantry and entered the Union army as a private. His military service seems to have consisted largely of guarding prisoners of war, and he apparently saw no direct battle action.

Following the war, Kelly's company was assigned first to Washington DC, where he had his first possible brush with the historically famous. In his memoir, Kelly describes standing in rank on Pennsylvania Avenue while a military parade passed in review: "I was but a recruit, and was unable to identify any of the famous warriors who moved so gallantly by, but I noted one dashing officer of high rank whose horse seemed to have gotten the bit and was bearing his rider at full speed along the line of march before he could curb him. It may have been Custer of the waving locks, although I am not sure" (6). Unlike Peter Bowen, who would have made much (and made *up* much) of this event, Kelly exercises restraint, reins in his imagination and memory, and locates this encounter within the realm of mere possibility. Later, Kelly's outfit was dispatched to the Dakota Territory, where Kelly distinguished himself as a young but skilled hunter and where he saw his first buffalo.

His three-year enlistment ended in 1868, and Kelly headed further west into Yellowstone country where he would literally make a name for himself. Here he came to know the trails of Wyoming and Montana and honed his talents as hunter and trapper. Here he came to educate himself in the culture and language of the Native tribes (particularly of the Sioux) and had his first encounter with Sitting Bull. Here, too, he began serving the American military, first as dispatch bearer and then as guide, attaching himself early on to Gen. George Forsyth's expedition to the upper Missouri and Yellowstone rivers. From 1876 to 1878, Kelly rode as chief scout for Gen. Nelson Miles, serving in numerous campaigns against the Sioux and Cheyennes and acquiring his nickname, "Yellowstone Kelly"; later, in 1880, Kelly scouted for the army again, in the Ute country in Colorado (Malone 309).

Kelly left the West in the early 1880s, making his way back East. He stopped in Detroit to court and to marry Alice May Morrison in 1885, then continued on to Washington DC, where he went to work for the War Department. His postings took him to Chicago, to Governors Island, and back to the Pension Bureau in Washington. In 1898, though, Kelly left the deskbound world of the War Department and took off again to the wilderness, acting as guide to Capt. Edwin Forbes Glenn's exploring expedition to Alaska. The next year, Kelly returned to Alaska, this time as guide to the celebrated Harriman expedition (of which John Muir was a part).

Kelly seemed unable or unwilling to avoid an often colorful involvement in the historical sweep of his time, including participation in the imperial impulse that drove so much of his country's political will. At the end of the century, Kelly turned up in the Philippines as captain of a company of volunteers and was eventually made commander of Post Dapitán, Mindanao. In 1903, while treasurer of the province of Surigao, Kelly led the inhabitants in a defense of their territory against attacking escaped convicts and outlaws; Kelly was picked out for special praise by President Roosevelt for his conduct in this action.

Kelly returned to the United States—and to the American West—in 1904 and became Indian agent at the San Carlos Reservation in Arizona, serving in this post until 1908. Heeding the sirens' song of quick and abundant wealth, Kelly became involved in the world of mines, supervising a gold mine near Lida, Nevada, and investing time and money in other unsuccessful mining ventures. Kelly then traveled to California where, in 1915, he started a fruit ranch at Paradise, California (near Chico), where he lived until his death on December 17, 1928 (Malone 309). Interestingly (and perhaps aptly) enough, Kelly was buried outside of Billings, Montana, on the old road to the Billings airport.

During those last years in Paradise, while not tending his orchards, Kelly composed and saw published a memoir, *"Yellowstone Kelly": The Memoirs of Luther S. Kelly,* a recollection of his days on the northern plains in the late 1860s and early 1870s. From this memoir comes the bulk of the detail concerning Kelly's early life. At the time of his death, Kelly was also finishing a manuscript about his work in Alaska and in the Philippines. Clearly, Kelly was interested in recording the "facts" of his own life and in constructing what might be conceived of as a *literary* life—a life of words, a life apart from the life lived, a life invested with a certain amount of cultural capital.

That literary life would be resurrected some thirty years later in 1957 with Clay Fisher's novel, *Yellowstone Kelly*, a work of popular genre fiction. In his preface to the novel, Fisher declares: "This book is based upon the memoirs of a remarkable old man who died twenty-nine years ago in Butte County, California. His story as told herein is fictional romance, not factual biography, yet it becomes a practical impossibility to elaborate on his real-life adventures" (vii). Fisher is not particularly interested in or concerned with the problems of writing historical fiction, and he assumes a clear-cut distinction between the fictional and the biographical (or factual). Yet Fisher does not feel bound to the memoir that he claims as his source; for example, he gives Kelly a sex life (with an American Indian woman), an element never mentioned by Kelly in his memoir. At the same time, Fisher is clearly intent on recovering and preserving the mythic resonance of the man and his name (vii–viii). Fisher has little regard for the "cynical" project that is history—or that is the writing of history—even while he advances Kelly as a crucial, catalytic figure in that history. Implicit in Fisher's critique still is the notion that history is a sort of drama and dramatic narrative, a stage piece enacted by personality.

Clearly, though, the most significant cultural "use" to which the life and times of Luther Kelly have been put is in the four novels by Peter Bowen—what might be called his Yellowstone Kelly tetralogy: *Yellowstone Kelly, Gentleman & Scout* (1987); *Kelly Blue* (1991); *Imperial Kelly* (1992); and *Kelly and the Three-toed Horse* (2001). Taking what we "know" about Kelly, taking what we consider to be the facts of his biography, Bowen revises and amends and imagines that life anew in these four works. With Bowen's help, Yellowstone Kelly moves through—and recalls and narrates—a history he knew, or might have known, but of which he was not always directly a part in his actual, historical life. So we see Kelly reliving his times in the nineteenth-century American West and in the Philippines and in Washington DC. But we also see Kelly in places he never apparently visited in his "real time": South Africa, for example, where he becomes involved first in the war against the Zulus and later in the Boer War. The fictional Kelly also rubs shoulders with other historical figures, most of whom Kelly never actually encountered. In South Africa, Kelly finds himself responsible for the young Winston Churchill and for the young Prince Imperial, the would-have-been Napoleon IV (Kelly manages to keep the former alive, the latter he does not), talks with, befriends, and ultimately defends the young Gandhi, and has a lively sexual encounter with Jennie Churchill.

Even in geographies Luther Kelly was known to inhabit, Bowen has him running into a very long list of folks he was not known to have known, including: in the West, Kit Carson, Jim Bridger (who educates Kelly), Tom Horn (whom Kelly educates), George Custer ("the most overblown actor ever carved from a hogg's butt"), Brigham Young, Pancho Villa, John Wilkes Booth (whom Kelly assassinates in Canada!), Crazy Horse, Sitting Bull, Buffalo Bill Cody, and even Oscar Wilde; and in the Philippines, Emilio Aguinaldo, Gen. Arthur MacArthur, and even Butch Cassidy and the Sundance Kid.

As suggested above, all of this is cast in the form of autobiography or memoir, with Kelly as the reflective, recollective narrator (and constructor) of his own life. We learn in the first book of the quartet, *Yellowstone Kelly, Gentleman & Scout*, that Kelly is provoked into authorship by the efforts of other, lesser writers to turn him into a literary character. One such effort is made by a George Hanks, a supposed writer for the Hartford *Courant* who has written (under Kelly's name) an "autobiography" of Kelly: "There were several hundred copies of a pulp tract supposedly authored by me, and I was to sign it. I wouldn't, because it was a pack of lies" (*Yellowstone Kelly* 68). Kelly later discovers that this book, and thereby Kelly himself, is known and recognizable even in South Africa. A second book has been written by a writer named James Blair, and Kelly's scorn for his work is just as virulent: "Took the train to Chicago via Minneapolis—and in Minneapolis I found a book written by a feller named James Blair. I was still in my leather and leggins and moccasins and hat, and every time I'd hoot with laughter the folks in the coach would all turn round and stare. Fortunately, the picture on the engraved cover (I was at least nine feet tall, if you scale me with the grizzly bear I was beating the bejesus out of with my bare knuckles) didn't resemble me in the slightest" (*Yellowstone Kelly* 52). To the best of my knowledge, neither Hanks nor Blair ever existed as Kelly here imagines them; neither book by or about Kelly ever came into publication.

But Kelly's most persistent and only *real* contemporary "autobiographer," and the writer Kelly reserves special contempt for, is Ned Buntline (pen name of E. Z. C. Judson), author of numerous dime novels about the American West and its less historical (or ahistorical) characters. It is Buntline who supposedly has given Kelly his moniker, in a book about Kelly's exploits, most of which Buntline gets wrong or distorts or makes up whole cloth: "'I should have shot that little bastard Ned Buntline. I didn't. I suffer for it.'" (*Imperial Kelly* 109). Despite Buntline's very real and prodigious output, however, such a book appears to be yet another figment of Peter Bowen's (and his hero's) imagination; nowhere, for example, in the catalogue of Buntline's works compiled by Jay Monaghan in his biography of Buntline, *The Great Rascal: The Life and Adventures of Ned Buntline* (321–33), is a Kelly title listed.

What is more important here, perhaps, is Kelly's urgent resistance to such biographizing efforts and to being transformed into a creature made of language. So Kelly sets about constructing his own life in and with his own words. As the tetralogy opens, Kelly is working in the War Office in Washington DC; the year is 1901, President McKinley has just been assassinated, and Kelly sits in a bar drinking to the late president's memory. The more he drinks the more he considers his own life, its excitements, and its literary possibilities. Spurred on by whiskey and by the desire to get it right, Kelly resolves to take pencil to foolscap and to "write a book" (9). So begins Kelly's writing life: as autobiographer, as historian, as chronicler and creator of a world made to compete with the historical record as it has come to exist in other narratives and other texts.

As Kelly learns, "the past can be a patient bushwhacker" (65). A highly self-conscious narrator, Kelly understands the tense relationship between "auto" and "biography" and the ways in which narratives of the (personal) past can reshape themselves over time. He begins his own narrative in 1877, midway through his two-year service as scout for Gen. Nelson A. Miles; as it will be throughout the tetralogy, Kelly's voice and perspective are decidedly cynical. Kelly occupies a precarious position as storyteller and historian. He is a narrator with a consciousness (and conscience) in at least two worlds. Employed by the U.S. Army to scout "hostiles," Kelly purposely distances himself from the actions of that army and declares his sympathies and empathies with the Indians they hunt: he is (or desires to be), at once, both engaged and disengaged. Kelly is a man possessed of an unusually high degree of negative capability, able to understand and to serve multiple ideologies, both as historian and as participant in that history.

Of course, it is possible that the ideology espoused by Kelly here is rooted in the authorially espoused ideology of Peter Bowen, or that the narratives of both Bowen and Kelly are (in the words of Robert Mayer) part of "a process shaped by an ideologically and tropologically determined 'prefiguring' of the narrative in the initial response to the historical record" (90). Certainly, Kelly promotes an ideology throughout the history he creates in his narrative, an ideology informed by skepticism toward the notion of historical process and progress and by a kind of historical subjectivity in which he is a maker of the history he constructs. Indeed, Kelly is, in a way, responding to the dominant "historical record" by creating an alternative to that record.

Much of that record is infused with a nostalgia that highlights a spirit of loss in Kelly's narrative: the loss of place and time, the loss of spirit and a sense of promise. Kelly is acutely aware—even in 1877—of how much of the West and its attendant, guiding mythology is in the process of passing. When the young Tom Horn laments the fact that the West—the pre-railroad, pre-sheep, and pre-cattle West, the West as it had (and has) been known in the popular American imagination—will be gone before he gets there, Kelly reflects to himself: "There wasn't anything I could say to that, except maybe the only thing that was worse was having to *watch* the Big Lonesome shorn of its buffalo, Indians, and openness" (*Yellowstone Kelly* 116). With a certain amount of anguish, Kelly plays witness to the death of a culture; his narrative provides a kind of ironic, elegiac testimony to the historical sweep of time and place through which he passes.

At the same time, Kelly participates in the artifice of a (re)constructed West when he briefly and reluctantly joins Buffalo Bill and Texas Jack Omonhundro in entertaining the visiting Duke of Ironheath with a "re-enactment": "Bill had hired a few tame Indians, and they was to make a mock attack on the Pullman cars. They was to swoop down just as Bill and Jack and I rode up, and we were to playfully fire blank cartridges at them, eventually knocking all of the savages off their horses—some sort of re-enactment of something or other. Well, hell, here it was the wild west" (130). With patent sheepishness, Kelly takes part in this artifice, this constructed drama; at the same time, however, he also deconstructs that artifice with the force of his historical narrative. Kelly is aware of the simulacrum—and we, as readers, are aware of the simulacrum-within-the-simulacrum that is Kelly's history—so that when the ahistorical Duke is shot by the historical Liver-Eating Johnson, the artifice(s) is attenuated before giving way to a kind of historical reality. The Old West strikes back, if only in a fanciful, semiconstructed way.

Bowen permits Kelly an "Epilogue" to this opening volume, wherein we find Kelly returned from a difficult sojourn among the Zulus in South Africa and finishing up his history on the shore of Lake George. He is fifty now, weary of "scribbling," wary of his memory's accuracy, and full of despair at the turning of the age: "This new century stinks of blood" (279). Still, he remains painfully conscious of his ambiguous status as participant-historian. When questioned by a Boston "blue stocking" about the morality of what he has done, of his participation in "the brutal and unjust destruction of the American Indian," Kelly replies with characteristic irony and self-awareness: "I never once forgot this—that it was wrong. The kind of wrong [that] happens when one big bunch of mean folks needs land for farms and homes. So they kill the weaker folks that was already there. And at least all the Indians I killed died clean and quick, and didn't perish of misery and boredom listening to the kind of pinch-faced god-wallopers descended on them later. I was a killer, but I warn't cruel" (280).

It's a difficult position that Kelly carves out for himself here and that he attempts to defend; his discomfort is palpable, his logic more like equivocation and moral squirming. While Kelly manages to keep his hands fairly clean of blood—both Indian and non-Indian—he does involve himself in the historical acts of which he is such an unforgiving critic. Culpability attends the life. Hope fades in the face of overwhelming force; power operates ineluctably in the colonial and imperial projects; the historical narrative, as unfortunate and tragic as it may be, tells itself over again. And Yellowstone Kelly is there—pseudohistorically, at times—to give us that story.

In the second volume of the tetralogy, *Kelly Blue,* Bowen indulges the same sort of playful revisionist sensibility and the same sort of political intention. The narrative is again recollective, and again it is precipitated by a significant death: this time, the death of Buffalo Bill Cody. The year is 1917, and Kelly has been called to Denver to attend Cody at his hospital bedside and to witness, alone, Cody's passing—a largely farcical scene that occurs only in Bowen's fictional history. Returning by train to his California ranch (as already noted, a historical aspect of Kelly's life), Kelly turns reflective once more ("I began to think of how I came to be here at all") and begins narrating his earlier history, the twenty-five years or so that led up to the life described in *Yellowstone Kelly*. Here, too, Bowen makes somewhat loose use of the biographical content of Kelly's lived life: his birth and his growing up in central New York (Bowen places Kelly in Oneida, when in fact he was born and raised in Geneva—one Finger Lake town being as good as the next, apparently—and changes his birth year to 1851), and his subsequent post–Civil War posting to Minnesota where he begins his exploits in "the meat hunter business." When Kelly leaves the army and heads West, Bowen's (and Kelly's) narrative turns much more fictional and much less historical, or at least much less (auto)biographical.

Much of *Kelly Blue* deals with the western education of Yellowstone Kelly as a scout and as a hunter, and one of the central relationships in the novel is that between Kelly and the near-archetypal scout and hunter, Jim Bridger (an event never mentioned by the historical Kelly in his memoirs nor by any biographer of Bridger). Kelly essentially apprentices himself to Bridger at the age of fourteen, and through his mentor Kelly comes to know the ways of the country and of the Indians who tenuously inhabit that country. The lessons are sometimes difficult ones, as Kelly discovers after coming upon three white men left dead and mutilated by Indians: "For a cold moment I wondered how I had pulled the luck to stay alive. This was hard country and these was hard men. I started crying. I'd run from home, joined the army, been captured by Indians, and now I was in the Rockies like I always had wanted to be (or the South Seas) with a man I had been reading about since I could read at all. And I wanted my mother. And nothing else. I sobbed some" (49). Several things deserve noting here. First, we see that Kelly has come to know Bridger, initially, through some popular text, through (as we learn) several dime novels he has read about the famed mountain man. And Kelly, to some degree, falls into emulation of this textually created character; one of the lessons Kelly learns is that of the distance between the constructed man and the authentic man. Moreover, Bowen in fact uses Bridger as a model for his own fictional Kelly, giving Kelly biographical experience that properly belonged to Bridger. We wonder, then, if Kelly is not more like Bridger than we suspect when we learn that, in his old age, the mountain man could tell a tall tale upon occasion: "'If he was cornered and asked to talk, he would tell the most outlandish yarns and then chuckle to himself and wonder if his questioner had gotten what he wanted'" (quoted in Vestal 292). Clearly, we must wonder about Bowen and Kelly and their truth-telling abilities; clearly, we must measure the gap between the historical and the leg-pulling.

Bridger was also a good friend of the great Shoshone chief, Washakie, and it is this friendship upon which Bowen draws in delineating Kelly's (fictional) relationship with the Shoshone leader. In *Kelly Blue*, Washakie in a way supplants Bridger and offers Kelly an alternative education, one that supplements the knowledge gained from the white mountain man. Perhaps more important is the fact that Kelly ends up marrying Washakie's daughter, Eats-Men-Whole, a name earned (as one might guess) by virtue of her strong "feminist" will and nature. Eats-Men-Whole is one of several powerful women Kelly will meet and usually bed (in *Yellowstone Kelly*, this role is filled by the young Boer woman, Marieke Uys, who reappears in *Imperial Kelly*), and Kelly's marriage to her suggests the degree to which he has "gone native" and provides some basis for his sincere and energetic defense of the Native American cultures later on in the novel. So extensive is this change in Kelly that alienation sets in: "I was changed forever and I knew it. I was a stranger to myself" (87).

Nor is this the only form of alienation experienced by Kelly. Part of his education has involved a reimagined relationship with the landscape itself. Having encountered the "hard country," Kelly has somehow to fashion an identity more in alignment with the country inhabited by that identity. Already distanced from the self he has known, Kelly also must first separate himself from the geography through which he travels. After he is captured by Spotted Tail and the Brulé Sioux, Kelly declares: "This was the very last spot in life when I ever trusted the land I was moving through again" (99). Once again, Kelly undergoes a sort of defamiliarization—of self, of landscape—in order to position himself as autobiographer and as historian.

For, of course, it is not only physical landscape that Kelly traverses; he is also a pilgrim through time and through history, and Bowen gives his Kelly more than enough history to handle. In the space of the novel, Kelly meets Crazy Horse and Custer; witnesses the Fetterman Massacre and the Sand Creek Massacre (where both his wife and unborn child are killed); helps guide the Mormons to Salt Lake City and later becomes entangled in a Mormon intrigue that puts him on the wrong side of Brigham Young; meets Buffalo Bill Cody and Ned Buntline; engages himself in the Black Hills problem (where he finds a mastodon fossil, hinting at events to come in the fourth Kelly novel); and, in perhaps Peter Bowen's most audacious act of pseudohistory, assassinates the assassin, hunting down and killing John Wilkes Booth in Canada! But the book's most intriguing instance of ahistoricism is probably the trip Kelly makes to Washington DC, accompanying the several Indian chiefs (including Red Cloud and Kelly's fictional nemesis Spotted Tail) who did meet with Pres.

Ulysses S. Grant in 1872 to discuss the matter of the white incursion into the Black Hills. Grant is painted sympathetically by both Bowen and Kelly, and in doing so they seem to reflect the developing historical consensus on Grant and his presidency—or at least on Grant as man and president (see, for example, Jean Edward Smith's *Grant*). Bowen also thereby further seeds the grounds for Kelly's own sympathies with the Native peoples and recalls his recommendation for Indian political activism at the end of *Yellowstone Kelly*.

Significant in all of this authorial manipulation is the fact that while the historical Luther Kelly occupied the temporal space—and parts of the physical, geographical space—described by Bowen in *Kelly Blue*, Bowen imagines the potentiality of such historical presence: what was possible, not probable; what could have been, not what might have been. It is a variety of fiction that E. L. Doctorow has called "speculative history, perhaps a superhistory" (Trenner 25); and as one who pursues the "imaginative truth" of that (super)history, Peter Bowen orchestrates a fiction that "criticizes history while cannibalizing it" (Lowenthal 228). Bowen is the artful comic cannibal, playfully devouring historical space and time to construct a reimagined western world.

Of course, Yellowstone Kelly himself is a storyteller full of the revisionist sensibility and ever conscious of the irony of his position as participant-historian. At one point in *Kelly Blue*, Kelly recalls the earliest and less respectable days of Salt Lake City:

> There was forty or so saloons each one cruder than the last, bedraggled whores working out of canvas cribs, restaurants that served rotten food where the only healthy things in the pies was the maggots and weevils, who'd died in the oven. (Years later, when I'd get roped into listening to speeches about our valiant pioneer forebears, I'd think of all the riffraff and scum what done the original work. Riffraff like me, scummily hiding out here from the consequences of misunderstandings with folks back East. We seemed to be greedy of gold, but if any of us made money we fair threw it away.) (119)

Kelly could pass for a contemporary western American historian in his demythification project here, stripping away the faded layers of historicized varnish to reveal the rather shabby truth of things. Kelly has no patience with those "jingo historians" (as he calls them) who gild and glorify the legacies of conquest (to paraphrase the eminent new West historian, Patricia Limerick); he is clearly conscious of historiography and of the varieties of historical narratives available to the historian. Yet as he looks back from the vantage point of the first quarter of the twentieth century, Kelly again is elegiac and lamentative: "It was fine country back then, and I don't like it so good now" (12). Kelly's relation to the western landscape—a landscape he continues to inhabit—continues to alter itself, remains tense and bittersweet. In some ways, Kelly remains an alien to that landscape, at least to the landscape recalled through the sometimes hazy medium of memory.

As its title suggests, Bowen's third Yellowstone Kelly novel takes up the problem of the imperialist impulse in landscapes distinctly non–North American. Whereas the first two books in the series certainly operated with an anti-imperialist subtext, *Imperial Kelly* makes its ideological statements more clearly and more directly, tracking its hero as he witnesses and testifies to a series of imperialist, genocidal acts in several foreign geographies. Kelly's involvement in these projects, however, originates mainly with his own country's political desires abroad, as Kelly understands: "America had imperial ambitions—all done for the moral improvement of whoever's land we wanted, mind you—and so it seemed that Cuba and the Philippines was in need of us" (1). And those desires are roundly, vigorously embodied in Kelly's persistent nemesis, Theodore Roosevelt. It is men like Roosevelt who, according to Kelly, insist on engaging Kelly in the unsettling sweep of history. Again, Kelly imagines himself as an (objecting) object of historical force, carried along against his will (such as it is) by events and personages greater and stronger than he. Kelly is the eternal "scout" of the historical record, a kind of anti–Ned Buntline reporting the ironic, inglorious history through which he is made to ride.

Appropriately enough, Kelly rides first in Cuba (a place not visited by the historical Kelly), where he has been sent by the then assistant secretary of the navy to scout out—to *spy* on—the Spanish in Santiago. Even before he leaves, Kelly knows what his report will say: "'The war is unnecessary, the report's unnecessary . . .'" (23). Kelly knows well his skeptical, anti-imperial sensibility, but he does participate in the project; that his participation is extorted by Roosevelt and by other men (and women) of power is meant somehow to mitigate Kelly's involvement and to provide him with some moral distance from the acts that take place. It also allows him to express once more his strong and consistent antiwar sentiment: "The Spanish-American War was the easiest to avoid of any war we ever had. It was fought for other reasons, for promotions in the Army and Navy, for Theodore and Hearst, for the Sugar Trust, for money. As a war, it is damned hard to brag on it. Any of 'em ain't much to brag on, you ask me" (23). Kelly is a remarkably acute revisionist historian, identifying as he does here the naked economic impulses that drive so much of the imperial effort.

The peripatetic Kelly is allowed little rest in his world—indeed, one of the informing spirits of Bowen's series is that of the picaresque—and he is (again) ordered to the Philippines, where the Spanish-American War has extended itself and engaged American interests. As William Howard Taft laments to Kelly: "'I'm ashamed of my country.... For the first time we grab land and the people on them when it isn't necessary. We defeat the Spanish and the Filipinos love us as liberators. Then we announce that we are here to stay and extend the pleasures of democracy to our little brown brothers. Stuff and nonsense. We want the Philippines for the markets of China and to block Japan from taking them'" (109). Taft's sentiments are essentially echoes of Kelly's own, who comes to this landscape (and the historical Kelly did serve in the Philippines, but not in the way Bowen imagines it here) again as an outsider, as one who finds that landscape forbidding, ambiguous, and almost unknowable; the island itself Kelly finds to be "the most dangerous place I had ever been in," yet the "jungle is beautiful." The place is as paradoxical as the political spirit that puts Kelly (and other non-Natives) in that place. And Kelly here again serves as a kind of reluctant emissary to the native peoples in this territory, encountering their world, listening to their stories, risking his hide, and reporting back to a generally uninterested, imperially disposed world. The news rarely is good. Kelly leaves the Philippines with his cynicism more deeply entrenched than ever.

The America—or the American West—to which he returns in the new century is in the midst of historical flux. Kelly hastens to the Wind River Range of Wyoming to witness the death of his old friend and mentor—his "father"—Washakie; his passing is just another reminder of the concurrent passing of an age and of an era, of a West (and a westerner) that once was and that will never be again. Back in the Yellowstone country, Kelly finds his familiar landscape now unfamiliar and despoiled by change; this is not the territory Kelly knew first and firsthand in 1872 and which gave him his nickname. Even his wife's miscarriage seems in keeping with the tenor of the times and of the landscape, as Kelly makes his continued passage through a geography of tragicomic loss.

A similar sense of loss pervades the fourth and final novel in the series, *Kelly and the Three-toed Horse*, though the loss here operates on several levels: personal, cultural, historical, scientific. The novel begins at one of the great confluences in the historical moment: the meeting at Promontory Point, Utah, in 1869 of the Union Pacific and the Central Pacific railroads. It is, of course, a moment of economic and physiographic conquest and expresses one of Bowen's dominant concerns: the plutocratic spirit that underlies so very much of American political and cultural life. Once again, we see Bowen critiquing the historical imagining of America—and of the American West—as an idyllic, paradisical landscape meant to be explored, excavated, and exploited, and once again we find Yellowstone Kelly centered and swept along on the high tide of the historical events.

In this novel, Bowen grounds his novelistic vision in what might be called the "great bone rush" of the nineteenth century—on the wave of fossil hunters who rushed to various parts of the West, infused by the spirit of a kind of paleontological manifest destiny—and on the scientific debates that emerged from that rush. In Bowen's imagining of the event, however, varieties of desire warp the scientific spirit; what was once, perhaps, a "disinterested science" becomes an opportunistic, territorial endeavor rife with intrigue, suspicion, cynicism, and even threat. Egos become particularly involved; reputations are at stake; wealth is to be had. Science itself becomes a cult.

This is why Bowen takes special aim in this novel at the "great man" theory of history, at the idea that the historical process is created and driven by the overlarge individual-in-time. As he has done at moments all along in the Kelly novels, Bowen here concentrates on dismantling the consciously and culturally constructed images of the American hero upon which we have hung our national story. Bowen apprehends the risks and the follies of turning history into biography, particularly when that biography is as ineluctably flawed as the man or woman it seeks to capture in its language. Our historical vision, our hindsight, says Bowen, is tragicomically myopic. We see no better than we understand, and we understand woefully little.

In the context of *Kelly and the Three-toed Horse*, those constructed images are embodied specifically in the two scientists (and characters) most intimately involved with the bone rush: Othniel Charles Marsh and Edward Drinker Cope, nineteenth-century America's preeminent paleontologists. Kelly finds himself employed as a scout for Cope (whom Bowen renames or misnames "Jonathan"), who comes to Wyoming in pursuit of fossils and looking to "out-fossil" Marsh, his scientific competitor—and the bone-hunting is undoubtedly a competition. Thrown into the mix is a woman (Bowen's creation) accompanying Cope, Alys de Bonneterre, ostensibly a scientific artist but who, as we learn in the unfolding mystery of the novel, is a very "interested" and willful scientist in her own right. (She also becomes another in the series of strong women for whom Kelly develops an affection, with whom he engages in bouts of "heroic" sex, and for whom Kelly eventually suffers the pangs of tragedy and loss.) As de Bonneterre explains the matter to an uninstructed Kelly, the world of nineteenth-century science was inalterably altered when Charles Darwin pronounced the Word: "When Mister Darwin opened the box . . . he changed the way we think about the world. The Bible became nothing more than some good poetry and suspect history. Science is God now, Kelly, and Jonathan and Othniel both seek to be the Prophet. They haven't got a scruple between them. . . . Othniel and Jonathan would kill for a good specimen, just so long as they didn't have to *do* it" (36–37). Science ascends to the level of religious faith and supplants it as a source of knowledge, at least in the rationalistic minds of nineteenth-century thinkers, and comes replete with physical forms of evidence. Science becomes, in essence, another type of historical narrative. Of course, there are those like Brigham Young who, in this novel, uses the fossil finds to support his preachings and to strengthen his role as prophet to the Mormon faithful. But at heart, the concern here is with the ways in which science torqued the intellectual enterprise and eventually contributed to the dominant, extractive, exploitative ideology that ruined so much of the geography and culture of the American West. In the destruction of the landscape, argues Bowen, we see the destructive capabilities of these dominant, determinant texts or myths. We see the appropriation of one text (science) for the expropriation of another (land and resource), and the construction of more than one exploitative narrative for political and economic gain. It is historical intertextuality at its very worst.

Admittedly, Kelly is not a disinterested commentator or observer. Indeed, one of Bowen's contentions through this novel is that the quality of disinterestedness—for the historian as well as for the self-in-history—is nothing more than myth in and of itself. Such is the problem of participation: as we move through the historical moment, we inevitably lose a measure of distance and instead attach ourselves to elements of the experience that subsequently warp our narratives of that moment. We develop a sense of ownership, as it were, about our part in what we come to think of as the historical process. Kelly himself possesses a very proprietary affection for *his* West. A familiar sense of loss and a familiar elegiac tone hang about this novel; Kelly had been a part of this landscape "when it was good," when it was still untouched, virgin, "and now it was to be chawed up like the whites had done everything else" (256). Kelly's nostalgia is undercut, of course, by his own participatory role in the ruining of this landscape.

Nor does Bowen's historical imagination ever lose its focus on the ways in which this historical *and* fictional character—this Luther "Yellowstone" Kelly—embodies so many of the potent forces of his age. In Bowen's telling of the life, Kelly becomes both object and subject, both active and passive participant in the currents of historical event; Bowen extends the historical presence of Kelly, a man who took part in many of the dominant domestic and global expansionist projects of his day, to geographies and to actions that accord (sometimes comically, almost always ironically) with the logic (if not with the biographical facts) of his lived life. So that in the end, what may be metafiction and what may be metabiography does clearly transform itself into a complex, ambiguous, and happy brand of metahistory.

WORKS CITED

Bowen, Peter. *Imperial Kelly*. New York: Crown, 1992.

———. *Kelly and the Three-toed Horse*. New York: St. Martin's Press, 2001.

———. *Kelly Blue*. New York: Crown, 1991.

———. *Yellowstone Kelly: Gentleman & Scout*. Ottawa IL: Jameson Books, 1987.

Fisher, Clay (pseud. Henry Wilson Allen). *Yellowstone Kelly*. Boston: Houghton Mifflin, 1957.

Foley, Barbara. *Telling the Truth: The Theory and Practice of Documentary Fiction*. Ithaca NY: Cornell University Press, 1986.

Grossman, Lionel. *Between History and Literature*. Cambridge MA: Harvard University Press, 1990.

Henderson, Harry B., III. *Versions of the Past: The Historical Imagination in American Fiction*. New York: Oxford University Press, 1974.

Herzberger, David K. *Narrating the Past: Fiction and Historiography in Postwar Spain*. Durham NC: Duke University Press, 1995.

Kelly, Luther S. *Yellowstone Kelly: The Memoirs of Luther S. Kelly*. Ed. M. M. Quaife. New Haven CT: Yale University Press, 1926; reprint, Lincoln: University of Nebraska Press, 1973.

Lewis, Nathaniel. *Unsettling the West: Authenticity and Authorship*. Lincoln: University of Nebraska Press, 2003.

Lowenthal, David. *The Past Is a Foreign Country*. Cambridge: Cambridge University Press 1985.

Malone, Dumas, ed. *Dictionary of American Biography*. Vol. 10. New York: Charles Scribner's Sons, 1933.

Mayer, Robert. *History and the English Novel: Matters of Fact from Bacon to Defoe*. New York: Cambridge University Press, 1997.

Monaghan, Jay. *The Great Rascal: The Life and Adventures of Ned Buntline*. Boston: Little Brown, 1951.

Nye, Russel B. "History and Literature: Branches of the Same Tree." *Essays on History and Literature*. Ed. Robert H. Brenner. Columbus: Ohio State University Press, 1966. 123–59.

Trenner, Richard. *E.L. Doctorow: Essays and Conversations*. Princeton NJ: Ontario Review Press, 1983.

Vestal, Stanley. *Jim Bridger, Mountain Man*. New York: William Morrow, 1946; reprint, Lincoln: University of Nebraska Press, 1970.

White, Hayden. *Metahistory: The Historical Imagination in Nineteenth-Century Europe*. Baltimore: Johns Hopkins University Press, 1973.

PART V Hugo-Land

CHAPTER ELEVEN

Richard Hugo's Montana Poems: Blue Collars, Indians, and Tough Style

STEVE DAVENPORT

It is fitting that *The Triggering Town*, Richard Hugo's collection of essays on the practice and teaching of creative writing, ends with the story of a squatter dispossessed of the land he and his wife had lived on for five years, a narrow strip of Boeing property between the company fence and the Duwamish River. In "The Squatter on Company Land," the poem that came of that story, the speaker voices the company claim:

> We had to get him off, the dirty elf—
> wild hair and always screaming at his wife
> and due to own our land in two more years—
> (*Making Certain* 96)

Here is the favored Hugo figure, a character living sometimes noisily, sometimes quietly, always rawly in the margins, and usually a double for the poet. In "How Poets Make a Living," the essay that closes *The Triggering Town*, Hugo includes the texts of two letters transcribed from the squatter's "near-illegible, primitive scrawl," a voice that refuses to go quietly into the night, the one we use "only in the most unguarded moments, in the wildest, most primitive phrases we shout alone at the mirror" (106, 109). About the Boeing squatters and the human condition they express in their reaction to forced removal, Hugo writes, "[W] e are all going into the dark. Some of us hope that before we do we have been honest enough to scream back at the fates. Or if we never did it ourselves, that someone, derelict or poet, did it for us once in some euphonic way" (109). In *Ten Tough Trips: Montana Writers and the West*, William Bevis describes Hugo's voice: "The basic subject of Hugo's poetry—locating the dispossessed—was personal enough, obsessive enough to deserve a passionate style" (143). As poet, essayist, and teacher, Hugo deepened our understanding that poetry might improve lives by doing some necessary, and necessarily poetic, screaming of his own.

In the process, he broadened our definition of poetry by admitting dispossessed figures like the squatter, known as The Admiral because of his incongruous yachting cap. Hugo gives us plenty of these derelict-poets, doubles for himself, who teach us about human conduct and spirit in the face of corporate or class power, who make a music, euphonic or not, that critiques the center from the margins. Consider "Mad Sam, the nutty preacher ring[ing] the bells" in "No Bells to Believe" (*Making Certain* 51) or the "hermit in the trailer at the field's / forgotten corner" and the "perfect solo on a horn he cannot play" in "At the Stilli's Mouth" (*Making Certain* 53) or the beer-drinking "fat man [who] plays a vicious clarinet / all night" along the river in "From the Rain Forest Down" (*Making Certain* 60) or the fat man "crude as a loon on land" in "The Swimmer at Lake Edward," forced by his unruly "tongue" to sing "alone in his mind, tunes he connected with rain" and who one day became a local legend:

> The first warm day, he dove from the sky
> into the lake we named for the king. We stood
> on the shore and marveled at his wake.
> When we applauded, he flashed away,
> his dorsal fin the only point in the glare.
> What was his name? . . .
> (*Making Certain* 252)

The Fat Man's other name, like The Admiral's, Mad Sam's, or the Hermit's, is Poet, and poems like "The Squatter on Company Land," "The Swimmer at Lake Edward," "From the Rain Forest Down," "No Bells to Believe," and "At the Stilli's Mouth" map Hugo territory, a bar or a dead-end Northwest town, a strip of land or a river where such a poet might sing or play his song, however sad and private or public and unruly the music might be. Hugo agrees: "Certainly I was Mad Sam, ringing bells no one responded to, remaining on the scene of a shameful past hoping in time to be accepted" (*The Real West* 11).

That these figures are male is also fitting, for in Hugo's universe, derived from American culture in general and his Depression-era, rough-and-tumble Northwest upbringing in particular, a man's masculinity is always in question. Looking back, William Matthews pointed to Hugo's lack of masculine self-worth, especially as it manifested itself in an early appreciation of "local toughs for their violent courage" or, as he got older, "sardonic movie stars, detective heroes, and British Royal Air Force flyers, who seemed to have a stylish, right manhood" (Hugo *The Real West* xv). Though Hugo becomes an accomplished athlete, he never sheds his self-image as a lonely failure sentimentalized by sexual timidity, a soft body, too much liquor, and tears that come too often and easily. The derelict-poet that Hugo finds in bars and dead-end Northwest towns is himself, as he puts it in "December 24 and George McBride Is Dead," "up from the grime" (*Making Certain* 87).

Not surprisingly, then, squatting at the center of Hugo's aesthetic are class and gender anxieties that he calls on to produce his blue-collar poetry. "That is the crude self I've come to," Hugo writes in "Places and Ways to Live." "The man who says / suffer, stay poor and I can create" (*Making Certain* 235). In "Self-Interview," a sober Hugo expresses some regret: "I began to see that a lot of my grief was old and shopworn and only the booze had kept it alive" (*The Real West* 198). What he also sees is a poet who, like many of his peers, "grew up in poor, often degrading circumstances. . . . We have had to struggle with memories of a working class past and acceptance of a middle class present. . . . The Depression, threats of poverty and dispossession, loyalty to defeated people we still love and desire not to be like, and then a feeling of having violated our lives by wanting to be different—oh, very complicated matters" (*The Real West* 193–94). Even as he maintains the old hurts that are essential to his portraits of "poverty and dispossession," the guilt associated with his having abandoned his past is considerable. He cannot go home again, and he is both bothered and relieved.

If the Northwest provided Hugo with the "anxious fields of play" he needed (ball diamonds, rivers, White Center, rivers, vast Montana and its lonely towns) to do the hard emotional work of finding his place in the world, poetry as Hugo came to practice it—getting, in his words, "tough in the poem" (*The Real West* 110)—gave him a masculinized vocational identity he could live with. To get at that process, the masculinization of an art form an eighth-grade Hugo secretly enjoyed but knew to be girls' stuff, and its product, the body of tough and not-so-tough poetry he left behind, I organize this essay around the three parts of its subtitle: Hugo's blue-collar worry, the economic and emotional or spiritual poverty of Montana Indians, and the tough style he leavened over time with sentiment.

The interrelatedness of these three elements helps us read Hugo's primary "fields of play," the poems that taught him "writing is a slow, cumulative way of accepting your life as valid, of accepting yourself over a lifetime, of realizing that your life is important" (*The Real West* 30). Whatever Hugo lost in leaving White Center, he multiplied in gain as he developed a voice that made him and the University of Montana's creative writing program inseparable and important. *The Lady in Kicking Horse Reservoir* (1973), *What Thou Lovest Well Remains American* (1975), and *31 Letters and 13 Dreams* (1977) form the core of a body of Montana literature that resonates today with a mix of anxiety and play, craft and concern that profits readers, writers, and the region itself.

BLUE COLLARS

By now Hugo's blue-collar credits are as "shopworn" as the grief he amplified with alcohol to reopen wounds, the feelings of being cheated by history and circumstance, of being abandoned, isolated, dispossessed. It is an old story that Hugo self-consciously repeated. A teenage mother, abandoned by her husband, leaves her twenty-month-old son to be raised in a tough neighborhood at the edge of a big city by her strict, quiet parents. The combination of a Depression-era household in which next to nothing was said; a tough, nearly rural Seattle neighborhood, White Center, which "had the reputation of being just outside the boundary of the civilized world" (*The Real West* 8); and the Northwest, which the son also experienced as being "near the edge of civilization, almost out of it" (quoted in Pinsker 55), left him with a highly developed sense of isolation that was intensified by his proximity to the "sources of felt debasement"—the loud steel mill, the polluted river, and the mixed immigrant population—that he shared with classmates from Riverside and Youngstown, who could actually see from their homes the "middle class paradise" of West Seattle, the hill of privilege where they all went to high school (*The Real West* 8). Years later, in his early forties and successful enough as a poet to be hired at the University of Montana, Hugo began experiencing class-bound isolation once again. Feeling like a stranger in the English Department, he found himself a more familiar haunt: "I was going back to an existence I'd known years before. I'd come from plain, naïve working class (even peasant class) people, the kind of people who came into the bar, and it was in that bar I felt at home" (*The Real West* 138).

Hugo's bar makes a very particular kind of home. His drinkers are not the stuff of bootstrap stories, heroically pulling themselves up and into the light of a middle-class paradise. His drinkers generally stay where they are, nursing their sense of isolation together. Consider the "love" and "honest drunks" available at "The Milltown Union Bar." "You were nothing / going in," the speaker says, "and now you kiss your hand" (*Making Certain* 166). Or these lines from "The Only Bar in Dixon":

Home. Home. I knew it entering.
Green cheap plaster and the stores
across the street toward the river
failed. . . .

This is home because some people
go to Perma and come back
from Perma saying Perma
is no fun. . . .
(*Making Certain* 212)

Or this one, "Death of the Kapowsin Tavern," which marks the power of art to reconstruct the lost thing, producing in this case a memory of home that endures:

Nothing dies as slowly as a scene.
The dusty jukebox cracking through
the cackle of a beered-up crone—
wagered wine—sudden need to dance—
these remain in the black debris.
Although I know in time the lake will send
wind black enough to blow it all away.
(*Making Certain* 102)

Erased by time, the Kapowsin Tavern remains every bit as real, Hugo insists, as the first home, the one that complicates matters, that makes escape and success both necessary and difficult. Referring to the West in "Letter to Gale from Ovando," he might as well be talking about White Center: "the brutal part we wave goodbye to / gladly and the honest part we hate to lose" (*Making Certain* 298). Because Hugo himself makes biographical detail, as demonstrated in the essays that comprise *The Triggering Town* and *The Real West Marginal Way*, central to explanations of his poetic work, it makes sense to revisit key details to get at the conflicted feelings played out in poems like "Letter to Gale."

Hugo first left White Center two years out of high school, not long after he legally switched last names, exchanging his biological father's (Hogan) for his mother's married name (Hugo). With a five-year stint in the Army Air Corps under his belt, the first two years of which he spent flying thirty-five missions as a bombardier during World War II, he returned a decorated veteran in 1948 and moved back into his bedroom at his grandparents', in his words, "as if the war represented only an interruption in a life that would know no change"

(*The Real West* 70). Wartime brushes with death, coupled with an absence of sexual experiences that might have encouraged him to move forward with his adult life, reinforced his desire to stay home, play semipro baseball, drink in the evenings, and go to school on the GI Bill instead of getting a job and settling down as his grandfather expected him to: "As it was, I tried to recapture the past. I even played cowboys and Indians with a little boy who lived across the street" (*The Real West* 70). Still, by the time his grandfather died and less than a year before he turned thirty in 1953, Hugo showed all of the signs of settling down into middle-class security: a wife, two college degrees (BA and MA from the University of Washington, where he studied poetry under Theodore Roethke), and a job as a technical writer at Boeing that he was to hold for twelve years.

During this time, he worked at being a poet, something that would have made even less sense to his grandfather, and found enough success publishing in little magazines that by the time he and his wife quit their jobs to spend a year in Italy, ostensibly to revisit the country where he fought in World War II, he had one book of poetry, *A Run of Jacks* (1961), published with the University of Minnesota Press and a second about to be published by Norton as *Death of the Kapowsin Tavern* (1965). This kind of mobility was unusual for Hugo. Years later the poet James Wright, an old friend, drunkenly assailed a university speaker for presuming "that workingclass [*sic*] people enjoyed the same cavalier mobility as upper-middle-class people. That they could change jobs with no emotional complications" (*The Real West* 230). Hugo understood all too well, and had Wright made the working-class claim back during Hugo's first year at the University of Montana, he would have understood the irony of his having quit a secure job to spend his and his wife's life savings for a year abroad without having a job lined up back home afterward. True to his social class, he came to feel anything but "cavalier" about the "mobility" he was exhibiting. The last two months were awful: "My wife and I had grown apart in Italy. The fault was mine. I couldn't hold myself together that far from friends, that uncertain of ever finding employment again. I drank too much, sullen the last two months, walked the streets of Florence in a hopeless state of depression that bordered on psychotic withdrawal" (*The Real West* 135). The marriage would break up and his wife would leave soon after they returned and moved to Missoula so he could take the job.

Though he had the stability of employment and the opportunity for professional success as university poet-professor, he suffered feelings of inadequacy as a teacher, he did not handle single life well, and the English Department failed to deliver the sense of home or familiar honesty he sought out in "plain" or "working class (even peasant class)" bars. In the powerful "Letter to Levertov from Butte," Hugo provides the most direct, extended poetic expression of the "ambiguous feelings" plaguing him. "On one hand," he writes, "no matter what my salary is / or title, I remain a common laborer." From that position, he tells Levertov, he maintains the feelings of humility and inadequacy that keep him connected with those damaged by the world.

> I know the cruelty of poverty, the embittering ways
> love is denied, and food, the mean near-insanity of being
> and being deprived, the trivial compensations of each day
> recapturing old years in broadcast tunes you try to recall
> in bars, hunched over the beer you can't afford, or bending
> to the bad job you're lucky enough to have. How, finally,
> hate takes over, hippie, nigger, Indian, anyone you can lump
> like garbage in a pit, including women. And I don't want
> to be part of it. I want to be what I am, a writer good enough
> to teach with you. . . .
> (*Making Certain* 308)

Caught between two worlds, Hugo's speaker knows where he wants to be, but damaged repeatedly by failed love affairs, bouts of drink, and the sad loneliness that he attributes to blue-collar drinkers, he stays with what he knows or thinks he needs, if only for his art. In "Statements of Faith," a *Triggering Town* essay, Hugo explains the problem with an anecdote about Faulkner. When asked why he keeps drinking, Faulkner responds, "For the pain." Hugo's reading of that response is not that alcohol numbs the pain but that it might "keep it alive" (*Triggering Town* 72). Hugo tries to do just that.

INDIANS

Before ending the Levertov letter-poem with apologies and assurances, the speaker makes one last stark admission that nods to the pain-for-profit anecdote:

> And I want my life
> inside to go on long as I do, though I only populate bare
> landscape with surrogate suffering, with lame men
> crippled by more than disease, and create finally
> a simple grief I can deal with. . . .
> (*Making Certain* 308)

Hugo depends on "suffering" for the "simple grief" he creates out of the psychologically or emotionally crippled figures, the derelicts who double for the suffering poet. Reconsider the scene in "The Only Bar in Dixon," one of Hugo's most famous Montana poems, and notice the Indians:

> Home. Home. I knew it entering.
> Green cheap plaster and the stores
> across the street toward the river
> failed. One Indian depressed
> on Thunderbird. Another buying
> Thunderbird to go. . . .
>
> This is home because some people
> go to Perma and come back
> from Perma saying Perma
> is no fun. . . .
> (*Making Certain* 212)

As Donna Gerstenberger writes, "In the Montana book [*The Lady in Kicking Horse Reservoir*], Indians become central symbols for the dispossessed and despairing" (25). To Gerstenberger's critique, Sanford Pinsker adds that the Montana Indians are "grotesque extensions" of Hugo (78). In "A Night at the Napi in Browning," what Hugo sees is degradation, human waste:

> Two pass out
> unnoticed on the floor. One answers to a cop
> for children left five hours in a car.
> (*Making Certain* 208)

Beaten by his aunt, a "brave . . . grovels now / in puke and odd hymns at [the speaker's] feet." The Napi is not the inviting bar in Dixon. The speaker, however well-intentioned, may walk into the Napi for what he assumes are the right reasons. He may think that he and the other drinkers share a sense of dispossession, a class wound that will make him feel at home, but he learns quickly that he is wrong, that this bar is not his home and will never be, that the derelict-poet's puke-ridden "odd hymns" are more desperate, more beaten down, that all dispossessions are not the same, that terms like "blue collar" or "working class" are not synonyms for "Indian."

Although the speaker finds common ground ("It never ends, this brutal way we crack / our lives across our backs. With luck / we'll be soft derelicts. . . ."), he also knows that he is white ("the first words spoken 'white man' / split my tongue") and has become middle class and can do nothing to reverse the process:

> And I, a Mercury outside, a credit card,
> a job, a faded face—what should I do?
> Go off shaggy to the mountains,
> a spot remote enough to stay unloved
> and die in flowers, stinking like a bear?
> (*Making Certain* 208)

The imagined self-removal in the last three lines, the poet going derelict, emulates the actual movement of the squatter and his wife, via company truck and driver, to a "remote country road in the dark" of the Monroe Valley, where the squatter claims to own land he cannot find (*Triggering Town* 108). The dream of refusal, of rejecting privilege or trading one advantage (financial security) for another (raw honesty), is the dream of return to the original home, a gesture as empty as it is self-indulgent. It is too late for Hugo's speaker to get "shaggy" like the homeless, wild-haired Admiral, too late to scream "the wildest, most primitive phrases" of class injustice anywhere but "alone in the mirror" or isolated in mountain flowers. The Admiral might as well have been talking about Hugo's speaker when he wrote the letters to his evictor: "You may be making millions of dollars but there will be a day when you won't be. I am still suffering from some of your dirty work. I know the kind of man you are and the rest of your so-called class. I don't like white-collared folks very well. I've mostly been with Navajo Indians and Mexicans when I was a kid amongst the Eskimos. All this I can prove" (*Triggering Town* 106). In the eyes of the squatter, social markers like the Mercury, the credit card, and the job would all register as white collar, not the blue collar of the speaker's (and Hugo's) self-image. The squatter has earned the credentials the speaker wants, the ticket that would get him into every "green cheap plaster" Northwest bar, Indian or not, he can find.

In "Letter to Welch from Browning," Hugo reworks the material in "A Night at the Napi in Browning." The speaker has traveled north to find a woman he knows. What he finds instead is a tavern with no other white in it:

> A scene of raw despair. Indians
> sleeping on the filthy floor. Men with brains scrambled in wine.
> A man who sobbed all night, who tried in strangled desperation
> to articulate the reason. . . .
> (*Making Certain* 299)

Whether this derelict language constitutes the "wildest, most primitive" poetic phrasing of all, body noise as protest song that needs no words, or it fails miserably because it cannot finger the cause or causes of its inarticulation, here is Hugo at his most articulate, using a derelict-poet double to voice his concern about "the cruelty of poverty" and what comes of it: "the mean near-insanity of being / and being deprived." Here is the cause of their pain, and the best they can do is make their separate noises as they go into the dark.

To Hugo's credit, he understands his attraction to figures like The Admiral and the Napi poet just as he recognizes the qualitative differences in the noises of deprivation each of them, Hugo included, make. All derelict-poets are not equal. While the roster Hugo compiles of those damaged by disadvantage and isolation is open to all, some are more prominently featured on the list than others, their pain more deeply engrained, less easily bandaged by formal education and the offer of a white-collar job, a credit card, and the keys to a Mercury. At the top of Hugo's list is the Indian, and despite the plea in "Letter to Hill from St. Ignatius" ("Friend, let me be Indian" [*Making Certain* 292]), Hugo rarely goes native. He consistently maintains an honest distance from which he might glean pieces of truth about the particularities of Indian history and the attendant pain. In "Indian Graves at Jocko," for instance, Hugo's speaker takes the position of sympathetic white tourist as he observes and mourns the dead in unsentimental language:

> A forlorn lot like this, where snow
> must crawl to find the tribal stones,
> is more than just a grim result of cheat,
> Garfield's forgery, some aimless trek
> of horses from the stolen Bitter Root.
> Dead are buried here because the dead
> will always be obscure, wind
> the one thing whites will always give a chance.
> (*Making Certain* 180)

In "Bear Paw," wind, "infantile and cruel," continues to have its way with the landscape while the speaker advises us to "study" the battlefield's "books" and "plaques," to read both Indian and white names, to appreciate the difference, to "[l]earn what you can. The wind / takes all you learn away to reservation graves" (*Making Certain* 215).

Hugo's treatment of Indians deepens in the Montana poems. Although Indians make an occasional appearance in his first two books, they do so as faceless figures indistinguishable from each other. The Indians he gives us in *The Lady in Kicking Horse Reservoir* and the books that follow take on a "sense of cultural and historical identity" (Gerstenberger 25). As he does in poems like "Bear Paw" and "With Ripley at the Grave of Albert Parenteau," in which he locates specific Indians (Chief Joseph, Parenteau) in specific historical time, he locates real Indians in "The Only Bar in Dixon," "A Night at the Napi in Browning," and "Letter to Welch from Browning," giving them characteristics that allow us to see them as members of a community, as individuals experiencing their dispossession separately and together. Ironically, "The Only Bar in Dixon" was born over drinks with a Blackfeet/Gros Ventre Indian, friend and former student James Welch, whom Hugo lovingly addresses at the end of "Letter to Welch from Browning" as Chief Boiling Whiskey:

> [O]ne afternoon, they went on an ice fishing trip together with J. D. Reed. They stopped by a bar in the town of Dixon afterwards, and under the influence of a few drinks, they exuberantly challenged one another to write a poem about the bar. They set a deadline of two weeks, and pledged that the three poems had to be published simultaneously in one magazine. "The title of the poems was 'The Only Bar in Dixon,'" Welch recalls. "Somehow we sent it out to *The New Yorker* on a fluke, and they took them and printed all three in the same issue." Thus began Welch's somewhat improbable career as a poet. (Lee 194)

James Welch's success as a novelist adds a layer to Hugo's treatment of Montana and its Indians that has deepened over time. The intimacy and unflinching humor implicit in the address of James Welch as Chief Boiling Whiskey marks a toughness in Hugo's style that admits "emotional need" (Allen 40).

TOUGH STYLE

"A Map of Montana in Italy," which opens *The Lady in Kicking Horse Reservoir*, draws a picture of the "state thick as a fist / or blunt instrument" (*Making Certain* 165). The Italians watching Westerns in "A Map" do not see that Montana. The one they see has already disappeared into the Hollywood imaginary that Hugo denies in "Letter to Gale from Ovando" when he writes, "I, not John Wayne, put the villains away / to rest, mark the headstones 'no one' and start another poem" (*Making Certain* 298). Refusing to let Montana go Western in the usual Cowboy-and-Indian way, Hugo describes an updated violence:

> With so few Negroes and Jews we've been reduced
> to hating each other, dumping our crud
> in our rivers, mistreating the Indians.
> (*Making Certain* 165)

Hugo's Montana is a tough place, vast ("When your sister's raped / help is out of range" [*Making Certain* 209]), harsh ("Last night, 20 below" [*Making Certain* 301]), abusive ("[They] get hurt early. Degraded by drab homes. Beaten by drunken / parents, by other children" [*Making Certain* 307]), and economically depressed ("The principal supporting business now / is rage" [*Making Certain* 216]). Even when a town experiences some success, the result is predictably dispiriting:

> The two biggest towns are dull deposits
> of men getting along, making money, driving
> to church every Sunday, censoring movies and books.
> (*Making Certain* 165)

If Montana, like White Center, is brutal, it is also honest and offers the potential for community. In "Letter to Goldbarth from Big Fork," Hugo describes:

> Montana at its best, lake
> next to town, lovely mountains close by, and independent
> people, friendly, generous, always a discernible touch
> of the amateur I like. Nothing slick. Montana is
> the rest of America 50 years back. . . .
> (*Making Certain* 310)

It is also a state dotted with "forlorn towns / just hanging on" that remind the speaker of the 1930s (*Making Certain* 311). Hugo is, as Michael S. Allen describes him, a product of the Great Depression and arguably its finest poet: "Opposing the self-confidence of Thoreau and the unquenchable optimism of Whitman, the underside of Hugo's American town is marked by fear, need, and neglect, where even the failed romantic notions of the past have given way to the hardness of historical, economic, and physical facts" (20).

"Letter to Goldbarth" paints the picture of Depression-era poverty and pain that we expect from Hugo. These Montanans have had "nothing from the beginning, never expected a thing, / accept cruelty, weather and man, as normal." Yet, as Allen points out, it is in this poem that Hugo calls them "my women, my men" and declares his Montana citizenship:

And I, who came from the seacoast,
who love the salmon, the damp air of Seattle, finally
have come to call this home. . . .
(*Making Certain* 311)

Hugo's Montana, like Hugo, is rooted in a Depression ethic that makes toughness necessary. It is that toughness that attracts Hugo and becomes an essential part of his aesthetic.

His anxiety, established in boyhood, over what constituted masculine and feminine behavior—women, for instance, liking church and men basketball (*The Real West* 21)—affected the way he thought about poetry. His early (and, to his mind, girlish) love of Tennyson's "The Brook," with its sentimentality and rippling rhythms, becomes his later manly love of Bernard Spencer's "poetic roughness" and "simple, direct validation of his relations with the world, often made crudely but honestly" (*The Real West* 153–54). In "Small Waters and Tiny Worlds," Hugo follows a poem of his own, "Northwest Retrospective: Mark Tobey," with this claim: "A space traveler would write the poem. An Indian. But above all, a tough man, who opted for reality over sentimentality" (*The Real West* 171). About "1614 Boren," Hugo writes, "What a tough guy speaks in the poem. You wouldn't fool with anyone who says, 'The world has water and the world has sperm.' He's right there, engaged with the real all the way" (*The Real West* 174). Poetry then was risky business not just because it might forfeit a White Center boy his blue-collar union card but also because it might make him a sissy.

The case of Wallace Stevens, modernist forefather and subject of the *Triggering Town* essay "Those Days I Was and Wasn't Wallace Stevens," is instructive. Although Stevens came from a different class and region than Hugo, he would have understood Hugo's reservations. About the effects of similar anxiety on Stevens, Frank Lentricchia points out that even though Stevens must have understood that "great," or canonized, poetry was primarily a masculine pursuit, he feared his practice of it was unmasculine. In a letter to his future wife, Stevens describes his behavior as effeminate: "I sit home o' nights. But I read very little. I have, in fact, been trying to get together a little collection of verses again. . . . There is something absurd about all this writing of verses; but the truth is, it elates and satisfies me to do it. It is an all-round exercise quite superior to ordinary reading. So that, you see, my habits are positively lady-like" (quoted in Lentricchia 138). The implications are clear. During the day he leaves to make money as other men do; in the evening he stays home to make verses as some ladies make doilies. Although the last line might be read ironically—the pride in his evening work neutralizing, if not overpowering, the self-deprecation—Stevens's anxiety is real. His evening practice of poetry threatens to undo the daily maintenance of his masculinity.

The response of Hugo to his own fear that art, or the practice of it, feminizes men is to masculinize it as many of his literary forefathers (e.g., Jack London and Ernest Hemingway) had done, by developing a tough style and linking it to a set of practices (traveling, fishing, playing ball) that make him a tough guy. One of those is modernist writing, in Hugo's (and Stevens's) case poetry, the aesthetic typically pitched as "firm, hard, dry, terse, classical masculinity, over against the messy, soft, vague, flowery, effusive, adjectival femininity of the late Victorians" (DeKoven 176). Anxious about his masculinity, Hugo fantasized about being a tough guy like Humphrey Bogart, "strong" and "in control." "My urge to be someone adequate," Hugo writes in "Ci Vediamo," an essay collected in both *The Real West Marginal Way* and *The Triggering Town*, "didn't change after the war. . . . A sissy in life, I would be tough in the poem." The example he gives is "Index," an early poem with a voice he calls "definite" and "strong": "And I even took a private pride in the difficulty of the poem" (*The Real West* 110–11; *Triggering Town* 79–81). Note the past tense. Hugo "took." In an early poem like "Duwamish," he used "language hard enough to prohibit wallowing in melancholy" (*The Real West* 17). And about "Duwamish No. 2," he admits, "I don't like the poem much, but the last stanza demonstrates a tough way of addressing myself. Those 'vague eyes' I wanted to escape were the eyes of nineteenth century sentiment I'd inherited from my grandparents" (*The Real West* 13).

It is, in fact, the failure of his flight from sentiment, his self-imposed prohibition against melancholy, that makes his poetry so powerful, so affecting, so human. In "Writing Off the Subject," a *Triggering Town* essay full of writing instruction, the mature Hugo makes a claim a young Hugo would not have: "All art that has endured has a quality we call schmaltz or corn. Our reaction against the sentimentality embodied in Victorian and post-Victorian writing was so resolute writers came to believe that the further from sentimentality we got, the truer the art. That was a mistake. As Bill Kittredge, my colleague who teaches fiction writing, has pointed out: if you are not *risking* sentimentality, you are not close to your inner self" (7). "Inner self" is what Hugo is after. During an interview in which he calls the opening lines of "The Lady in Kicking Horse Reservoir" "very nasty" and the speaker "very hard," he describes that moment in the poem when the voice changes: "Then, of course, and as so often happens in my poems, I get closer to what I really am, deeper in the poem; a couple of stanzas later I'm saying, 'Sorry. Sorry. Sorry' and I become the soft slob I really am at heart" (quoted in Allen 36).

Recall his charge that "writing is a slow, cumulative way of accepting your life as valid" (*The Real West* 30). Part of that acceptance in Hugo involves the inevitability of, even the desire for, tears, the unmanly, un-Bogartlike activity that, at the end of "Ci Vediamo," becomes what he needs, "a good cry," an exchange of "sob for strangulated sob" (*The Real West* 129). About Elia Kazan's *Man on a Tight Rope* (1952), he writes, "I've seen the movie about twenty-five times, more than any other, and I'm not ashamed to admit that I cry every time I see it" (*The Real West* 84). A cold war film pitting a circus of "freaks, outcasts, forlorns" against "Communist bureaucracy" (*The Real West* 88, 84), *Man on a Tight Rope* is also a perfect example of what Tom Lutz calls a "male weepie," a subgenre of filmic melodrama especially popular in the 1950s when so many men felt they were being hemmed in by the corporatization of America (194). The tears Hugo sheds at the movies, like those he sheds in "Ci Vediamo," do him good both because they allow the release of pent-up emotion and because they help him develop an emotional style more expressive of his need than the hard masculinity he once imagined to be the solution to his problems.

Hugo's West is not Owen Wister's, Frederic Remington's, or Theodore Roosevelt's, easterners all. Hugo's are not the "tough, emotionless, cowboy figures who inspired American fighting men during World War II" (Allen 84). Consider the scene at the end of "December 24 and George McBride Is Dead," a poem from Hugo's second collection:

> I get along, write my poems. Essentially
> a phony, I try my feelings now
> and know I fail. George, it's Christmas eve
> and the bells are caroling. I'm in the kitchen,
> fat and writing, drinking beer and shaking.
> (*Making Certain* 87)

Compare the treatment of feelings, the "shaking," to the admission he delivers in his sixth book in "Letter to Peterson from the Pike Place Market":

> Today, I am certain,
> for all the terrible mistakes I did the right thing
> to love places and scenes in my innocent way and to spend
> my life writing poems, to receive like a woman

the world in its enduring decay and to tell
that world like a man that I am not afraid to weep
at the sadness, the ongoing day that is draining our life
and is life. Sorry. Got carried away. . . .
(*Making Certain* 289)

Less interested in hard surfaces, Hugo commits himself in his later books to a voice that admits feeling, honest emotion, and tears and exhibits, according to Donna Gerstenberger, "a greater ease and acceptance of the world than one finds in the earlier ones." Hugo's speaker, Gerstenberger adds, "no longer seems so much to be the lonely and tough Western traveler, the searcher obsessed by a need to lay claim to a territory and people it with the ghosts of its difficult past" (29). Indeed, Hugo seems more interested in unpeopling the troubled parts of that territory, in making amends with his past, in opening up. One such ghost is his grandfather's. Not long after the old man dies, Hugo happens to spot his old Model A while commuting from work in someone else's car. Had he been traveling alone, he would have pulled over and taken it all in: "I would have tried to dream back a lot of moments and relive them without shame, fear or anger. And I would have abandoned any idea of separating the sentimentality I'd inherited and knew was crippling from the honest affection for life I knew I didn't ever want to lose. If I found I couldn't weep, I would have waited and remembered until I could because I believe some things and some moments deserve our tears" (*The Real West* 81). In those tears that did not come, in the "sob for strangulated sob" exchanged with the old Italian acquaintance from World War II, in the "strangled desperation" of the Napi derelict-poet's all-night sobbing, in all this sentimental risk resides the potential for release and repair, what Michael S. Allen describes as Hugo's belief in "the importance of human connection" (88).

NOT SO TOUGH AFTER ALL

Hugo is a complex case. Looking back at a magazine that published some of his early poems, he takes a "perverse delight" in the picture of himself on the cover in his "Boeing All-Star softball shirt," positioned as it is among "the pictures of the other contributors, some of them terribly affected (face half hidden by smoke in the coffeehouse gloom)" (*The Real West* 45). Yet, as readily as he does not want to look like a poet, he wants thoroughly to be one. Pointing to the self-contradiction, he admits that "inside the magazine [his] poems, along with reproductions of the paintings that had triggered them, were by far the artiest items there" (*The Real West* 45–46). As he explains in "Letter to Levertov," he wants to "remain a common laborer." He wants to maintain the feeling of inadequacy caused by the class "hurt" ("the mean near-insanity of being / and being deprived") he incurred while young even as he maintains his adult position as a university poet-professor hobnobbing with the likes of Levertov and Isaac Bashevis Singer.

Drawn to failure because of the human connections failure engenders in Montana's blue-collar bars and restaurants (think of the young waitress who, in "Degrees of Gray in Philipsburg," "serves you food / is slender and her red hair lights the walls" [*Making Certain* 217]), he also finds failure interesting because it is so often experienced in isolation. He explains: "The dignity and self sufficiency I longed for, I found on the baseball and softball fields, or when I was alone" (*The Real West* 5–6). He found them also in the poems he wrote while "standing off, sort of at the edge of things" (*The Real West* 162). A few years before his death, while revisiting his old neighborhood with director Annick Smith for the film *Kicking the Loose Gravel Home* (1977), Hugo found himself standing outside his grandparents' old house and talking to the tenant, a sad man he saw as the drunk he might have become had he never left. In "Doing the House," Hugo melds with the tenant who lives in disconnect, another derelict-poet, and serves as the perfect vehicle for Hugo's aesthetic. Girding the poem with the hard language of "last night's bad wine," "scrub hawthorne," and "every ten minutes / fresh diesel fumes," Hugo earns the soft he delivers so powerfully in the poem's middle:

> It's nice of the last man here
> to let me come in. I want to tell him
> he's me, menial job at the door plant,
> table set just barely for one. . . .
> (*Making Certain* 325–27)

Former student Larry Levinger writes,

> Every now and then Richard Hugo came across as a man in want of forgiveness and a man in earnest to forgive. This vulnerability registered at deep levels, and I believe his students thrived for their unconscious accessibility to it. One poet told me his whole orientation to his work and its purpose changed the day Hugo, during a workshop, described a group of homeless people thrown off Boeing Company land, where he had worked for many

> years. Telling this story to a workshop of some twenty writers, Hugo began to sob, and dismissed the class. One poet remarked: "Hugo's workshops are like church." (50)

Hugo makes a similar claim in "Self-Interview": "We need writing classes the way we once needed churches, because, simplistic as it sounds, that's where we can reveal our feelings and admit they are important to us" (*The Real West* 193). It is there, in the sentiment, or tears, that Hugo folds into his early tough style, into his Montana of blue collars and troubled Indians, that his not-so-tough poetry works, its power not weakened by the addition of naked emotion but strengthened by it. "All art that has endured," Hugo still teaches us, "has a quality we call schmaltz or corn." Hugo endures because he risked failure.

WORKS CITED

Allen, Michael S. *The Poetry of Richard Hugo*. Fayetteville: University of Arkansas Press, 1982.

Bevis, William W. *Ten Tough Trips: Montana Writers and the West*. Seattle: University of Washington Press, 1990.

DeKoven, Marianne. "Modernism and Gender." *The Cambridge Companion to Modernism*. Ed. Michael Levenson. New York: Cambridge University Press, 1999. 174–93.

Garber, Frederick. "Fat Man at the Margin: The Poetry of Richard Hugo." *The Iowa Review* 3, 4 (1972): 58–67.

Gerstenberger, Donna. *Richard Hugo*. Western Writers Series 59. Boise: Boise State University Press, 1983.

Hugo, Richard. *Making Certain It Goes On: The Collected Poems of Richard Hugo*. New York: Norton, 1984.

———. *The Real West Marginal Way: A Poet's Autobiography*. Ed. Ripley S. Hugo, Lois Welch, and James Welch. New York: Norton, 1986.

———. *The Triggering Town: Lectures and Essays on Poetry and Writing*. New York: Norton, 1979.

Lee, Don. "About James Welch: A Profile." *Ploughshares* 20, 1 (1994): 193–99.

Levinger, Larry. "Poet Richard Hugo: The Open Field Beyond." *Ploughshares* 18, 1 (1992): 33–58.

Lutz, Tom. "Men's Tears and the Roles of Melodrama." *Boys Don't Cry?: Rethinking Narratives of Masculinity and Emotion in the U.S.* Ed. Milette Shamir and Jennifer Travis. New York: Columbia University Press, 2002. 185–204.

Pinsker, Sanford. *Three Pacific Northwest Poets: William Stafford, Richard Hugo, and David Wagoner*. Twayne's United States Authors Series 506. Boston: Twayne, 1987.

CHAPTER TWELVE
Semicolonial Moments: The History and Influence of the University of Montana Creative Writing Program

LOIS M. WELCH

What do you *do* out there?
—Mark Strand

"Why Does Montana Have So Many Good Writers?" asked a 2002 Internet review of Judy Blunt's memoir *Breaking Clean*. The reviewer, not surprisingly, didn't answer this frequently asked question. While there may be no good answer,[1] several possibilities converge to sketch a picture of the University of Montana creative writing program as a strong influence on Montana writing, and as a nexus for writers—local, regional, nationally recognized—at conferences, workshops, and readings. Growing visibility of its writing faculty and the success of its graduates have brought the program increasing recognition: in the 1997 *US News and World Report* national ranking of creative writing programs, the University of Montana's ranked among the top ten.[2]

My focus here is on the influence of the program on *Montana* writing,[3] but that influence extends so far that I would conclude with a discussion of the French fascination with Montana writers, were there space to do so. The very category, "Montana writing," has fuzzy edges. Montana may epitomize the West in the national imagination, but it is hard to distinguish between, say, Terry Tempest Williams's writing (Utah based) or Kim Barnes's (Idaho based, University of Montana trained) and Judy Blunt's eastern Montana-based writing. Further, while my focus is on the creative writing program as a unit, that program's influence derives from individual writing faculty, from its students, and from an ambiance established early on. Additionally, some Montana writers graduated from the program and taught frequently in it (e.g., David Long) and some never (Ford or Doig); either sort may be part of the writing community. Many so-called Montana writers (like Bill Kittredge) are not *from* Montana; some Montana writers (like Ivan Doig) *no longer* live here; some Montana writers publish only in Montana *for* Montanans (for example, Rick Newby); some *never* published in Montana (such as Hugo and Welch). Some nationally recognized writers live in Montana but don't mingle with local writers (e.g., Jeff Shaara).[4] Several nationally recognized writers lived here for a time, then left (Richard Ford, Beverly Lowry, William Pitt Root; Lowry and Root taught in the program). As the creative writing program has gained national reputation, fewer and fewer of its students are native Montanans, so its influence is inevitably becoming more national and more difficult to categorize.[5] Further, an important effect like the Hugo House, a nonprofit community center for writers and readers in Seattle, must be credited directly to their native son Richard Hugo's influence, and only indirectly to that of the University of Montana's creative writing program. Whether we discuss direct or indirect influence, however, it's a good story. It is a story with two semicolonial beginnings, rather than just one, and a lot of good stories along the way.

My claim is that the University of Montana's creative writing program is now and has been since its inception a complex positive influence on both the university and the state, providing a welcoming community for writers and one of several cultural bridges between Montanans and their university, itself part of national intellectual culture.[6] The university's creative writing program is of particular interest, I believe, because it is older than most, and thus imbricated in the state's culture.[7] Faculty and graduates of the program have helped shape new generations of writers and readers in Montana, around the country, perhaps even internationally.[8] The gauge of influence must, of course, include more than publications and personal connections. Many graduates teach in high schools or universities, some teaching creative writing, some literature and writing. Graduates contribute to Montana literary culture by involvement in activities considered less "artistic," such as writing grants, computer programs, and academic reports.[9] Other graduates have day jobs and write on the side.[10] As a community, Missoula encourages and values its writers: witness the annual Montana Festival of the Book (offering sixty Montana writers to five thousand participants in 2006), numerous book groups, and public readings at the university, in bookstores, and at cafés. The Missoula Writing Collaborative, a nonprofit organization, sends writers into more than a dozen local schools each year; the majority of these writers are graduates or students in the MFA program. The *Missoulian* used to cover most literary events as front-page news; it still covers a few. Though there are writers in a city like Billings, for example, it lacks such a concentrated literary ambiance.[11] Until the 1970s, Garden City News, owned by Art and Mary Evans, served as an important downtown literary resource; Barbara Theroux's independent bookstore, Fact and Fiction, staunchly serves the same purpose, sponsoring regular readings, largely by regional writers. Shakespeare and Co. has recently joined the scene. Missoula is on the national and international map as a place with a far higher ratio of writers to citizenry than usual.[12] National attention to Montana writers increased dramatically in the 1970s, while intense international attention was a phenomenon of the 1990s. The University of Montana creative writing program always gets a portion of that attention.[13]

How did this reputation come about? While the University of Montana's creative writing program cannot take total credit for the books written by its graduates, it should take credit for creating an environment that nurtured them. Several Montana writers (Guthrie, McNickle, Welch) might not have become writers without that institutional support.[14] The program created a congenial institutional, and ultimately, a *cultural* space for those writers.[15] H. G. Merriam first carved out this space, Warren Carrier doubled its institutional proportions, Richard Hugo enlarged it, and Kittredge made it environmentally aware. Madeline DeFrees diversified it. The parties made it fun. Harold's Bar Cafe and Laundromat in Milltown and Eddie's Club (later Charlie's) in downtown Missoula became points of pilgrimage.

CULTURE AND MARGINALITY

> Who is Mildred Walker and what is she? The fine writing of *Winter Wheat* causes me to ask this for there are signs of a kind of culture in the writer—somewhat unusual.
>
> —Letter to Harcourt Brace & Co. from a Mrs. Olive Snider, 1944

My epigraph above from Mrs. Snider at the Vanderbilt Hotel in New York City to Mildred Walker's publishers epitomizes a fairly common eastern condescension toward books written in the West about the West. Wheat and "culture" may have seemed antithetical in 1944; the contrasts are cloaked in more postmodern terminology these days. Mildred Walker was a nationally known writer, educated at Wells College and the University of Michigan, who married a doctor and moved to Montana where she published ten novels. She matters to this history both as a Montana writer and as Richard Hugo's mother-in-law. Such hybrid pedigrees abound.

Now is a good moment to examine the influence of the University of Montana creative writing program because we are all postmodern in our recognition of the constructedness of positions that have previously been accepted as "natural." Bill Kittredge regularly prefaces discussions with a reminder that our invented stories keep us going.[16] The image of Montana as the Wild West, all macho and cowboy boots, has been both a help and a hindrance to writers, as it has to most Montanans. On the one hand they can luxuriate in their bumpkinhood, scuff their shoes and say "aw shucks"—getting off the competitive hook. On the other, they can employ their reading, travel, and acquired culture to whatever end they choose.[17] Postcolonial double-consciousness haunts us all.

"The Last Best Place," title of the monumental 1988 anthology of Montana writing, expresses both the value of Montana as frontier and the fragility of its good qualities. It may not be remote *enough* any longer. Montana is remote from centers of power, sparsely populated, and poor (ranking 46th to 50th in most economic categories[18]). These factors lead outsiders to expect little in the way of sophistication and cultural achievement.[19] Hilarious examples abound.

For example, in 2002 a publicity person from her New York publisher tried to persuade Judy Blunt to wear *chaps* to her New York reading from her memoir *Breaking Clean*! In 2000, during a winter writing residency, non-Montana novelist Joy William was actually asked by her agent if she was seeing Marlboro men on Missoula streets—meaning cowboys on horseback. (Not in pickups, on horseback.) As recently as March 23, 2003, a reviewer from the *Baltimore Sun* described a writer now living in the state as having left "civilization" for Montana.[20]

Montanans live a constant counterpoint to the imagined West of outsiders. "The actual West and the imagined West are engaged in a constant conversation; each influences the other" (White 614–15). Montana regularly serves the country as a kind of cultural Timbuktu, an inland antipode, a repository of exotic escapes from "real" (read: hectic, noisy) metropolitan life. The more sophisticated the Montanan, the more self-conscious the counterpoint becomes: James Welch used a (brand-new) canvas fishing creel as attaché case on his 1974 trip to New York, something he would never have done in Missoula. In the case of Native Americans, this counterpoint is doubled: they cannot but be aware of the imaginary Indians they are expected to be, even as they try to make their way in a society that wishes they would disappear.[21] Isolation, on the other hand, leads people to develop their own culture, which in turn can lead to (unique) artistic expression.

We should not belabor stereotypes, however much fun they are; they preclude livelier analytical categories. Precisely because Montana is so sparsely populated, the university has been more influential than it might have been where there were more cultural institutions. Needless to say, the university serves the usual functions of providing a livelihood and intellectual companionship. Wallace Stegner, writer and founder of the Stanford Creative Writing Program (1947), suggested why, in the United States, a university is a good place to teach creative writing: "Within the academy, which is itself a sort of monastic sanctuary in the cultural darkness, [the writing teacher] can encourage—and perhaps create a substitute for the places that more developed societies have created: the Mermaid Taverns and Hampstead pubs. In a university, people of similar interests and comparable talents can get together and knock sparks off each other" (11).

Let us ignore for the moment the many publike venues in Missoula.[22] The University of Montana has served as a place to "knock sparks off each other" in "the cultural darkness" from its founding in 1893. One positive "spark": Prof. H. G. Merriam and his creative writing students started publishing Montana's first literary magazine, *Frontier*, in 1920. Sometimes the sparks flew among the university, the governor, or the Company (as the Anaconda Copper Company was often called), and political consequences ensued. For example, H. G. Merriam was summarily dismissed as a "troublemaker" in 1939; he returned after a year's teaching at the University of Oregon, when his dismissal was redefined as a "leave." Professor (1941–1964) and prolific writer Leslie Fiedler was called an "intellectual firecracker," even by his admirers, for his joyously iconoclastic views; Fiedler clearly loved the commotion that often ensued.[23] By definition, the university is a nexus, a place where people and influences come together—and *from which* influences and people disperse, radiating outward into that "cultural darkness"—or at least into the literal distance surrounding Missoula. Let us call the University of Montana a remote but sparky nexus.[24]

SPARKY NEXUS VS. ACADEMIC GULAG

> In 1941, straitjacketed in his new doctorate, the burly [Leslie] Fiedler was bundled by implacable Fate into the train that would haul him off kicking and fuming to the academic Gulag in Montana.
>
> —Hugh Kenner, "Who Was Leslie Fiedler," 69

While some might view the University of Montana in postcolonial terms, looking at Montana as a former colony of the eastern United States—a resource rather than a center of culture—others might use Ashcroft, Griffiths, and Tiffin's term, "settler colony."[25] Recent postcolonial theory (Bhaba, Spivak, et al.) suggests that the relations of center and margin are important to Empire; we could examine the development of Montana writing in a postcolonial light: as resistance to eastern hegemony, as primarily representational, as historically grounded, as reversing the relative advantages of center and margin. The fascination of the hegemonic (eastern, urban) culture with the indigenous and the remote (consider the Western Myth, Mythic Montana, and the Noble Savage) has increased from the 1970s through the end of the twentieth century. The sophistication of the westerner has increased apace.[26]

That Montana has been and still is considered a colony of sorts is indisputable. Not so long ago, *Newsweek* magazine called the six states of the Inland West "colonies," finding them subject to the whims of OPEC, wheat futures in China, and other forces beyond its control (October 9, 1988). Its real "subalterns" (the subordinated native population in postcolonialist parlance)—in this case, Montana's Native American population—had already been sidelined entirely by reservations, smallpox, and lack of education by 1893. The colonial predicament referred to by historians and, here, *Newsweek*, casts the current immigrant/settler population as subalterns, subject to economic forces beyond their control.

While it's handy to enumerate instances where Montana is considered absent or empty, neither the term *colonial* nor *postcolonial* quite applies to Montana. To talk of the influence of the university and its creative writing program is already to talk of a culture brought to the region after the defeat and forced sequestration of the indigenous inhabitants. Even the term *settler*—as in "settling the West"—suggests an emptiness just waiting to be filled. The Native people in the West, of course, did not consider their region empty, nor did they consider themselves uncivilized—since their cultural indicators weren't permanent dwellings, for example, or rolling wheat fields.

Historically, the lands west of the Mississippi River were Hispanic. The 1803 Louisiana Purchase added 828,000 square miles to the United States, though the Spanish territory still extended to what is now the southern boundary of Oregon, Idaho, and Utah. The Oregon country, claimed by the British, Russians, and Spanish, became part of the United States in 1848. Montana still figured on maps as "unorganized territory" until it became the Montana Territory in 1864. It became a state in 1889.

To regard Montana as a colony, either literally or metaphorically, has long been a habit among those analyzing the state's history. K. Ross Toole, historian and professor at the University of Montana for many years, wrote: "Nature, not the evil designs of men, decreed that Montana be a place with a colonial economy. The object of [white] men had been to trap it, mine it, shoot it, and get out. Every one of the salient industries has been extractive, from beaver through beef to copper. The capital required for frantic exploitation, whether of furs, cattle, silver, lumber, or copper, had to come from the East. And as eastern capital flowed westward, control and the bulk of the wealth flowed eastward" (9). The founding of the Montana University system in 1893 came in the middle of Montana's transition from wilderness to industrialization in the two decades from 1883 to 1900 (Toole 166). The university system was founded with four units to accommodate students from the various parts of the state. This step helped close the gap that educated folks perceived between Montana and the East Coast. It was also a quasi-colonizing move between center and margin, since the administration and faculty were of necessity imported from centers of learning (i.e., the East Coast). The first courses in creative writing were taught in 1919. The university then boasted 1,442 students, 205 from other states and 10 international students.

THE FIRST BEGINNING OF CREATIVE WRITING: THE MERRIAM YEARS, 1919–1954

Born in 1883 and raised in Colorado, Harold Guy "H.G." Merriam received a BA in science and the classics from the University of Wyoming in 1905. He went to Oxford for four years as part of the first class of Rhodes Scholars (BA 1907, MA 1911). In 1919 Merriam arrived to teach at the University of Montana.[27] His first creative writing class—"Practice in writing literary types, with instruction in literary conception and execution"—was taught that fall.[28]

While later creative writing teachers have considered their courses professional training, Merriam believed such courses primarily made students more aware and better readers. He wrote, "The teacher of creative writing is teaching that subject primarily in order to help students keep alert their senses, their feeling and thought, their awareness of life. He also helps them to see life in terms of expression. He is recognizing and helping students to realize that keeping the mind, the imagination, the senses agile is a most important objective for education. . . . The students of creative writing need most of all to be helped to *see*" ("Who" 465).

A tall, gaunt, affable man, Merriam chaired the English Department from 1919 until his retirement in 1954. He remained actively involved in literary and artistic affairs until his death in 1980. (Fittingly enough, during his first years in Missoula he and his wife lived in the very apartment where Bill Kittredge has lived for two decades.) Merriam was a persistent if not particularly gifted writer: he wrote four books, including a history of the university (1970), wrote many book reviews, edited eleven anthologies, and was an unremitting advocate for the cause of regional literature.

In the spring of 1920, the creative writing students inaugurated a literary magazine, first called *The Montanan* but immediately renamed *Frontier*. In 1929 it was expanded into the regional *Frontier and Midland*. This magazine, supervised by Merriam until its demise (for economic reasons) in 1939, published local, regional, and national writers. Guthrie, Stegner, Dorothy Johnson, and many other writers got their start on its pages.

Between 1930 and 1934, then again between 1948 and 1960, Merriam ran summer writers' conferences at the university, featuring nationally recognized authors such as Mary Austin, Struthers Burt, and Walter van Tilburg Clark. Montana writers including A. B. "Bud" Guthrie Jr., Mildred Walker, and Joseph Kinsey Howard often participated. It was an enjoyable way both for aspiring and published Montana writers to get to know their nationally respected peers.

While it now seems remarkable, in those days English Department faculty taught *both* literature and creative writing courses, then called "Imaginative Writing." Leslie Fiedler taught poetry writing along with American Literature and Humanities after his arrival in 1942.[29] The University of Montana was becoming a nexus for creative writing. Students were writing and publishing; faculty were gaining recognition. Always a New York Intellectual, Fiedler kept up a stream of publications in major national magazines. His book, *Love and Death in the American Novel* (1960), brought him national fame. More importantly, perhaps, for the role of the university, its graduates were also publishing. Bud Guthrie (BA 1923) published *The Big Sky* in 1947; he won a Pulitzer in 1950 for *The Way West*. Arguably a landmark in Native American writing, D'Arcy McNickle (BA 1925, then Oxford and the University of Grenoble) published *The Surrounded* in 1936. Whitefish native and UM Journalism graduate, Dorothy Johnson (BA 1928) did a writing and editing stint in New York City from 1935 to 1950, publishing western short stories in the meantime, such as "The Death of Liberty Valance," often made into movies. Less well known but still admired, Grace Stone Coates, who was associate editor of *Frontier* for many years, published in 1931 a still respected novel, *Black Cherries*.

SEMICOLONIALITY, CONTACT ZONES, AND INTERACTIVE UNDERSTANDING

In 1946 Prof. H. G. Merriam called the Northwest a "semi-colony," an apt description of the lively culture emerging far from American centers of power:

> Many Westerners know that the Northwest economic pattern is tied to the control of the East, making our region a semi-colony and ourselves only a little more than colonists. Leadership in the Northwest, backed by the people's support and will, could and should break the pattern. The Northwest has been like a young giant in serfdom so busy getting pioneer jobs done that he has not noticed his boss and the conditions of his labor. Like many Westerners, I want the young giant to rise and declare his freedom. . . . *Before, however, that young giant can declare himself, people in the region must learn to act together, having a recognized community of interests.* (159, emphasis mine)

To speak of the Northwest's, and more pointedly Montana's, condition as that of a "semi-colony" allows us to consider university faculty as colonists of a sort. Students (and by extension their families and communities) become the colonized (the supporting "people")—among whom this "giant" (writer/artist) may rise up when everyone shares a "recognized community of interests." Merriam's metaphor is based on the assumption that writers and artists emerge *after* art becomes a valued activity to that local community: artists and writers do not themselves set in motion the forces that create that indispensable sense of community.

In this statement of faith, Merriam clarifies why he worked so assiduously those many years to create a "recognized community of interest." While one cannot lay the entire credit for "so many good writers in Montana" at Merriam's door, he should get most of the credit for setting in motion many situations specifically designed to help the people develop their "community of interest." This would include his creative writing courses, his establishment of *Frontier* magazine in 1920, his founding of the Montana Institute of the Arts in 1948, his organizing of summer literary conferences, as well as his editing books, publishing articles, and giving speeches all over the Northwest. A very active semicolonist, he strongly believed that local people could write significantly of their lives, taking images from "life," rather than their reading.

Merriam was in the right spot to observe the tension between the canonical texts he taught and the material world of his students. His notion of semicoloniality allows us to interrogate the Montana writer's response to inevitable marginalization. Merriam roused the people to organize; Warren Carrier organized a program; Hugo embraced the program and the area; Kittredge looked at the consequences; faculty and students carry on. Distance from the center, or from centers, has the effect of isolating the state almost to the degree it would be if it were Mali or Paraguay. Paradoxically, that distance has become fascinating to those in the centers of power and culture, giving Montana writers a new intellectual éclat. More semicolonial moments.

What has this to do with the University of Montana creative writing program? Had Montana writers been entirely home-schooled, so to speak, had they written in the kind of vacuum often imagined to exist in these parts, they likely would not have earned the national and international success one finds: Guthrie's Pulitzer in 1950, Hugo's appointment as editor of the Yale Younger Poets series in 1978, Hugo's and Welch's invitations to the Carter White House in 1979, Kittredge's 1994 Charles Frankel Prize from President Clinton, Welch's Chevalier de l'ordre des artes et des lettres from the French government in 1995, the three Guggenheims to date (Hugo, Blunt, Earling). Their subject matter no longer seemed entirely alien to the rest of the country. John Benedict, Hugo's editor at Norton, exclaimed—on first reading Hugo—how did this man, so unlike him, write precisely what he had always felt?[30] That day at Norton in New York when the urbane Benedict read the "regional" Hugo is an important semicolonial moment. Technically, regional writing became accessible, probably even important, in that move from being written *about* (by outsiders) to writing well from and about one's own life. Benedict testifies to its power. On the other hand, it may be that the influence of a writer like Wallace Stegner, who is still largely unknown outside the West even after receiving his Pulitzer prize in 1972, is strongest inside creative writing programs and diffuses from there.

THE SECOND BEGINNING: WARREN CARRIER AND THE MFA IN CREATIVE WRITING

The university offered a vibrant semicolonial contact zone, to use Mary Louise Pratt's term, from the beginning.[31] The notion still obtains today. Merriam is the original poster boy for encouraging Montana writers and artists. But credit must also go to Warren Carrier, who actually founded the Master of Fine Arts in Creative Writing. Influenced by his own training at the University of Iowa's Writing Workshop, he shaped the program, got it approved (February 1965), and hired the first writers to teach graduate courses. His fortuitous hiring of the

Seattle poet Richard Hugo turned up the semicolonial volume and visibility. Though I will deal with these men in more detail later, I want here to suggest that each of them had exemplified that fruitful semicolonial tension: the youthful isolation from centers of power and culture, later the sophisticated cultural education (Oxford, Harvard, University of Washington, as well as significant foreign travel: England, France, Burma, Italy), then the return to the hinterlands where the double experience was put to work.[32]

Of the three, Carrier was probably the most urbane (or colonial) in attitude, lacking any interest in "regional" writing.[33] Hugo, by contrast, loved Montana for its abandoned towns, defeated people, and empty spaces because it gave the imagination such scope to work. A few years later, Kittredge followed a similar pattern. It was during his teaching here, specifically after a conference in Sun Valley in 1976, that he began to write of the West he knew and on which he had expected to turn his back. He has become a major voice for the new West in recent years.

I would suggest that the semicolonial turn in these writers has to do with each of these writers recognizing in himself both the self that appeared as the interesting, exotic marginal Other (for the eastern powers) as well as a more complicated, even sophisticated self that had absorbed an education in the Euro-American canon along with experiences in big cities and popular culture absorbed from the omnipresent media. While representational writing may be the expectation, most Montana writers understand how literature *refracts* life's multifariousness, responding to "referential realities by making inroads into them, thereby disrupting and rearranging their structure and semantics" (Iser 312). Needless to say, this is not a phenomenon limited to Montana.

When Hugo encouraged students to "write what they knew," he was doing it within a context and a tradition, not in some lonely garage in Butte. James Welch loved Spenser's "Faerie Queene" on first reading (in a class). Hugo's poets were encouraged to examine intimately the Other they found themselves to be through their contact with canonical literature: Jim and the Blackfeet, Ed Lahey and Butte, Rick DeMarinis and suburban California, Dee McNamer and the Highline. Bill Bevis carried on this tradition to good effect, most notably with Judy Blunt, in his popular Montana Writers course.[34]

In Merriam's terms, the young giant is striding across the world. The university may usefully be considered a semicolonial agency. It goes nearly without saying that its administration and faculty were eastern educated, since that is where the established universities were. Certainly, the English Department was stocked with eastern intellectuals. (The expression "western intellectuals" is still oxymoronic.) The curriculum, "naturally," consisted of the same disciplines and subject matter as that of the major eastern universities. The radical departure, for our purposes, was Merriam's introduction of creative writing into the English Department curriculum.[35] By 1929 a major in Creative Writing was an option for the bachelor's degree. Guthrie and McNickle were among the students who took H.G.'s courses. In later years, many English Department faculty—themselves writer/scholars—taught imaginative writing: Fiedler, Bier (Ph.D., Princeton, 1953), Moore.

THE HUGO YEARS, 1964–1982

> The world likes to think of Dick Hugo as a fine poet who played softball. That's jake. It lets me remember him as a fine softball player who wrote poems.
>
> —Bryan Di Salvatore, "Take Two, Hit to Right, and Lie About Your Batting Average," 99

Towering, glowering above the Montana writing scene looms the figure of Richard Hugo (born 1923) who taught poetry in the creative writing program from its inception in 1964 until his death in 1982. When Hugo came to UM, eleven students were enrolled in graduate creative writing courses; he said that by 1969 more than two hundred students were enrolled in the courses and "we are getting applications from graduate students all over the country."[36] Those numbers increased every year until a peak of six hundred applications in the 1990s.

It must also be remembered that MFAs in Creative Writing were rare in the 1960s. The University of Iowa's program was, of course, the granddaddy of them all. In 1975 there were still only fifteen such programs in the country. However remote and inconsequential UM was, it was in the vanguard of the graduate creative writing programs.[37]

Carrier, an Ohio native, a graduate of the Iowa Writing Workshop (founded in 1942, and where he taught 1949–52), with a Harvard master's degree and a PhD in Comparative Literature from Occidental College, was hired in 1963 to chair the English Department. His interest in the University of Montana had little to do with Montana, and nothing whatever to do with its tradition of encouraging regionalism. The fractious English Department was ready for new direction when its chief luminary, Leslie Fiedler, decamped for State University of New York–Buffalo. Carrier's expansion of the department came at what turned out to be the only period when Montana's university system was prospering. Further, creative writing was a new degree that wouldn't require hefty additions to the mediocre library. A handful of new faculty was all it took. After landing the respectably published poet Richard Hugo, Carrier looked to the Iowa Writer's Workshop and landed James Crumley, James Lee Burke, and Earl Ganz, newly minted MFAS—a Texan, a Louisianan, and a New Yorker. Ganz, with his BA from Cornell, was hired to direct the program. They arrived in 1966. Sr. Madeline DeFrees had come on board in 1967. Kittredge arrived in 1969.

The creative writing faculty may have been from out of state, but those first students, graduate and undergraduate, were Montanans. Ed Lahey from Butte, James Welch from Harlem (Montana), Rick DeMarinis from Havre, Carole Bubash and Denise Scanlon from Anaconda, Bill Velde from Missoula. Neither Carrier nor Hugo limited their reading of poets to the standard British and American fare. Of course they studied Yeats and Eliot, Pound and Stevens, but they also read Vallejo, Montale, Neruda, and Kawabata.

Often jovial, Hugo was the dominant personality in the program. Collegial, he played softball with other English Department faculty. Recently divorced and lonely, he socialized with faculty and students alike with an enthusiasm a family man might save for his family. He published continually, giving the program further recognition. He gave readings all over the country. Over the following decade, his students enjoyed success at conferences and with published books. All indicators of success combined during that period to make the program a nexus of creative writing—no longer merely regional. Writer friends of local writers, of varying degrees of fame, would come to participate in readings and conferences—Stafford, Kizer, Wagoner, Merwin, Piercy, Levine, Hawkes, James Wright, John Ciardi, Kesey, Wendell Barry, James Tate—and the "scene" was hot.

In other larger and older universities, especially those boasting doctoral programs, the English Department stars were scholars and critics. Given, first of all, Montana's fledgling library, a doctoral program in English was out of the question—forever. Its master's degree was adequate, never stellar. Consequently, the MFA in Creative Writing was the department's star graduate program. At UM, the nationally recognized stars in the English Department were all creative writers, after the critic Leslie Fiedler left for Buffalo.

Hugo's influence was probably stronger than that of many teachers because he had little private life at that time and consequently was happy for the company of students who shared his enthusiasm for baseball and poetry over a beer. Or two. Though insecure in his first teaching position, Hugo was clearly a remarkable teacher from the start. His classroom stance was one of camaraderie and humility. So he met his students with a combination of brilliance and earthiness that generated persuasive authority.

In a revealing letter to his parents, dated October 23, 1964, mere weeks after he started teaching, he first tells his parents that his wife has left him, then goes on:

> I'm amazingly popular as a teacher. Students bring wives, friends etc [*sic*] to hear my classes and yesterday I was told that everybody in the Freshman Comp course wants to take their second quarter under me. I have some good students.
>
> Gave a poetry reading too. Quite successful. Now I'm being asked to read or lecture here and there. . . . Here the school is close to the community and the community is not large, so I decided I'd better play ball and earn my money.
>
> Also I'm getting job offers, one to stay on here for another year and just yesterday a feeler came from the University of Victoria. I'm not sure what to do. The problem is will they love me in June as they do in October.[38]

Heartbreak and happiness were certainly intermingled at that point. As a teacher, Hugo had the knack of knowing from their first few poems what a student needed to do to take off and write his or her best poems. James Welch, himself a first-year graduate student of Blackfeet Irish descent, with a mediocre academic record, often told about having turned in some admittedly bad poems in his first Hugo workshop in 1966. Hugo, who always advocated writing about what one knows, asked Welch later, in his office, what he did know about, since he clearly didn't know about the topics of his current poems. Welch replied that he knew about the Blackfeet. Hugo said, "Write about them." Welch replied that no one would be interested—after all, what poem about Indians did anyone know since "Hiawatha"? Hugo said "Try it. *Make* them interested." Welch went home and wrote "In My First Hard Springtime," a poem that starts "Those red men you offended were my brothers." In the 1969 Yates interview, Hugo said that at that moment he knew he had nothing further to teach Welch.

While Hugo was the towering force during those years, other strong personalities were arising: Bill Bevis came in 1974 and soon began to teach his Montana Writers course. Ed McClanahan came for a year in 1974, a powerful personality, creating a vector around New Journalism. Both Stanford graduates, he and his wife were vectors—she for women writers like Maggie Crumley and Cynthia White. Kittredge was publishing but didn't hit stride until the 1976 Sun Valley conference that sent him toward nonfiction, and the Stegner Fellowship, which resulted in a new wave of visiting writers during the 1980s (whose names all began with *K* sounds): John Keester, Chuck Kinder, Max Crawford, and Ray Carver. That was the decade of "Meaty Dudes"—including students like Neil McMahon, Ralph Beer, Fred Haefele, all well over six feet tall—and the Buffalo (as Kittredge was then called). It was also the decade when writerly wags named their baseball team "The Montana Review of Books," boasting an outfield with twelve published novels.

THE FEMALE MUSE AND OTHER CLAPTRAP

> I wanted to read stories of this place I consider my home, to see my experience here reflected in the words of others to identify with characters whose experiences are very different from my own.
> —Melissa Kwasny

No one dares air any longer the view that there are no great women writers simply because the muse is female (ergo, women don't have a muse of their own); nor does anyone dare air the view that only the two Emilys were Major Women Writers—as we were told in 1973, the year Madeline DeFrees and I first proposed our Women Writers course. The Montana myth is male and macho. The Missoula Writing Scene myth is male and macho: all night at the bar and fishing stories. Listen again: Judy Blunt, Frances Kuffel, Mary Blew, Caroline Patterson, Dee McNamer, Kate Gadbow, Ripley Hugo, Sandra Alcosser, and Melissa Kwasny are telling another set of stories. Postcolonial theory can't explain these stories. Feminism obviously can. Semicoloniality has room for them. "As children, we could easily have believed that our mothers had no stories," say Kim Barnes and Mary Blew in their introduction to *Circle of Women*. "What we discovered as we grew older was that the women had kept their stories secret. . . . [W]e began to understand that our lives were not anomalies but rather a part of the vast web of common experience" (x–xi). Like Warren Carrier, DeFrees has slipped out of the myth. McNamer, Gadbow, Blunt, Debra Earling, Karen Volkmann, and Joanna Klink, currently teaching in the writing program, are nationally recognized writers, but not the stuff of myth. Clearly, it's time to look beyond the myth.

Semicolonial awareness remains, even self-conscious. The Rattlesnake Ladies' Writing Salon (deliberately so named) met regularly during the 1990s to give Missoula's women writers a community of camaraderie and criticism away from students and faculty, from stalwart husbands—and from fishing stories. Annick Smith, Chicago transplant, rancher, and widow of a UM English professor, perfectly exemplifies the semicolonial sophisticate. She has produced films (*Heartland*), organized Hellgate Writers and the splendid summer Yellow Bay Writers' Workshops, edited *The Last Best Place* anthology with Bill Kittredge, and is publishing steadily.

Madeline DeFrees was the first woman on the UM creative writing faculty. An Oregonian, a nun for thirty-eight years, a poet who studied with Karl Shapiro and John Berryman, she taught at Montana for twelve years, after seventeen at Holy Names College (now Fort Wright College) in Spokane. She left UM to head the creative writing program at the University of Massachusetts–Amherst in 1979, then retired in 1985 to Seattle where she writes, swims, and gives readings around the country still. By 2000 she had published seven books of poems and two of prose. She first composed poems, she told me once, while scrubbing the convent floors, slipping under the radar, as it were, of the vigilant keepers of the colonial/patriarchal order. In 2002 she won the Lenore Marshall Prize from the Academy of American Poets for her *Blue Dusk: New and Selected Poems, 1951–2001*, "the most outstanding book of poems published that year."

After 1970 more young women poets began to appear in creative writing classes; feminism was in the air; the ex-nun took assertiveness training and began telling senior faculty to let her talk rather than speaking for her. The change was on. Women poets—Nancy Schoenberger, Roberta Hill Whiteman, Kim Anderson, Caroline Patterson, and more—were praised and liked and loved and enjoyed success, but they never have become mythical. It doesn't matter. Joy Harjo, Tess Gallagher, Patti Ann Rogers, Dara Weir, Michele Glazer—there's a long list of successful women poets who have taught as visitors to the program. There is another, perhaps even longer list of visiting women fiction writers and nonfiction writers. Patricia Goedicke, on the faculty since 1982, published eleven books of poems before her death in 2006; her *As Earth Begins to End* placed among the top ten poetry books published in the country in 2000.[39] Women writers now are important voices in the Real West; that they still don't figure in the myth only damns the myth once again—even if it still sells glossy magazines like *Outside* and *Cowboys and Indians*.[40]

BRIGHT LIGHTS, NO CITY. STILL

Our most telling semicolonial moment may have occurred when the *Los Angeles Times* published a story in March of 1989 titled "Bright Lights, No City," which announced that Missoula was the new literary capital of the United States. Obviously an exaggeration, the designation nevertheless marked a shift in our place in the national imagination: no longer unorganized empty space, Montana became a place—sort of.[41] We may still be marginal, perhaps even exotic, but our own writers are reimagining our place, our landscape, its inhabitants—human and nonhuman—and reframing our stories. Not only are they reimagining Montana and the West, but they are being read—and honored. In April 2007 William Kittredge, professor emeritus for whom two endowed chairs are named, received the 2007 Robert Kirsch Lifetime Achievement Award from the *Los Angeles Times*. He was praised for nurturing young writers, helping build a community of writers *and readers*, and writing "his unflinching vision of the hardscrabble vision of the West and the people who survive and die in it."[42]

Other evidence abounds of a shift in Montana's place in the literary world. Montana native and a University of Montana fiction MFA herself, Kate Gadbow has directed the creative writing program for fourteen years. She suggests much of its success is due to the personal attention students still receive—despite the fact that the stipend for teaching assistants is half that of major universities.[43] Graduates of the program now turn up all around the country. The "spellbinding biography" of seventeenth-century artist and naturalist Maria Sibylla Merian by Kim Todd (MFA 1995, MS Environmental Studies) was reviewed briefly in the January 29, 2007, *New Yorker*. Missoula native Frances Kuffel appeared on *Good Morning America* in late 2003, talking about her new book *Passing for Thin*. She had studied under Hugo as an undergraduate in the late 1970s, then received her MFA from Cornell in the 1980s. A fifth novel by J. Robert Lennon (MFA 1995), *Happyland*, was serialized in *Harper's Magazine* in 2006. Two recent MFAS in fiction, Frances Hwang (2001) and Aryn Kyle (2004), received Rona Jaffe Foundation Writers' Awards in 2005. Kyle's first novel, *The God of Animals*, hit number 18 on the *New York Times* Bestseller List in April 2007. Montana's first poet laureate, Sandra Alcosser (MFA 1982), directs the MFA program at San Diego State University but lives south of Missoula half the year.

Montana writers are clearly a presence in the intellectual world, in public discourse beyond Montana. There's a lot of land out here; it's semiarid and sparsely populated. Should we turn it back to the buffalo or strip-mine it? The Association for the Study of Literature and the Environment, ASLE, was founded at the Western Literature Association in 1992. While, obviously, not all Montana writers are environmental writers, fruitful cooperation has developed between UM's creative writing program and the environmental studies program.

As I stated at the beginning of this essay, degrees of connection of Montana writers to UM's creative writing program vary. Writing faculty themselves are widely visible. Prageeta Sharma, a poet with three books and a Media Degree from the New School, became director in the fall of 2007. Nonfiction teacher Judy Blunt has a Guggenheim; Debra Earling was just awarded one for 2007–08. Professors Deirdre McNamer and Joanna Klink have forthcoming books. McNamer appears frequently on the op-ed page of the *New York Times*, commenting on issues relating Montana to the national scene. Klink won a Rona Jaffe Foundation Writers' Award in 2003. Three of Kevin Canty's books have been named as Notable Books by the *New York Times Book Review*.

Missoula may not be the literary capital of the country, but the per-capita concentration of writers remains high; you're as likely to meet a young writer/bartender today as you were in 1970 when David Quammen (fresh from Yale and Oxford) worked at The Stockman's. The university's creative writing program may not be the principal cause of all this literary activity, but it is still a lively nexus for aspiring and accomplished writers. Writers can no longer escape theoretical debates over representation/simulation, regional difference, imagination, authenticity, and the like. Most cannot escape, either, environmental concerns and their practical consequences. There are bears in our back yards. Sometimes, these days, the subalterns teach the colonists and the tension proves fruitful. We may be semicolonial still, but we now understand that the helix twists and that certain advantages devolve from semimarginal status. That may or may not be why there are so many good writers in Montana; to paraphrase Hugo's last book title, the University of Montana's creative writing program remains committed to "making certain it goes on."

NOTES

I came to the University of Montana in the fall of 1966 to teach Literary Criticism and Comparative Literature. As English Department Lecture Committee chair, then director of Creative Writing, with an office sandwiched between Hugo's and DeFrees's, I regularly associated with writers. In the spring of 1967, I met and began dating James Welch, then a graduate student in poetry (*never* a student of mine). We married in 1968. This essay is deliberately not anecdotal, not a memoir; it is an attempt to integrate the scholarly and the experiential. Were I to adopt a more distant tone, I would falsify my relation to this material.

1. The very fact that this question is asked suggests that Montana remains empty space in the American imaginary. Other states have more writers, obviously, though

not necessarily more per capita. To my knowledge, there are no writer-per-capita statistics.

2. *US News* has ceased its rankings of graduate programs in the arts.
3. My discussion will be limited to poetry, fiction, and creative nonfiction by Montanans or about Montana. Books on bears or geology, however splendid, fall outside my purview.
4. *The Glorious Cause, Rise to Rebellion*, and other historical novels. Some "Montana writers" have never even lived in Montana, such as the British Nicholas Evans, whose best-selling novel (and movie) *The Horse Whisperer* takes place in Montana. In fairness, Evans did spend a few weeks in Choteau. Once, to a *Missoulian* reporter, Richard Ford—then living in Missoula—even denied the existence of a "Missoula writing community."
5. Andrew Sean Greer, recently recognized by John Updike in the *New Yorker* (January 26, 2004, and May 5, 2008), publicly acknowledges the importance of the university's creative writing program to his career.
6. Other University of Montana programs, of course, bring in music and drama and visual arts.
7. Undergraduate instruction in writing began in 1919, when no one but Harvard was teaching it.
8. A list of faculty and student publications, even for the past decade, is obviously too long to include here.
9. See, for example, Joyce Brusin, MFA, with the Rural Institute; Kim Anderson, BA in Creative Writing , running the book festival and other programs for the Montana Committee for the Humanities; Kathy Witkowski, a journalist often heard on NPR. Caroline Patterson is an editor with Farcountry Press in Helena. Sandra Alcosser is not only Montana's first poet laureate but also Poet-in-Residence at Poet's House and the Wildlife Conservation Society in New York, as well as director of the San Diego State Creative Writing Program. Mandy Smoker-Broaddus (MFA 2004) is the Indian Education Achievement Specialist for the Montana Office of Public Instruction.
10. Neil McMahon and Kim Zupan work as carpenters; Jon Jackson used to. Fred Haefele was a tree surgeon until recently.
11. Rick Newby and Suzanne Hunger's anthology *Writing Montana: Literature Under the Big Sky* reminds readers that Missoula may hog the limelight but does not have a corner on Montana writing.
12. See Brandon Griggs, "Montana Tradition Beckons Creative Writers," from a *Salt Lake Tribune* article reprinted in the *Missoulian* November 27, 1995, C-2. See also, Jean-Sebastien Stehli in *Le Point*, July 29, 1995.
13. The entire creative writing faculty was invited to the Etonnants Voyageurs book festival in St. Malo, France, in 1999. This festival, which draws fifty thousand people in a mid-May weekend, regularly brings Montana writers. The session on the teaching of creative writing was packed to overflowing. This was particularly notable because the French don't believe creative writing can be taught.

14. Guthrie, like Deirdre McNamer later, was a journalism major who took creative writing courses.
15. The waxing and waning of the popularity of the Western, of western and nature writing, is a whole separate subject. See, particularly, Richard White's *It's Your Misfortune and None of My Own* (1991) for a very readable account of the issue.
16. Kittredge often begins discussions with something like:

    Each morning we wake and start telling a story about our lives, an act almost as involuntary as breathing. We listen as long as we live, and if we're lucky, we discover terms that make us feel whole and safe, even useful. . . . A society capable of naming itself lives within its stories, inhabiting and furnishing them. . . . We ride stories like rafts, or lay them out on the table like maps. They always eventually fail and have to be reinvented. The world is too complex for our forms ever to encompass for long. (*Nature of Generosity* 8–9)

17. See Rick Newby's charming essay, "The Montana-Paris Axis, or Unpacking My Grandfather's Library: On the Track of a Bookish Tradition" (Newby and Hunger 300–328).
18. Montana scored 50th among states for average wage in 2003 (*Missoulian* May 25, 2003). In a *Forbes* magazine listing "Best Small Places for Business and Careers," Missoula ranked 139th of 168 in housing affordability, 36th in job growth (*Missoulian* May 14, 2003). By 2007 Montana had risen to 42nd with per-capita income at $36,276.
19. "Montana is where male writers go to feel strong emotions and drive pickups." Claire Dederer, *Washington Post*, August 11, 2002, BW06.
20. Mike Chase, *Baltimore Sun*, March 23, 2003, probably in the *Missoulian*.
21. Louis Owens addresses this issue often. See, for example, "As if an Indian Were Really an Indian," 217.
22. A recent airline magazine article announced Missoula has 370 drinking establishments for its 58,000 inhabitants. I have not verified this figure.
23. John K. Hutchens, "Literary Montana," *Herald Tribune*, August 6, 1961; from HG Merriam Archival Box 17 in the UM Mansfield Library. He also notes that Montana had the highest per-capita book use rate among all western and midwestern states.
24. To consider any university a "monastic sanctuary" seems wishful thinking these days.
25. The term *settler colony* used by Ashcroft, Griffith, and Tiffin in *The Empire Writes Back* might seem apropos, given the need of the settlers in the West generally to adapt their native English language to terrain and climate, unlike the British. However, Ashcroft et al.'s discussion of how settlers develop their "indigenous" culture completely ignores the fact that the indigenous inhabitants already had a culture of their own. To that degree, Leslie Fiedler may have been right in his "Montana Face" essay (1949), stating that Montanans could never develop a serious—meaning tragic—literature of their own until they came to terms with how they had treated Native Americans.

26. That is, Missoula now has a wine bar and several excellent restaurants, measures of increasing if not perfected sophistication.
27. Merriam had already taught at Reed, Whitman, and Beloit, and studied briefly at Harvard as an Austin Fellow.
28. Course description in the 1919–20 University of Montana catalog.
29. "Techniques of Poetry" described in the catalog as "guidance in writing."
30. Recounted to me at the Hugo Memorial Conference in Seattle in 1984.
31. Contact zone:

    [T]he space of colonial encounters, the space in which peoples geographically and historically separated come into contact with each other and establish ongoing relations, usually involving conditions of coercion, radical inequality, and intractable conflict . . . often synonymous with "colonial frontier." . . . [A]n attempt to invoke the spatial and temporal co-presence of subjects previously separated by geographic and historical disjunctures, and whose trajectories now intersect. (7)

32. Such isolation, according to Fiedler's "Montana Face" essay, leads to "poverty of experience" unredeemed by "art museums, ballet or even a movie in any language not their own" (165). Note that he did not assume these isolated souls had grown up utterly bookless.
33. By the time of this writing, Carrier, a retired university chancellor, had written seventeen books—poetry, novels, translations. He was a founder and original editor of the *Quarterly Review of Books*.
34. The precursor to his *Ten Tough Trips*. Judy Blunt went on to publish an enormously popular memoir, *Breaking Clean*. Compare with paragraph 1, above.
35. Writing ("creative" or otherwise) was not taught in American universities until the 1900s. At Harvard (founded, by the way, in 1636) Dean Le Baron Russell Briggs began teaching a class that required a daily theme (Stegner 45). "Charles Townsend Copeland, also at Harvard, followed Dean Briggs's lead. Between the two, they must have trained half the American writers of their time" (46). Stegner himself studied writing as a student at the University of Utah in the 1920s. H. G. Merriam studied with Briggs during his year at Harvard (see archival letter).
36. Interview with Rebecca Yates (May 21, 1969). Personal copy.
37. Not enough has been written about the importance of the New Criticism in the growth of creative writing in academe. Philology was the dominant scholarly approach to literature through the 1920s. In the 1930s, poet/scholars like John Crowe Ransom, Allen Tate, Brooks, and Warren emerged in the South, insisting on the autonomy of art, loosening poetry from the authority historical and linguistic approaches. New Criticism was also democratizing, in the sense that close reading was not dependent on a long background of training in the classics, and consequently higher education became a possibility for soldiers back from WWII. One read all poems in terms of unity, complexity, ambiguity, and formal elements; once one read Chaucer and Frost with the same criteria.

38. Richard Hugo to Esther and Herbert F. Hugo. Letter dated 23 October 1964. Richard Hugo Papers. University of Washington Libraries, Seattle.
39. American Library Association ranking. She also recently won the H.G. Merriam Prize for Distinguished Contribution to Montana Literature.
40. One dreary winter day, Kittredge, an avid golfer when weather permits, proposed starting a glossy magazine titled *Montana Indoors*.
41. The hilarious local writer Bill Vaughn designed a popular T-shirt with the logo "Missoula, a place. Sort of." He is a contributing editor for *Outside* magazine; his article "Skating Home Backwards" was included in the *Best American Magazine Writing for 2001*.
42. David L. Ulin, book editor of the *L.A. Times*. Cited in the *Missoulian*, April 8, 2007.
43. In 2007 the program received more than four hundred applications: three hundred in fiction, one hundred in poetry, and sixty in nonfiction.

WORKS CITED

Barnes, Kim, and Mary Blew. *Circle of Women: An Anthology of Contemporary Women Writers*. New York: Penguin, 1994.

Bevis, William W. *Ten Tough Trips: Montana Writers and the West*. Seattle: University of Washington Press, 1990.

Di Salvatore, Bryan. "Take Two, Hit to Right, and Lie About Your Batting Average." *Cutbank* 40 (1993): 99.

Fiedler, Leslie. "The End of Jean Jacques Rousseau or the Montana Face," originally published in *The Partisan Review* vol. 16, July 1949. Reprinted in *The Art of the Essay*. Ed. Leslie Fiedler. New York: Crowell, 1958.

Hugo, Richard. *The Triggering Town: Lectures and Essays on Poetry and Writing*. New York: Norton, 1979.

Howard, Joseph Kinsey. *Montana: High, Wide, and Handsome*. 1949. Reprint, Lincoln: University of Nebraska Press, 1983.

Iser, Wolfgang. "Do I Write for an Audience?" *PMLA*, 115, 3 (May 2000): 310–14.

Kenner, Hugh. "Who Was Leslie Fiedler?" *Harper's* (November 1982): 69–73.

Kittredge, William. *The Nature of Generosity*. New York: Knopf, 2000.

Kittredge, William, and Annick Smith, eds. *The Last Best Place: A Montana Anthology*. Helena: Montana Historical Society, 1988.

Kuffel, Frances. *Passing for Thin: Losing Half My Weight and Finding My Self*. New York: Broadway Books, 2004.

Kwasny, Melissa. "Why Have There Been No Great Women Writers in Montana?" *Writing Montana: Literature under the Big Sky*. Ed. Rick Newby and Suzanne Hunger. Helena: Montana Center for the Book, 1996. 188–91.

Merriam, H. G. "Does the Northwest Believe in Itself?" *Northwest Harvest: A Regional Stock-Taking*." Ed. V. L. O. Chittick. New York: Macmillan, 1948. 291–304.

———. "Who Can Teach Creative Writing?" *English Journal* (1947): 464–69.

Myers, D. G. *The Elephants Teach: Creative Writing Since 1880*. Englewood Cliffs NJ: Prentice-Hall, 1996.

Newby, Rick, and Suzanne Hunger, eds. *Writing Montana: Literature Under the Big Sky*. Helena: Montana Center for the Book, 1996.

Owens, Louis. "As if an Indian Were Really an Indian: Native American Voices and Postcolonial Theory." *I Hear the Train: Reflections, Inventions, Refractions*. Norman: University of Oklahoma Press, 2001. 207–226.Pratt, Mary Louise. *Imperial Eyes: Travel Writing and Transculturation*. New York: Routledge, 1992.

Spurr, David. *The Rhetoric of Empire: Colonial Discourse in Journalism, Travel Writing and Imperial Administration*. Durham NC: Duke University Press, 1993.

Stegner, Wallace. *On the Teaching of Creative Writing: Responses to a Series of Questions*. Ed. Edward Connery Latham. Hanover NH: Montgomery Endowment, Dartmouth College, 1988.

Toole, K. Ross. *Montana: An Uncommon Land*. Norman: University of Oklahoma Press, 1959.

White, Richard. *It's Your Misfortune and None of My Own: A History of the American West*. Norman: University of Oklahoma Press, 1991.

Williams, Patrick, and Laura Chrisman. *Colonial Discourse and Post-Colonial Theory: A Reader*. New York: Columbia University Press, 1994.

SELECT BIBLIOGRAPHY OF MONTANA WRITING

Abbott, E. C., and Helena Huntington Smith. *We Pointed Them North; Recollections of a Cowpuncher*. Norman: University of Oklahoma Press, 1955.

Alderson, Nannie T., and Helena Huntington Smith. *A Bride Goes West*. 1942. Reprint, Lincoln: University of Nebraska Press, 1969.

Bevis, William W. *Shorty Harris, or, The Price of Gold*. Norman: University of Oklahoma Press, 1999.

Blew, Mary Clearman. *All but the Waltz: A Memoir of Five Generations in the Life of a Montana Family*. New York: Penguin, 1992.

———. *Balsamroot: A Memoir*. New York: Viking, 1994.

———. *Bone Deep in Landscape: Writing, Reading, and Place*. Norman: University of Oklahoma Press, 1999.

———. *Lambing Out and Other Stories*. Norman: University of Oklahoma Press, 2001.

———. *Runaway: A Collection of Stories*. Lewiston ID: Confluence Press, 1990.

———. *Sister Coyote: Montana Stories*. New York: Lyons Press, 2000.

———. *Writing Her Own Life: Imogene Welch, Western Rural School Teacher*. Literature of the American West. Vol. 14. Norman: University of Oklahoma Press, 2004.

Blunt, Judy. *Breaking Clean*. New York: Knopf, 2002.

———. *Not Quite Stone*. Missoula: Merriam-Frontier Award/University of Montana, 1992.

Bowen, Peter. *Coyote Wind and Specimen Song: The First Two Montana Mysteries Featuring Gabriel Du Pre*. New York: St. Martin's, 2000.

———. *Imperial Kelly*. New York: Random House, 1993.

———. *Kelly Blue*. New York: Crown, 1991.

———. *Kelly and the Three-toed Horse*. New York: St. Martin's, 2001.

———. *Yellowstone Kelly*. New York: Bantam, 1990.

Brinig, Myron. *Copper City*. London: Cobden-Sanderson, 1931.

———. *Singermann*. London: Cobden-Sanderson, 1930

———. *The Sisters*. New York: Grosset & Dunlap, 1937.

———. *Sons of Singermann*. London: Cobden-Sanderson, 1932.

———. *The Sun Sets in the West*. London: Cobden-Sanderson, 1935.

Canty, Kevin. *Honeymoon and Other Stories*. New York: Doubleday, 2001.

———. *Into the Great Wide Open*. New York: Doubleday, 1996.

———. *Nine Below Zero*. New York: Doubleday, 1999.

———. *A Stranger in This World*. New York: Doubleday, 1994.

———. *Winslow in Love*. New York: Nan. A. Talese, 2005.

Cates, David. *Hunger in America*. New York: Simon and Schuster, 1992.

Cates, David Allan. *X Out of Wonderland: A Saga*. Hanover NH: Steerforth Press, 2005.
Charlo, Victor A. *Swift Current Time*. Dixon MT: Charlo Press, 2002.
Clark, William, and Meriwether Lewis. *Travels to the Source of the Missouri River and Across the American Continent to the Pacific Ocean. Performed by Order of the Government of the United States, in the Years 1804, 1805, and 1806*. Ed. Thomas Rees. London: Longman, Hurst, Rees, Orme & Brown, 1814. Rpt of *History of the Expedition under the Command of Captains Lewis and Clark, to the Sources of the Missouri, thence Across the Rocky Mountains and Down the River Columbia to the Pacific Ocean. Performed During the Years 1804–5–6*. Ed. Paul Allen. 2 vols. Philadelphia: Bradford & Inskeep; New York: Abm. H. Inskeep, J. Maxwell, printer, 1814.
———. *The Original Journals of the Lewis and Clark Expedition, 1804–1806; Printed from the Original Manuscripts in the Library of the American Philosophical Society and by Direction of Its Committee on Historical Documents, Together with Manuscript Material of Lewis and Clark from Other Sources, Including Note-Books, Letters, Maps, etc., and the Journals of Charles Floyd and Joseph Whitehouse*. 8 vols. Ed. Reuben Gold Thwaites. New York: Dodd, Mead, 1904–1905.
———. *The Journals of Captain Meriwether Lewis and Sergeant John Ordway, Kept on the Expedition of Western Exploration, 1803–1806*. Ed. Milo M. Quaife. Madison WI: The Society, 1916.
———. *Westward with Dragoons; the Journal of William Clark on His Expedition to Establish Fort Osage, August 25 to September 22, 1808; a Description of the Wilderness, an Account of the Building of the Fort, Treaty-Making with the Osages and Clark's Return to St. Louis*. Ed. Kate L. Gregg. Fulton MO: Ovid Bell, 1937.
Coates, Grace Stone. *Black Cherries*. New York: Knopf, 1931.
Crumley, James. *Bordersnakes*. New York: Mysterious Press, 1996.
———. *Dancing Bear*. New York: Random House, 1983.
———. *The Final Country*. New York: Mysterious Press, 2001.
———. *The Last Good Kiss: A Novel*. New York: Random House, 1978.
———. *The Mexican Tree Duck*. New York: Mysterious Press, 1993.
———. *The Muddy Fork and Other Things: Short Fiction and Nonfiction*. Livingston MT: Clark City Press, 1991.
———. *One to Count Cadence*. New York: Random House, 1969.
———. *The Right Madness*. New York: Viking, 2005.
———. *Whores*. Missoula MT: Dennis McMillan Publications, 1989.
———. *The Wrong Case: A Novel*. New York: Random House, 1975.
Cushman, Dan. *Stay Away Joe*. New York: Viking, 1953.
DeFrees, Madeline. *Blue Dusk: New and Selected Poems, 1951–2001*. Port Townsend WA: Copper Canyon Press, 2001.
———. *Double Dutch*. West Sacramento CA: Red Wing Press, 1999.
———. *Imaginary Ancestors: Poems, 1978*. Revised ed. Seattle: Broken Moon, 1990.

———. *The Light Station on Tillamook Rock*. Corvallis OR: Arrowood Books, 1990.
———. *Magpie on the Gallows*. Port Townsend WA: Copper Canyon Press, 1982.
———. *Possible Sibyls: New Poems*. Amherst MA: Lynx House Press, 1991.
———. *When Sky Lets Go*. New York: Braziller, 1978.
DeMarinis, Rick. *Apocalypse Then: Stories*. New York: Seven Stories Press, 2004.
———. *The Art & Craft of the Short Story*. Cincinnati: Writer's Digest, 2000.
———. *Borrowed Hearts: New and Selected Stories*. New York: Seven Stories Press, 1999.
———. *The Burning Women of Far Cry*. New York: Arbor House, 1986
———. *Cinder*. New York: Farrar, Straus, Giroux, 1978.
———. *The Coming Triumph of the Free World: Stories*. New York: Norton, 1991.
———. *Jack and Jill: Two Novellas and a Short Story*. New York: Dutton, 1979.
———. *A Lovely Monster: The Adventures of Claude Rains and Dr. Tellenbeck*. New York: Simon & Schuster, 1976.
———. *The Mortician's Apprentice*. New York: Norton, 1994.
———. *Poems*. San Diego: Transparent Communications, 1974.
———. *Scimitar*. New York: Dutton, 1977.
———. *Under the Wheat*. Pittsburgh: University of Pittsburgh Press, 1986.
———. *The Voice of America*. New York: Norton, 1991.
———. *The Year of the Zinc Penny*. 1989. Reprint, New York: Seven Stories Press, 2004.
Dimsdale, Thomas J. *The Vigilantes of Montana, or Popular Justice in the Rocky Mountains*. Virginia City MT: M. T., D. W. Tilton, 1866.
Doig, Ivan. *Bucking the Sun*. New York: Simon & Schuster, 1996.
———. *Dancing at the Rascal Fair*. New York: Atheneum, 1987.
———. *Early Forestry Research*. Washington DC: U.S. Forestry Service, 1976.
———. *English Creek*. New York: Atheneum, 1984.
———. *Heart Earth*. New York: Atheneum, 1993.
———. *Mountain Time*. New York: Scribner, 1999.
———. *Prairie Nocturne*. New York: Scribner, 2003.
———. *Ride with Me, Mariah Montana*. New York: Atheneum, 1990.
———. *The Sea Runners*. New York: Atheneum, 1982.
———. *The Streets We Have Come Down*. Rochelle Park NJ: Hayden, 1975.
———. *This House of Sky: Landscapes of a Western Mind*. San Diego: Harcourt, 1978.
———. *Utopian America: Dreams and Realities*. Rochelle Park NJ: Hayden, 1976.
———. *The Whistling Season*. San Diego: Harcourt, 2006.
———. *Winter Brothers: A Season at the Edge of America*. San Diego: Harcourt: 1980.
Doig, Ivan, and Carol Doig. *News: A Consumer's Guide*. Englewood Cliffs NJ: Prentice-Hall, 1972.
Doig, Ivan, and Duncan Kelso. *Inside This House of Sky*. New York: Atheneum, 1983.
Dove, Mourning. *Cogewea, The Half Blood*. Lincoln: University of Nebraska Press, 1981.

———. *Mourning Dove*. Ed. Jay Miller. Lincoln: University of Nebraska Press, 1990.

———. *Coyote Stories*. Ed. Heister Dean Guie. Lincoln: University of Nebraska Press, 1990.

Dunsmore, Roger. *Blood House*. Vancouver: Arsenal Pulp Press, 1988.

———. *Earth's Mind: Essays in Native Literature*. Albuquerque: University of New Mexico Press, 1997.

Earling, Debra Magpie. *Perma Red*. New York: BlueHen Books, 2002.

Fiedler, Leslie. *Love and Death in the American Novel*. 1960. Revised ed, 1966. Afterword by Leslie Fiedler. Reprint, New York: Anchor Books, 1992.

———. *A New Fiedler Reader*. New York: Prometheus Books, 1999.

Ford, Richard. *Independence Day*. New York: Knopf, 1995.

———. *The Lay of the Land*. London: Bloomsbury, 2006.

———. *A Multitude of Sins: Stories*. London: Harvill, 2001; New York: Knopf, 2002.

———. *A Piece of My Heart*. New York: Harper, 1976.

———. *Rock Springs: Stories*. New York: Atlantic Monthly Press, 1987.

———. *The Sportswriter*. New York: Vintage, 1986.

———. *The Ultimate Good Luck*. Boston: Houghton Mifflin, 1981.

———. *Vintage Ford*. New York: Vintage, 2003.

———. *Wildlife*. New York: Atlantic Monthly Press, 1990.

———. *Women with Men: Three Stories*. New York: Knopf, 1997.

Gadbow, Kate. *Pushed to Shore*. Louisville: Sarabande Books, 2003.

Ganz, Earl. *Animal Care: Stories*. Amherst MA: Lynx House Press, 1990.

———. *The Confessions of a Unicorn*. [Salt Lake City]: Ganz, 1977.

———. *The Taos Truth Game*. Albuquerque: University of New Mexico Press, 2006.

Garcia, Andrew. *Tough Trip Through Paradise*. 1967. Ed. Bennett H. Stein. Reprint, Moscow: University of Idaho Press, 2001.

Gibbons, Mark. *Connemara Moonshine*. Seattle: Camphorweed Press, 2002.

Grinnell, George Bird. *Blackfoot Lodge Tales: The Story of a Prairie People*. 1962. Introduction by Thedis Berthelson Crowe. Reprint, Lincoln: University of Nebraska Press, 2003.

———. *By Cheyenne Campfires*. Foreword by Omer C. Stewart. Lincoln: University of Nebraska Press, 1971.

———. *The Cheyenne Indians*. 2 vols. Lincoln: University of Nebraska Press, 1972.

———. *Pawnee Hero Stories and Folktales*. Introduction by Maurice Frink. Lincoln: University of Nebraska Press, 1961.

———. *The Punishment of the Stingy and Other Indian Stories*. Introduction by Jarold Ramsey. Lincoln: University of Nebraska Press, 1982.

Goedicke, Patricia. *As Earth Begins to End: New Poems*. Port Townsend WA: Copper Canyon Press, 2000.

———. *Between Oceans: Poems*. New York: Harcourt, Brace & World, 1968.

———. *Crossing the Same River*. Amherst: University of Massachusetts Press, 1980.

———. *The Dog That Was Barking Yesterday*. Amherst MA: Lynx House Press, 1980.

———. *For the Four Corners*. Ithaca NY: Ithaca House, 1976.
———. *Invisible Horses*. Minneapolis: Milkweed Editions, 1996.
———. *The King of Childhood: A Sequence*. Lewiston ID: Confluence Press, 1984.
———. *Listen, Love*. Daleville IN: Barnwood Press, 1986.
———. *Paul Bunyan's Bearskin: Poems*. Minneapolis: Milkweed Editions, 1992.
———. *The Tongues We Speak: New and Selected Poems*. Minneapolis: Milkweed Editions, 1989.
———. *The Trail That Turns on Itself*. Ithaca NY: Ithaca House, 1978.
———. *The Wind of Our Going: Poems*. Port Townsend WA: Copper Canyon Press, 1985.
Guthrie, A. B. *Arfive*. Boston: Houghton Mifflin, 1970.
———. *The Big It and Other Stories*. Boston: Gregg Press, 1960.
———. *The Big Sky*. Boston: Houghton Mifflin, 1947.
———. *Big Sky, Fair Land: The Environmental Essays of A. B. Guthrie, Jr.* Ed. David Peterson. Flagstaff AZ: Northland Press, 1988.
———. *The Blue Hen's Chick: An Autobiography*. 1965. Afterword by David L. Peterson. Reprint, Lincoln: University of Nebraska Press, 1993.
———. *Fair Land, Fair Land*. Boston: Houghton Mifflin, 1982.
———. *A Field Guide to Writing Fiction*. New York: HarperCollins, 1991
———. *Four Miles from Ear Mountain*. Missoula MT: Kutenai Press, 1987.
———. *The Genuine Article*. Boston: Houghton Mifflin, 1977.
———. *The Last Valley*. Boston: Houghton Mifflin, 1975.
———. *Murder in the Cotswalds*. Boston: Houghton Mifflin, 1989.
———. *Murders at Moon Dance*. 1943. Introduction by William Kittredge. Reprint, Lincoln: University of Nebraska Press, 1993.
———. *No Second Wind*. Boston: Houghton Mifflin, 1980.
———. *Once Upon a Pond*. Missoula MT: Mountain Press Publishing, 1973.
———. *Playing Catch-Up*. Boston: Houghton Mifflin, 1985.
———. *These Thousand Hills*. Boston: Houghton Mifflin, 1956.
———. *The Way West*. New York: William Sloane, 1949.
———. *Wild Pitch*. Boston: Houghton Mifflin, 1979.
Hammett, Dashiell. *Red Harvest*. 1929. Reprint, New York: Vintage, 1992.
Harrison, Jim. *Legends of the Fall*. New York: Delta/Seymour Lawrence, 1989.
———. *The Shape of the Journey: New and Collected Poems*. Port Townsend WA: Copper Canyon Press, 1998.
Harrison, Jim, and Ted Kooser. *Braided Creek: A Conversation in Poetry*. Port Townsend MA: Copper Canyon Press, 2003.
Haste, Gwendolen. *Young Land*. New York: Coward-McCann, 1930.
Howard, Joseph Kinsey. *Golden River: What's to Be Done About the Missouri?* New York: Harper & Bros, 1945.
———. *Montana: High, Wide, and Handsome*. New Haven CT: Yale University Press, 1943.

———. *Montana Margins, A State Anthology*. New Haven CT: Yale University Press, 1946.
———. *Montana Twins in Trouble?* New York: Harpers Magazine, 1944.
Hugo, Richard. *31 Letters and 13 Dreams*. New York: Norton, 1977.
———. *Death and the Good Life*. New York: St. Martin's Press, 1981.
———. *Death of the Kapowsin Tavern*. New York: Harcourt, 1965.
———. *Duwamish Head*. Port Townsend WA: Copperhead, 1976.
———. *Five Poets of the Pacific*. Ed. Robin Skelton. Seattle: University of Washington Press, 1964.
———. *Good Luck Cracked Italian*. New York: World Publishing, 1969.
———. *The Hitler Diaries*. New York: Morrow, 1983.
———. *The Lady in Kicking Horse Reservoir*. New York: Norton, 1973.
———. *Making Certain It Goes On: The Collected Poems of Richard Hugo*. New York: Norton, 1984.
———. *Rain Five Days and I Love It*. Port Townsend WA: Graywolf Press, 1975.
———. *The Real West Marginal Way: A Poet's Autobiography*. Ed. Ripley S. Hugo, James Welch, and Lois Welch. New York: Norton, 1986.
———. *The Right Madness on Skye*. New York: Norton, 1980.
———. *Road Ends at Tahola*. Pittsburgh: Slow Loris Press, 1978.
———. *A Run of Jacks*. Minneapolis: University of Minnesota Press, 1961.
———. *Sea Lanes Out*. Story WY: Dooryard Press, 1983.
———. *Selected Poems of Richard Hugo*. New York: Norton, 1979.
———. *The Triggering Town: Lectures and Essays on Poetry and Writing*. New York: Norton, 1979.
———. *What Thou Lovest Well, Remains American*. New York: Norton, 1975.
———. *White Center: Poems*. New York: Norton, 1980.
Johnson, Dorothy M. *The Bloody Bozeman: The Perilous Trail to Montana's Gold*. 1971. Reprint, Whitefish MT: Mountain Press, 1983.
———. *The Hanging Tree*. 1957. Reprint, Lincoln: University of Nebraska Press, 1996.
———. *A Man Called Horse*. New York: Ballantine, 1970.
Keeler, Greg. *American Falls: Poems*. Lewiston ID: Confluence Press, 1987.
———. *Epiphany at Goofy's Gas: Poems*. Livingston MT: Clark City Press, 1991.
———. *The Far Bank*. Lewiston ID: Confluence Press, 1985.
———. *A Mirror to the Safe*. Boise ID: Limberlost Press, 1997.
———. *New, Improved Coyote!* Bozeman MT: Pumpernickel Press, 1990.
———. *Poetryman: Five Poems*. Bozeman MT: Bozarts Press, 1989.
———. *Sea Widow's Journal: To a Fisherman Drowned*. Toronto: Tapir Press, 2000.
———. *Spring Catch*. Lewiston ID: Confluence Press, 1982.
———. *Waltzing with the Captain: Remembering Richard Brautigan*. Boise ID: Limberlost Press, 2004.
Keeler, Greg, and Ricardo da Silveira Lobo Sternberg. *Close Before Striking: Poems*. [Pocatello ID]: G. Keller, 1972.

Kelly, Luther S. *Yellowstone Kelly: The Memoirs of Luther S. Kelly*. Ed. M. M. Quaife. Lincoln: University of Nebraska Press, 1973.
Kittredge, William. *Balancing Water: Restoring the Klamath Basin*. Photographs by Tupper Ansel Blake and Madeleine Graham Blake. Berkeley: University of California Press, 2000.
———. *The Best Short Stories of William Kittredge*. Port Townsend WA: Graywolf Press, 2003.
———. *Hole in the Sky: A Memoir*. New York: Knopf, 1992.
———. *The Nature of Generosity*. New York: Knopf, 2000.
———. *Owning It All: Essays*. Port Townsend WA: Graywolf, 1987.
———. *Southwestern Homelands*. Washington DC: National Geographic, 2002.
———. *Taking Care: Thoughts on Storytelling and Belief*. Minneapolis: Milkweed Editions, 1999.
———. *The Van Gogh Field and Other Stories*. Columbia: University of Missouri Press, 1979.
———. *We Are Not in This Together*. Ed. Raymond Carver. Port Townsend WA: Graywolf Press, 1982.
———. *Who Owns the West?* San Francisco: Mercury, 1996.
———. *The Willow Field*. New York: Knopf, 2006.
Kittredge, William, and Annick Smith, eds. *The Last Best Place: A Montana Anthology*. Helena: Montana Historical Society Press, 1988.
Klink, Joanna. *They Are Sleeping*. Athens: University of Georgia Press, 2000.
Kwasny, Melissa. *The Archival Birds*. Cohasset CA: Bear Star Press, 2000.
———. *Modern Daughters and the Outlaw West: A Novel*. San Francisco: Spinsters Book Co., 1990.
———. *Thistle: Poems*. Sandpoint ID: Lost Horse Press, 2006.
———. *Toward the Open Field: Poets on the Art of Poetry, 1800–1950*. Middletown CT: Wesleyan University Press, 2004.
———. *Trees Call for What They Need*. Minneapolis: Spinsters Ink, 1993.
Lahey, Ed. *The Blind Horses and Still More Poems*. Missoula: The Bookstore at the University of Montana, 2001.
Linderman, Frank Bird. *Big Jinny: The Story of a Grizzly Bear*. Lincoln: University of Nebraska Press, 2005.
———. *Henry Plummer*. Lincoln: University of Nebraska Press, 2000.
———. *Indian Old Man Stories*. Lincoln: University of Nebraska Press, 2001.
———. *Indian Why Stories*. Lincoln: University of Nebraska Press, 2001.
———. *Kootenai Why Stories*. Lincoln: University of Nebraska Press, 1997.
———. *Lige Mounts, Free Trapper*. Lincoln: University of Nebraska Press, 2005.
———. *The Montana Stories of Frank B. Linderman*. Lincoln: University of Nebraska Press, 1997.
———. *Old Man Coyote*. Lincoln: University of Nebraska Press, 1996.
———. *Plenty-coups*. Lincoln: University of Nebraska Press, 2002.

———. *Pretty-shield*. Lincoln: University of Nebraska Press, 2003.
Long, David. *Blue Spruce*. New York: Scribner, 1995.
———. *The Daughters of Simon Lamoreaux*. New York: Scribner, 2000.
———. *Early Returns*. Waldron WA: Jawbone, 1981.
———. *The Falling Boy*. New York: Scribner, 1997.
———. *The Flood of '64*. New York: Ecco Press, 1987.
———. *Home Fires*. Urbana: University of Illinois Press, 1982.
MacLane, Mary. *The Story of Mary MacLane*. Chicago: Herbert S. Stone, 1902.
Maclean, Norman. *A River Runs Through It and Other Stories*. 1976. Engravings by Barry Moser. Reprint, Chicago: University of Chicago Press, 1983.
———. *Young Men and Fire*. Chicago: University of Chicago Press, 1992.
Malone, Michael P. *The American West: A Twentieth-Century History*. The Twentieth-Century American West. Lincoln: University of Nebraska Press, 1989.
———. *The American West, as Seen by Europeans and Americans*. European contributions to American studies, 16. Amsterdam: Free University Press, 1989.
———. *The Battle for Butte: Mining and Politics on the Northern Frontier, 1864–1906*. Seattle: University of Washington Press, 1981.
———. *C. Ben Ross and the New Deal in Idaho*. Seattle: University of Washington Press, 1970.
———. *Historians and the American West*. Ed. Michael P. Malone. Lincoln: University of Nebraska Press, 1983.
———. *James J. Hill: Empire Builder of the Northwest*. The Oklahoma western biographies. Vol. 12. Norman: University of Oklahoma Press, 1996.
———. *Montana: A Contemporary Profile*. Helena MT: American & World Geographic, 1996.
———. *Montana Century: 100 Years in Pictures and Words*. Helena MT: Falcon, 1999.
Malone, Michael P., and Richard B. Roeder. *The Montana Past: An Anthology*. 2nd ed. Missoula: University of Montana Press, 1973.
Malone, Michael P., Richard B. Roeder, and William L. Lang. *Montana: A History of Two Centuries*. 1976. Revised ed. Seattle: University of Washington Press, 1991.
McGuane, Thomas. *The Bushwhacked Piano*. New York: Vintage, 1989.
———. *The Cadence of Grass*. New York: Vintage, 2002.
———. *Gallatin Canyon: Stories*. New York: Knopf, 2006.
———. *Nobody's Angel*. New York: Vintage, 1986.
McNamer, Deirdre. *My Russian*. Boston: Houghton Mifflin, 1999.
———. *One Sweet Quarrel*. New York: HarperCollins, 1994.
———. *Red Rover*. New York: Viking, 2007.
———. *Rima in the Weeds*. New York: HarperCollins, 1991.
McNickle, D'Arcy. *The Hawk and Other Stories*. Ed. Birgit Hans. Tucson: University of Arizona Press, 1993.
———. *Indian Man: A Life of Oliver La Forge*. Bloomington: Indiana University Press, 1971.

———. *The Indian Tribes of the United States: Ethnic and Cultural Survival.* New York: Oxford University Press: 1962.
———. *Indians and Other Americans: Two Ways of Life Meet.* New York: Harper & Row, 1959.
———. *The Legacy of D'Arcy McNickle: Writer, Historian, Activist.* Norman: University of Oklahoma Press, 1996.
———. *Native American Tribalism: Indian Survivals and Renewals.* New York: Oxford University Press, 1993.
———. *Runner in the Sun: A Story of Indian Maize.* 1954. Afterword by Alfonso Ortiz. Reprint, Albuquerque: University of New Mexico Press, 1987.
———. *The Surrounded.* 1936. Reprint, Albuquerque: University of New Mexico Press, 1978.
———. *They Came Here First: The Epic of the American Indian.* Philadelphia: J. B. Lippincott Co., 1949.
———. *Wind from an Enemy Sky.* New York: Harper & Row, 1978.
Meloy, Ellen. *The Anthropology of Turquoise: Meditations on Landscape, Art, and Spirit.* New York: Pantheon, 2002.
———. *The Last Cheater's Waltz: Beauty and Violence in the Desert Southwest.* New York: Holt, 1999.
———. *Raven's Exile: A Season on the Green River.* New York: Holt, 1994.
Murphy, Clyde. *Glittering Hill.* New York: Dutton, 1944.
Newby, Rick. *Old Friends Walking in the Mountains.* Helena MT: Bedrock Editions, 1994.
———. *The Suburb of Long Suffering.* Helena MT: Riverbend Publishing, 2002.
Pape, Greg. *American Flamingo.* Carbondale IL: Crab Orchard Review, 2005.
———. *Black Branches.* Pitt Poetry Series. Pittsburgh: University of Pittsburgh Press, 1984.
———. *Border Crossings.* Pitt Poetry Series. Pittsburgh: University of Pittsburgh Press, 1978.
———. *Little America.* Maguey Press Poetry Chapbook Series, #3. Tucson AZ: Maguey Press, 1976.
———. *Storm Pattern.* Pitt Poetry Series. Pittsburgh: University of Pittsburgh Press, 1992.
———. *Sunflower Facing the Sun: Poems.* Iowa City: University of Iowa Press, 1992.
Smith, Annick. *Homestead.* Minneapolis: Milkweed, 1995.
Stegner, Wallace. *Angle of Repose.* New York: Doubleday, 1971.
———. *Collected Stories of Wallace Stegner.* New York: Random House, 1994
———. *Where the Bluebird Sings to the Lemonade Springs: Living and Writing in the West.* New York: Viking, 1992.
———. *Wolf Willow: A History, a Story, and a Memory of the Last Plains Frontier.* New York: Viking, 1962.
Stegner, Wallace, Stuart Page Stegner, and Eliot Porter. *American Places.* New York: Dutton, 1981.

Thomas, David A. *Fossil Fuel*. Missoula: Montana Writer's Cooperative, 1977.
———. *Buck's Last Wreck*. Missoula MT: Wild Variety Books, 1996.
———. *The Hellgate Wind*. Seattle: Camphorweed Press, 2004.
Thon, Melanie Rae. *First, Body: Stories*. Boston: Houghton Mifflin, 1997.
———. *Girls in the Grass: Stories*. New York: Random House, 1991.
———. *Iona Moon*. New York: Poseidon Press, 1993.
———. *Meteors in August: A Novel*. New York: Random House, 1990.
———. *Sweet Hearts*. Boston: Houghton Mifflin, 2000.
Two Leggings, Peter Nabokov, and William Wildschut. *Two Leggings: the Making of a Crow Warrior*. New York: Crowell, 1970.
Volkman, Karen. *Crash's Law*. New York: Norton, 1998.
———. *Spar*. Iowa City: University of Iowa Press, 2002.
Walker, Mildred. *The Body of a Young Man*. 1960. Introduction by Sharon Bryan. Reprint, Lincoln: University of Nebraska Press, 1997.
———. *The Brewers' Big Horses*. 1940. Introduction by David Budbill. Reprint, Lincoln: University of Nebraska Press, 1996.
———. *The Curlew's Cry*. 1955. Introduction by Mary Clearman Blew. Reprint, Lincoln: University of Nebraska Press, 1994.
———. *Dr. Norton's Wife*. 1938. Introduction by David Budbill. Reprint, Lincoln: University of Nebraska Press, 1996.
———. *Fireweed*. 1934. Introduction by Annick Smith. Reprint, Lincoln: University of Nebraska Press, 1994.
———. *If a Lion Could Talk*. 1970. Introduction by James Welch. Reprint, Lincoln: University of Nebraska Press, 1995.
———. *Light from the Arcturus*. 1935. Introduction by Mary Swander. Reprint, Lincoln: University of Nebraska Press, 1995.
———. *Medical Meeting*. 1949. Introduction by Robert Giroux. Reprint, Lincoln: University of Nebraska Press, 1997.
———. *A Piece of the World*. New York: Atheneum, 1972.
———. *The Quarry*. 1947. Introduction by Ripley Hugo. Reprint, Lincoln: University of Nebraska Press, 1995.
———. *The Southwest Corner*. 1951. Foreword by Mildred Walker. Reprint, Lincoln: University of Nebraska Press, 1995.
———. *Unless the Wind Turns*. 1941. Introduction by Deirdre McNamer. Reprint, Lincoln: University of Nebraska Press, 1996.
———. *Winter Wheat*. 1944. Introduction by James Welch. Reprint, Lincoln: University of Nebraska Press, 1993.
Welch, James. *The Death of Jim Loney*. New York: Harper, 1979.
———. *Fools Crow*. New York: Viking, 1986.
———. *The Heartsong of Charging Elk*. New York: Doubleday, 2000.
———. *The Indian Lawyer*. New York: Norton, 1990.
———. *James Welch*. Lewiston ID: Confluence Press, 1986.

———. *Killing Custer: The Battle of the Little Bighorn and the Fate of the Plains Indians.*
New York: Norton, 1994.
———. *Riding the Earthboy 40: Poems.* New York: World Publishing, 1971.
———. *Winter in the Blood.* New York: Harper, 1974.

CONTRIBUTORS

WILLIAM W. BEVIS is professor emeritus of English at the University of Montana–Missoula; author of *Mind of Winter*, *Ten Tough Trips*, *Borneo Log*, and *Shorty Harris, or The Price of Gold: A Novel*; and coeditor with William E. Farr of *Fifty Years After the Big Sky*. He has published widely on American poetry and the literatures of the American West.

NANCY COOK is associate professor of English at the University of Montana–Missoula. She has published work on a variety of western writers and issues, as well as on book history. She teaches courses on ecocriticism, place studies, and the West. Her current project examines women in the twentieth-century American Outback, with an emphasis on wives of park rangers.

STEVE DAVENPORT is associate director of creative writing at the University of Illinois–Urbana-Champaign and the nonfiction editor of *Ninth Letter*. He is the author of *Uncontainable Noise*, winner of the Transcontinental Award for Poetry; a dozen short stories in magazines such as *Black Warrior Review* and *Fiction International*; and "Murder on Gasoline Lake," which received a Notable listing in *Best American Essays* 2007.

TAMAS DOBOZY is associate professor in the Department of English and Film Studies at Wilfrid Laurier University. He has published on John Coltrane, Charles Bukowski, Richard Ford, Raymond Carver, and Mavis Gallant in venues such as *Genre*, *Modern Fiction Studies*, *Critical Survey*, and *Canadian Literature*. He has also published two collections of short fiction, *When X Equals Marylou* (Arsenal Pulp) and *Last Notes and Other Stories* (HarperCollins). He lives in Kitchener, Ontario, Canada.

ROGER DUNSMORE taught humanities, wilderness studies, and American Indian literature at the University of Montana–Missoula from 1963 to 2003. He was one of the founding members of the Round River Experiment in Environmental Education at UM, 1971–74. During the academic year 1988–89 he trained teachers at the largest American Indian high school in the United States, at Tuba City on the Navajo Reservation. In 1991 and 1997 he was the Faculty Exchange Fellow between UM and Shanghai International Studies University, China. He has published three volumes of poetry as well as a collection of essays, titled *Earth's Mind: Essays in Native Literature*, and he edited *The Poetics of Wilderness*, the "Proceedings" of UM's 2001 Wilderness Lecture Series. He teaches literature and writing at the University of Montana–Western in Dillon.

BRADY HARRISON is professor of English at the University of Montana–Missoula. He is the author of *Agent of Empire*, editor of a Broadview edition of Richard Harding Davis's *Soldiers of Fortune*, and coeditor with Tamas Dobozy of a special issue of *Short Story* on Canadian short fiction set in the United States. His work has appeared in scholarly journals and books in the United States, Mexico, Puerto Rico, and Australia, and he teaches courses on American and Canadian literature, with a particular interest in the literatures of the North American West.

MATTHEW L. JOCKERS is consulting professor and Academic Technology Specialist in the Department of English at Stanford University. His research interests are in Irish Studies, the American West, and Humanities Computing. Jockers is secretary of the American Conference for Irish Studies and executive director of the Western Institute of Irish Studies. His recent publications focus on the literary work of Irish Americans who lived and wrote west of the Mississippi.

GREGORY L. MORRIS teaches at Penn State Erie, the Behrend College, where he is professor of American literature. He is the author of *Talking Up a Storm: Voices of the New West* and has contributed two titles to the Western Writers Series. His essays on western American writing have appeared in journals such as *Western American Literature*, *Great Plains Quarterly*, and *South Dakota Review*.

KARL OLSON is a native of Idaho. He lives in Missoula, Montana, and works for the Missoula Public Library. In 2008 he was cocurator of Montana's first Out at the Library exhibit and series devoted to lesbian and gay literature and history.

ANDREA OPITZ received her PhD in comparative literature from the University of Washington. She teaches American and contemporary literature at the University of Rhode Island. Her previous work on James Welch has appeared in *American Indian Quarterly* and *Studies in American Indian Literatures*.

JIM RAINS, a member of the Creek Nation of Oklahoma, earned a doctorate in English from the University of Michigan. He teaches in the departments of English and Native American Studies at Montana State University–Billings.

LOIS WELCH is a professor emerita of the University of Montana–Missoula, having taught comparative literature and theory in the English Department at UM for thirty-seven years, retiring in 2001. She directed the creative writing program for eight years and the department for three. Among her publications are articles on Aristotle, Dostoevsky, Richard Hugo, and Eudora Welty. She is at work on a memoir about her deceased husband, the author James Welch.

O. ALAN WELTZIEN is professor of English and department chair at the University of Montana–Western in Dillon. He teaches a range of American, regional, and environmental literature. His most recent book is a memoir, *A Father and an Island: Reflections on Loss*. Weltzien spends too much time reading. In the summers, he likes to climb mountains, although he is not very good at it.

INDEX

Page references in *italics* indicate a photograph; the first part of the reference indicates the page of text the photograph section follows; the second part of the reference indicates the page within the photograph section.